Class Struggle
in the Pale

CLASS STRUGGLE IN THE PALE

*The Formative Years
of the Jewish Workers' Movement
in Tsarist Russia*

BY

EZRA MENDELSOHN

CAMBRIDGE
AT THE UNIVERSITY PRESS
1970

Published by the Syndics of the Cambridge University Press
Bentley House, 200 Euston Road, London N.W.1
American Branch: 32 East 57th Street, New York, N.Y.10022

331,0947
MS37c
1970

Printed in Great Britain
at the University Printing House, Cambridge
(Brooke Crutchley, University Printer)

Contents

v

Acknowledgements

I wish to thank the Russian Institute of Columbia University for sponsoring this work for publication, and Mrs L. Solotaroff for her efforts to improve the style of the manuscript. Among my teachers and friends at Columbia University, where this book was begun, I am particularly grateful to Professor Alexander Erlich, who took a personal as well as a scholarly interest in my progress and was a source of great encouragement. I must also record my debt to the staff of the Bund Archives, New York City, and especially to its devoted archivist Mr Hillel Kempinsky, whose help was invaluable to me.

Parts of this book have appeared, in different form, in the *International Review of Social History*, *Jewish Social Studies*, and the *YIVO Annual of Jewish Social Science*.

E. M.

Jerusalem, 1970

Introduction

Autonomous Jewish political movements, which aimed at solving the 'Jewish question' by mobilizing the Jewish population in support of a particular program, were the product of Eastern Europe. It was there, and particularly in the Russian Empire, that the necessary conditions for the creation of such political movements were to be found. That is, there existed an enormous, unassimilated Jewish community which was clearly distinguished, linguistically and otherwise, from other ethnic groups, and a secularized Jewish intelligentsia which, though at least partly assimilated, found it difficult to enter the gentile world. This situation differed sharply from that of Western and Central Europe, where Jews were much less densely settled and where, by the end of the nineteenth century, assimilation had all but destroyed the distinctive Jewish life of medieval times. If the rate of assimilation may be regarded as an index of modernity, the very backwardness of East European society encouraged the emergence of independent Jewish political movements.

The massive Jewish settlement of Eastern Europe originated in the flight of German Jews to Poland during the persecutions of the Middle Ages. The secular intelligentsia, however, was the creation of the nineteenth century. Early in that century the Jewish 'Enlightenment' ('Haskalah') movement penetrated Eastern Europe from its country of origin, Germany. The 'Haskalah' stood for a general purification and reform of Jewish life, particularly in the cultural sphere; it also insisted that Jews become good and loyal citizens of the state. The impact of this movement, though largely restricted to the middle class, was such as to provide a number of willing recruits for the state gymnasia (high schools) and universities, which were opened to Jews during the course of the century. And many who could not gain entrance to these schools studied secular subjects on their own, or in modern Jewish schools, or possibly abroad. Thus was born a small but vitally important Jewish secular intelligentsia.

The history of Jewish politics in the Russian Empire is largely the story of how members of this intelligentsia forged an alliance with the Jewish masses to create specifically Jewish political movements. Such an alliance was, at first, rather unlikely. For many Russian Jewish intellectuals were, by their very nature, estranged from the Jewish masses, having abandoned both the language of the masses, Yiddish, and religious orthodoxy. As they themselves had left traditional Jewish life behind, their most natural inclination was, often enough, to advocate the integration of Jews into Russian society and to participate in general political movements. This inclination, however, was sorely tested by the all-pervasive nature of Russian anti-semitism and the 'Chinese wall' which separated Jew from gentile. While some Jewish intellectuals continued to hope and work for integration, and became active in Russian socialist and liberal movements, others advanced new ideologies which contained specifically Jewish solutions to the 'Jewish question'.

Such ideologies were based on the idea that the Jews were a nation, and that among their tasks was to preserve themselves as a nation. The bearers of the national culture were, of course, the unassimilated Jewish masses, and by articulating national ideologies the intelligentsia signaled its return 'to the people'. Just as Polish or Russian-educated Ukrainians became the champions of the Ukrainian renaissance, and German-educated Czechs became the leaders of Czech nationalism, so many russified Jewish intellectuals found their identity as leaders of Jewish nationalism.

Of these national ideologies the best known (because it has proved the most successful) is Zionism. Russian Zionism, the backbone of the world Zionist movement, proclaimed that Russian Jewry had no future within the Empire and insisted that the only viable alternative was organized mass emigration. The Zionist position, however, was overshadowed in its mass appeal, at least until 1905, by a Jewish social democratic party known as the Bund. The 'General Jewish Workers' Union ("Bund") in Russia and Poland' ('Lithuania' was added later) was founded in Vilna in 1897. Its history illustrates the pattern discussed above. The progenitors of the party were russified Jewish intellectuals, who originally intended to dedicate their lives to the Russian Marxist movement. As we shall see, their confrontation with Russian reality led them to create an all-Jewish movement by allying themselves with the Jewish proletariat. This alliance eventually obliged the intellectuals to voice not only socialist slogans, but specifically Jewish demands. These demands were initially restricted to equal rights for Jews, but soon were expanded into a full-blown national program.

The Bund's national ideology, unlike that of Zionism, was based on the concept of national cultural autonomy. The Russian state of the future, based on socialist principles, would guarantee to all nationalities, including the Jews, the right to maintain their national life through the creation of national cultural institutions. Thus the Jews, while lacking a clearly defined territory, would be permitted to maintain Yiddish schools and promote Yiddish culture in areas of dense Jewish settlement.

The Bund's mixture of nationalism and socialism, not untypical of Eastern Europe, was naturally rejected by the Palestine-oriented Zionists. It was also rejected by the Russian Social Democratic Labor Party, of which the Bund had been a charter member. The Russian Marxists refused to recognize the Jews as a separate nation, and opposed the Bund's claims to absolute jurisdiction over the Russian Jewish proletariat. At the second congress of the Russian party, held in 1903, the Bund's national program was condemned and the Jewish organization found itself isolated within the Russian Marxist camp. Despite Zionist and Russian Marxist hostility, however, the Bund remained a potent force in Russian Jewish life until the Bolshevik revolution ended its legal existence.

A history of the Bund would naturally place considerable emphasis on the development of its ideology and its relations with other political parties, both Jewish and non-Jewish. This study is emphatically not concerned with such questions.[1] Rather, it concentrates on the mass labor movement itself, which took place under the auspices of the Bund but which was not always con-

---

[1] A number of studies, many still unpublished, deal with these problems. See 'Unpublished Sources' in the Bibliography.

trolled by the party. To be sure, the Jewish labor movement cannot be entirely disassociated from certain ideological developments; it was, for example, the theoretical decision to advance from propaganda to agitation which inaugurated organized class warfare between Jewish workers and their employers. This book, however, will focus not on the policies of the party but on the activities of the thousands of workers attracted to the labor movement. Among the questions it will attempt to answer are the following: What did the Jewish workers hope to attain by their adherence to the movement, and to what extent were these hopes realized? How did they set about to improve their economic and cultural situation? How did their aspirations coincide with those of the leadership? Finally, it will try to explain the reasons for the very distinct evolution of the Jewish labor movement within the Russian Empire.

Chronologically, the book deals with the Jewish labor movement from its origins up to, but not including, the revolutionary events of 1905–6. By that time its major characteristics had become clearly manifest. Geographically, it is chiefly concerned with the three Belorussian and three Lithuanian provinces (Minsk, Vitebsk, Mogilev, Vilna, Grodno and Kovno) which constituted the so-called northwest region of the Russian Empire. In Russian-Jewish parlance the area was often referred to simply as 'Lithuania'; (all of these provinces had been part of the Lithuanian segment of the old Polish-Lithuanian Commonwealth). It was in this area that the Jewish labor movement, as an organized phenomenon, originated; it was there, too, that it attained its greatest influence over the Jewish proletariat and intelligentsia.

One explanation for this was demographic. Jews lived in great numbers in the Russian Ukraine and in Russian Poland as well as in 'Lithuania', but while the urban proletariats of the former two regions were chiefly Christian, in the northwest the Jewish element predominated. In addition, the Jewish intelligentsia of the northwest, which was a buffer area between Russian and Polish culture, was subject to weaker assimilationist pressures than were its counterparts in the Ukraine and Russian Poland. This combination of a dominant Jewish proletariat and an intelligentsia more likely than elsewhere to be sensitive to its needs made possible the emergence of a specifically Jewish labor movement.[1] The movement eventually spread beyond the frontiers of Belorussia–Lithuania—and material from other areas has been included—but its leadership remained chiefly of 'Lithuanian' stock, and the primacy of Vilna, the movement's birthplace and the Jewish cultural capital of the region, was never challenged.[2]

A Note on Spelling and Transliteration. With regard to place names, I have used those forms which (1) were employed during the period under discussion, and (2) will be most familiar to the reader. Thus Kovno, not Kaunas; Grodno, not Gardinas. These forms correspond to both Yiddish and Russian usage. Where Yiddish and Russian usage disagree, I have again chosen the more familiar form. Thus Brest-Litovsk, not Brisk.

Yiddish orthography was not consistent at the turn of the century, and therefore my transliteration system is also inconsistent. Thus the word 'worker', for instance, is occasionally written 'arbeter', and occasionally 'arbayter'. At all times I have tried to distinguish clearly between Yiddish and German.

[1] See Moshe Mishkinsky, 'Regionale faktorn bay der oisforemung fun der yidisher arbeter-bavegung in tsarishn rusland', available in mimeographed form in the YIVO Institute for Jewish Research, New York City.

[2] It should be noted that the administrative frontiers of the Russian northwest region did not always coincide with the frontiers of 'Jewish Lithuania'. The Province of Suvalki, for example, which was included in the Kingdom of Poland (after 1863 known as the 'Vistula lands'), was in all other respects an integral part of Belorussia–Lithuania, and the Jewish labor movement in that province was indistinguishable from that of the above-mentioned six provinces. On the other hand, the city of Bialystok, included in Grodno Province, resembled more a Polish than a Lithuanian city, and its labor movement was far more similar to that of Lodz (in Russian Poland) than to that of other cities in the northwest.

CHAPTER 1

The Jewish Proletariat

> If the Russian people suffer more than other peoples, if
> the Russian proletariat is more exploited than any other
> proletariat, there exists yet another class of workers who
> are still more oppressed, exploited, and ill-treated than
> all the others; this pariah among pariahs is the Jewish
> proletariat in Russia.   KARL KAUTSKY, 1901

The last third of the eighteenth century witnessed the collapse of
the Polish Commonwealth as its territory and population were
absorbed by Austria, Prussia, and Russia. If the dismemberment
of Poland was bound to affect European history, it had no less of an
impact on Jewish history, certainly on that of East European
Jewry. For, ironically, the acquisition of Polish territory resulted
in what Russia had long attempted to prevent: a mass influx of
Jews into the Russian Empire. To be sure, there were Jews in
Russia before the Polish partitions. During the Kievan period they
had constituted a not unimportant community. But the seventeenth and eighteenth century rulers were hostile to the idea of
Jewish settlement, Empress Elizabeth going so far as to order a
general expulsion of the Jews in 1742. Consequently there were
relatively few Jews in Russia until after the first partition of
Poland in 1772. Thus the collapse of Poland marks the beginning
of modern Russian Jewish history.[1]

In Western Europe, traditionally, Jews were a highly urbanized
element which specialized in trade. In Eastern Europe the situation
was more complex. The Polish Jews absorbed into the Russian
Empire lived in cities, small towns, and villages, and their
economic activities were accordingly more varied. In urban areas
they were engaged not only in trade but also in craft production;
in the countryside they administered the estates of the 'szlachta'

[1] Salo W. Baron, *The Russian Jew under Tsars and Soviets* (New York, 1964), Chapter 1,
Iulii Gessen, *Istoriia evreiskago naroda v Rossii* (Petrograd, 1916), I, Chapters 1–3.

(the Polish nobility), and in general played an important but unenviable role as the economic link between landlord and peasant.[1] An English traveler in Eastern Europe in the early nineteenth century noted that 'The entire petty trade in Poland and Lithuania is controlled by Jews...', while an eminent historian of Lithuanian Jewry wrote that in 1792 'All the trade and industry of Lithuania was controlled by this population'.[2] The Jewish practice of leasing a landowner's property and administering it was so widespread that in the southwest provinces the census confused the concept of leaseholder ('arendator') with that of Jew and instead of describing a village as having no Jews, stated: '...in the village there is no leaseholder'.[3] The sale of liquor in rural areas was an especially important Jewish profession: in the villages of Zhitomir Province 73·7 per cent of the Jews earned a living by leasing distilleries and selling the product at inns.[4]

During the nineteenth century the demographic and economic situation changed considerably. Thousands of Jews left the Empire in search of better opportunities elsewhere in Europe or in the New World. Others migrated to the economically promising regions of 'New Russia', where new centers of Jewish life emerged in such cities as Odessa and Ekaterinoslav. More important, for our purposes, was the urbanization of Jewish life

---

[1] Jacob Leschinsky, 'Di antviklung fun idishen folk far di letste 100 yor', in Jacob Leschinsky (ed.), *Shriftn far ekonomik un statistik* (Berlin, 1928), I, 55. On the early economic activities of Russian Jewry see also Y. Yakhinson, *Sotsial-ekonomisher shtayger ba yidn in rusland in XIX y"h* (Kharkov, 1929), 1; Israel Sosis, *Di sotsial-ekonomishe lage fun di ruslendishe yuden in der ershter helft fun 19-ten yorhundert* (Petrograd, 1919), 3. More precise data on specific areas is available in Kh. Korobkov, 'Perepis' evreiskago naseleniia vitebskoi gubernii v 1772 g'., *Evreiskaia starina*, v, No. 2 (April–June 1912), 176–7; 'Die Berufsgliederung der Juden im Kreise Zhitomir im Jahre 1789', in S. B. Weinryb, *Neueste Wirtschaftsgeschichte der Juden in Russland und Polen* (Breslau, 1934), 219.

[2] The quotations are from Robert Johnston, *Travels through parts of the Russian empire and the country of Poland* (London, 1815), 436; S. A. Bershadskii, *Litovskie evrei* (St Petersburg, 1883), 3.

[3] See I. Kamanin, 'Statisticheskiia dannyia o evreiakh v iugo-zapadnome krae vo vtoroi polovine proshlago veka (1765–91 gg.)' *Arkhiv iugo-zapadnoi Rossii*, Part V, Vol. II (1890), 63.

[4] See the appendix to Weinryb, *Neueste Wirtschaftsgeschichte*, 221–2; and for general information, A. Margolis, *Geshikhte fun yidn in rusland* (Moscow-Kharkov-Minsk, 1930), 6 ff.; Korobkov, 'Ekonomicheskaia rol' evreev v Pol'she v kontse XVIII v.', *Evreiskaia starina*, III, No. 3 (July–September 1910), 377.

in the traditional areas of Jewish settlement. This was partly the work of government intervention. Alleging that the Jews were a major cause of poverty and discontent among the peasants, the Russian authorities made various attempts to force the Jews out of the villages by prohibiting their employment as administrators of estates and as liquor salesmen. The 1804 'Statute Concerning the Jews', the first comprehensive law on the Jews enacted in Russia, stipulated that they were to leave the countryside within three years. While the expulsion proved impossible to enforce, a legislative precedent had been established; other expulsions followed. For example in the 1820s the Jews were expelled from the villages of Mogilev, Vitebsk, and Grodno provinces.[1] Moreover, the government took steps to remove Jews to a 50-verst (roughly 35 miles) radius from the western frontier in order to halt smuggling operations.[2] In 1845 the war against the village Jews was resumed with a decree forbidding them to manufacture or sell liquor in rural areas.[3] This policy culminated in the 'May Laws' of 1882, which prohibited Jewish resettlement in rural areas.[4]

Jews ousted from rural areas were not allowed to migrate to the cities of the Russian interior, but were rather obliged to remain within the 'Pale of Settlement', a special area first clearly defined in 1835. Roughly speaking, the Pale included the regions of 'New Russia', the Ukraine, Belorussia–Lithuania, Polish territories added to the Empire after the Napoleonic wars, and some areas in the Baltic Provinces. Hence, the extremely limited mobility of the Jews within Russia contributed to their growing concentration in those cities where Jewish residence was permitted.[5]

[1] V. O. Levanda (ed.), *Polnyi khronologicheskii sbornik zakonov o polozhenii kasaiush-chikhsia evreev* (St Petersburg, 1874), 119–20, 216–17; the effects of this expulsion are described in Yakhinson, *Sotsial-ekonomisher shtayger*, 30. For early charges to the effect that Jews were responsible for peasant poverty, see Iulii Gessen, *Evrei v Rossii* (St Petersburg, 1906), 21, 37, 109. The text of the 'Statute' is published in Levanda (ed.), *Polnyi khronologicheskii sbornik zakonov*, 54–60. On the history of the first expulsion see Gessen, *Evrei v Rossii*, 315 ff.

[2] See M. I. Mysh, *Rukovodstvo k russkim zakonam o evreiakh* (St Petersburg, 1904), 94 ff.

[3] Levanda (ed.), *Polnyi khronologicheskii sbornik zakonov*, 621.

[4] For the 'May Laws' see Mysh, *Rukovodstvo k russkim zakonam*, 109 ff.

[5] On the emergence of a clearly-defined 'Pale of Settlement', see 'Zhitel'stvo i peredvizhenie evreev po russkomu zakonodatel'stvu', *Evreiskaia entsiklopediia* (St Petersburg, 1906–13), VII, 590–4.

1-2

If urbanization was a function of governmental intervention, it was also a function of the general economic decline of Jewish life in the villages. Dependent upon the landowners for employment, Jews were severely hurt when the emancipation of the serfs brought increasing impoverishment to the gentry. The village Jew could welcome neither the emancipation nor the gradual economic development of the countryside that came with railroad construction, for both tended to undermine his security as a middleman. The crisis generated by their loss of the 'old sources of livelihood' compelled many rural Jews to seek employment in the cities.[1]

Statistical evidence confirms the marked process of urbanization that occurred in Russian Jewish life. In Vitebsk Province, for example, the number of urbanized Jews in 1772 was 2,997, as compared with 9,812 Christians; by 1815 the population figures for the two groups were 17,856 and 17,336 respectively.[2] The following table illustrates the growth of the Jewish urban communities in several major cities of Belorussia–Lithuania:[3]

City	Year	Jewish pop.	Year	Jewish pop.	Year	Jewish pop.
Minsk	1802	2,716	1847	12,976	1897	47,562
Kovno	1797	1,508	1847	2,013	1897	25,448
Brest–Litovsk	1766	3,157	1847	8,136	1897	30,608
Dvinsk	1805	749	1847	2,918	1897	32,400
Pinsk	1801	1,600	1847	5,050	1897	21,065
Grodno	1816	8,422	1859	10,300	1897	22,684
Gomel	—	—	1864	9,730	1897	20,385

By 1897 the percentage of Jews in twelve major cities of the region was as follows:[4]

[1] See Kotik, as quoted in Yakhinson, *Sotsial-ekonomisher shtayger*, 174; Weinryb, *Neueste Wirtschaftsgeschichte*, 60; Margolis, *Geshikhte*, 23 ff. I. G. Orshanskii, *Evrei v Rossii, Ocherki i izsledovaniia* (St Petersburg, 1872), 13, remarks that 'general economic progress of Russian life was harmful to the Jewish population'.

[2] Korobkov, 'Perepis'', 177.

[3] From Leschinsky, *Dos idishe folk in tsifern* (Berlin, 1922), 74–5.

[4] From data in *Evreiskoe naselenie Rossii po dannym perepisi 1897 g. i po noveishim isotochnikam* (Petrograd, 1917).

City	Jewish pop. (%)	City	Jewish pop. (%)
Minsk	52	Gomel	55
Kovno	36	Bialystok	63
Brest–Litovsk	65	Bobruisk	60
Dvinsk	44	Mogilev	50
Grodno	48	Vitebsk	52
Pinsk	74	Vilna	41

By the end of the century Jews comprised 52 per cent of the entire urban population of Belorussia–Lithuania. The Russian element composed the second largest urban group (18·2%) and the balance was made up of Poles, Belorussians, and Lithuanians.[1] Among the many nationalities in that region, then, the Jews were the dominant urban group. In a sense, the cities were their 'territory'.

Those Jews who flocked to the cities found a limited choice of occupation open to them. As one Russian observer noted, they gathered in the urban areas to engage 'in trade and crafts'.[2] Those who chose to become artisans were continuing an old, established Polish Jewish profession. As early as 1389 Grand Duke Vitovt (Witold) of Lithuania granted a 'Privilege' to the Jews of Grodno expressly permitting them to engage in craft work. By the fifteenth century there were Jewish glass-makers, furriers, painters, leadsmiths, and goldsmiths, while a comprehensive list of jobs performed by Polish Jewish artisans in the eighteenth century numbers over sixty crafts.[3]

---

[1] Leschinsky, *Dos idishe folk*, 60. See also 'Naselenie', *Evreiskaia entsiklopediia*, XI, 538–39. The figures given in *Sbornik materialov ob ekonomicheskom polozhenii evreev v Rossii* (St Petersburg, 1904), I, xxiv, show an even higher Jewish urban population in Belorussia–Lithuania.

[2] Margolis, *Geshikhte*, 38 and also 45, 236.

[3] The 'Privilege' is published in Bershadskii (ed.), *Russko-evreiskii arkhiv, dokumenty i materialy dlia istorii evreev v Rossii* (St Petersburg, 1882), I, 26–8. Originally, Jewish craftsmen produced mainly for the Jewish market, but according to one authority they were already concentrating on the peasant market in the fourteenth century; see B. Mark, 'Rzemieślnicy żydowscy w Polsce feudalnej', *Biuletyn żydowskiego instytutu historycznego*, Nos. 13–14 (January–June 1954), 16. See also R. Notik, 'Tsu der geshikhte fun hantverk bay litvishe yidn', *YIVO bleter*, IX, No. 1–2 (January–March 1936), 116. On the eve of the Polish partitions 30–33 per cent of the urban Jewish population in Crown Poland engaged in craft production. See Raphael

During the early years of Russian rule Jews constituted some 50 per cent of the artisan class in the cities of Minsk Province, a representative area in Belorussia–Lithuania.[1] By the end of the century urbanization had so increased the number of Jewish craftsmen that two-thirds to three-fourths of the entire artisan class within the Pale of Settlement (excluding Poland) was Jewish.[2] This Jewish dominance of craft production is extremely important, but no less important is the fact that, within the Jewish proletariat itself, the vast majority of workers were artisans. Thus in Belorussia–Lithuania 90 per cent of the 200,000 Jewish workers were craftsmen.[3] The Jewish proletariat of the northwest, then, was overwhelmingly a proletariat of artisans.

The Russian Jewish artisan of the late nineteenth century resembled in many ways the Jewish artisans of the old Polish Commonwealth. As had always been the case, Jewish craftsmen concentrated on the preparation of clothing (over 25 per cent were tailors).[4] And, also traditionally, the Jewish artisan shop was a tiny establishment. The majority of Jewish artisans in Belorussia-

---

Mahler, *Yidn in amolikn poylen in likht fun tsifern* (Warsaw, 1958), 98, 169. Higher estimates (for all of Polish Jewry) are given by Mark Wischnitzer, *Yidishe bal melokhe tsekhn in poyln un lite* (Berlin, 1922), 26, and Mark, 'Rzemieślnicy żydowscy', 88. For a convenient survey of Jewish crafts in Poland, see Wischnitzer, *A History of Jewish Crafts and Guilds* (New York, 1965), Chapters 19–21.

[1] Leschinsky (ed.), *Shriftn far ekonomik un statisk*, 58.

[2] *Sbornik*, I, 190–2. The figures refer to the year 1898. To cite several specific examples, an official report from the city of Minsk in 1877 (Margolis, *Geshikhte*, 258) noted that all the artisans of the city were Jews, while A. P. Subbotin, *V cherte evreiskoi osedlosti* (St Petersburg, 1888), Part I, 127, notes that in the 1870s 73 per cent of all artisans in Kovno Province were Jews. The preponderance of Jews in the artisan class of the small towns was especially marked. In Vileika, for example, a town of 2,225 inhabitants in Vilna Province, twenty of the twenty-two artisans were Jews; see *Ekonomicheskoe sostoianie gorodskikh poselenii Evropeiskoi Rossii v 1861–62 g.* (St Petersburg, 1863), Part I: 'Vilenskaia Guberniia', 9.

[3] *Sbornik*, I, 194; II, 215. Avraham Menes, 'Vegen der industrie-bafelkerung ba idn in rusland, 1897', in Leschinsky (ed.), *Shriftn*, 255–6, claims these figures are too low but he does not himself provide any estimates for Belorussia–Lithuania.

[4] Shoemakers made up the second major group (14·4%), followed by carpenters (6%), bakers (4·6%), and butchers (4·4%). See the list in *Sbornik*, I, 197. The percentage of tailors among eighteenth century Jewish artisans in Poland was even higher (see Mahler, *Yidn in poyln*, 115 ff.). The preponderance of Jewish tailors can be explained in part by the fact that Jews were forbidden to wear clothing made of more than one fabric (according to the religious ordinance known as *sha'atnez*), and, in order to ensure this, had recourse to their own artisans. Religious custom also accounts for the large number of Jews engaged in the preparation of foodstuffs, which had to be prepared in a ritually acceptable fashion.

Lithuania were self-employed, and those who did not work alone or with the help of their families seldom hired more than a few assistants (journeymen or apprentices). The average artisan's establishment (in Belorussia) consisted of two people, a master and a journeyman or apprentice.[1] This held true even for a major urban center like Minsk where it was uncommon for a master to hire more than one journeyman. Similarly in Gomel, another important city, 800 artisans were distributed among numerous shops of two to three men each.[2]

In many of the shops the relationship between masters, journeymen, and apprentices had scarcely changed since medieval times. The latter were used chiefly as servants, and had little opportunity to learn their trade properly.[3] On the other hand, the journeyman and master maintained their solidarity, as they had centuries before, through membership in the craft guild, known in Hebrew (and Yiddish) as the 'hevrah ba'alay melakhah' ('artisans' association'). Jewish guilds had emerged in sixteenth and seventeenth century Poland when competition from Christian artisans necessitated that the Jews form societies of their own, modeled on those of their rivals, to protect their common interests. The societies aimed to ensure a decent livelihood for each master, and to satisfy the artisans' social and religious needs.[4]

Interestingly, the Jewish guilds continued to flourish throughout the nineteenth century. Though in a state of decline economically, they nevertheless fulfilled an important cultural need in the daily life of the Jewish artisan. Thus in 1882 a German traveler in Vilna remarked on the existence of over twenty of these

---

[1] *Sbornik*, I, 255.

[2] 'K voprosu o polozhenii evreev remeslennikov', *Nedel'naia khronika 'Voskhoda'*, XX, No. 39 (21 June 1901), 13 ff.; 'Gomel'skoe rabochee dvizhenie', in Sh. (S) Agursky (ed.), *Di sotsialistishe literatur of yidish in 1875–97* (Minsk, 1935), 364.

[3] See *Sbornik*, I, 210 ff. For accounts of how apprentices were treated see Sholem Levin, 'Di ershte yorn fun der revolutsie', *Royte bleter* (1929), 2; Ezriel Presman, *Der durkhgegangener veg* (New York, 1950), 22 ff.

[4] See, in general, Perla Kramerówna, 'Żydowskie cechy rzemieślnicze w dawnej Polsce,' *Miesięcznik Żydowski*, II, No. 7–12 (July–December 1923), 259–98; Mark, 'Rzemieślnicy żydowscy', 36 ff.; Moshe Kremer, 'Le-heker ha-melakhah ve-hevrot ba'alay ha-melakhah etsel yehuday polin ba-maot ha-17-ha-18', *Zion*, II, No. 3–4 (July 1937), 294–325; Notik, 'Tsu der geshikhte fun hantverk', 107–18. Several of the guilds' minutes have been published; for a partial bibliography see Isaac Levitats, *The Jewish Community in Russia, 1772–1844* (New York, 1943), 231.

guilds.[1] The wealthier guilds maintained their own synagogues, where members would congregate to pray and study; others, with more limited means, would raise enough money to purchase a Torah scroll (a hand-written copy of the Pentateuch) which symbolized the guild's independence within the community and the unity of its members. The latter enjoyed the use of the guild's library of religious books and benefited from its sick-fund.[2]

Jewish socialists were fond of using the term 'paternalistic' to describe the nature of the master-journeyman relationship. Indeed, the journeyman was often regarded as a member of the master's household (a single man, particularly if he was from out of town, often lived with his employer); as such he became the object both of paternal affection and of wrath. Doubtlessly some of the workers were genuinely attached to their 'bread-givers', as they were called, and the Dvinsk artisans who drank to the health of their master and his wife every Saturday may well have been sincere.[3] But on the whole employers were inclined to abuse the unlimited power they had over their journeymen and apprentices. A well-informed observer, commenting on the crude treatment dealt these workers, noted that 'there were insults, sometimes blows'.[4] Numerous instances of such cruelty, often the cause of long and costly strikes, were reported in the socialist press of the period. Indeed, the absence of well-defined obligations on

---

[1] J. Rülf, *Drei Tage in Jüdisch-Russland* (Frankfort a/M, 1882). The author notes that 'the Jewish Russian craftsman is very religious, and is certainly no layman when it comes to biblical-talmudic knowledge. In order to demonstrate his piety...he founds a guild (Verein) and erects a synagogue (Klaus) where he devotes himself to the service of God and the study of the law' (p. 5). See also Pinkhas Kan, 'Idishe tsekhn in vilne onhayb XIX-tn yorhundert', in Leschinsky (ed.), *Shriftn*, 89 ff. For the existence of numerous guilds in Mogilev at the turn of the century see Sara Rabinowitsch, *Die Organisationen des jüdischen Proletariats in Russland* (Karlsruhe, 1903), 47 ff.

[2] See the description of the artisans' society in Minsk in Shmuel K. Tsitron, 'Kehilat yisrael be-minsk', *Knesset yisrael* (Warsaw, 1886), I, 738; see also Israel Halperin, 'Hevrot ba'alay melakhah yehudim be-poylin ve-lita', *Zion*, II, No. 1 (October 1936), 70 ff. for a description of a tailors' guild in Bialystok.

[3] L. Berman (Leibetshke, pseud.), *In loif fun yorn, zikhroynes fun a yidishn arbeter* (New York, 1945), 68. For other examples see Levin, 'Di ershte yorn'; Frants Kursky, *Gezamlte shriftn* (New York, 1952), 133; *Der bialystoker arbayter*, No. 4 (April 1901), 4; *Tsu ale lodzer arbayter-shuster*, October 1904 (a proclamation of the Jewish Bund). See also the remarks in Boris Frumkin, 'Ocherki iz istorii evreiskago rabochago dvizheniia v Rossii (1885–97 g.)', *Evreiskaia starina*, VI, No. 1 (January–March 1913), 108 ff.

[4] A. Litvak, pseud. (Helphand), *Vos geven* (Vilna, 1925), 122.

the part of the artisan master toward his hired hands—those a modern, capitalist system takes for granted—was to become one of the major grievances of the Jewish worker during the period of mass strike activity.

Nonetheless, it should be emphasized that the Jewish journeyman by no means considered himself permanently a wage earner. As he saw it, were he compelled to suffer the insults of his master one day, the next he himself might become an employer, the master of his own shop. For such changes in status were fairly common practice. A report from Vilna notes that the hired artisans 'are themselves future employers...', while according to another observer an apprentice no sooner learns a bit about his trade than he begins to 'dream of independence, and at the first opportunity...will leave his master and open his own shop or become a journeyman'.[1] It was this tendency of the journeymen to become employers, their failure to recognize the class struggle, that made the early socialist leaders despair. Feliks Kon, the Polish socialist, disparagingly characterized the Jewish artisans as 'journeymen who dream of becoming masters', while S. Gozhanskii, whose role as a pioneer in the Jewish socialist movement in Vilna will be discussed in some detail, was dismayed to learn that in some crafts there was no clear-cut distinction between employers and workers: an artisan might be a worker one summer and an employer the next.[2] As though to confirm Gozhanskii's apprehensions, some of the workers who had participated in early socialist movements in Minsk later opened their own shops, thus becoming (in the eyes of the socialists) 'exploiters'.[3]

The tiny shops, the guilds, the constant fluctuations in workers' status, all this harkened back to an earlier era, and was somewhat anachronistic in an age when even Russia was industrializing. Yet changes were taking place. For one thing, the traditional community of interest between master and journeyman was occasion-

[1] Ab. Cahan, 'Bildung un sotsialistishe propaganda bay yidishe bale melokhes in di litvishe shtet', *Historishe shriftn* (Vilna-Paris, 1939), III, 397; *Sbornik*, I, 211.
[2] Feliks Kon, *Za piat'desiat let* (Moscow, 1936), II, 217; S. Gozhanskii, 'A briv tsu di agitatorn', *Historishe shriftn* III, 633.
[3] E. A. Gurvich, 'Evreiskoe rabochee dvizhenie v Minske v 80-kh gg.', in S. Dimanshtein (ed.), *Revoliutsionnoe dvizhenie sredi evreev* (Moscow, 1930), 57.

ally challenged. In the 1820s, for example, a feud arose in Lodz between the master tailors and their employees, the latter threatening to leave the city unless working conditions improved.[1] In Minsk in 1841 the journeymen tailors broke away from the guild to form their own association, and there is evidence that a similar society of journeymen tailors was established in Bialystok.[2] More important was the fact that, in some crafts, the number of employees increased considerably. Although the typical shop, as we have seen, consisted of a master and one helper, by the century's end there were many exceptions. Using Minsk as an example once again, in 1901 thirty-one shops employed ten or more workers, the two largest engaging twenty-four men each. Similarly in Vitebsk the average shop hired only a few persons, yet some employed as many as fifteen or twenty men; in Vilna small shops existed side by side with tailors' establishments staffed by as many as thirty or forty men.[3]

Since employer–staff relationships were more clearly defined in the larger establishments, workers naturally found it more difficult to alter their status. Martov, the future Menshevik leader who was active in Vilna in the 1890s, noted that the tendency to concentrate the majority of crafts in the hands of larger firms was the wave of the future, and that Jewish artisans would become more and more 'proletarianized'. His prognosis was confirmed, at least with regard to the Vilna carpenters, by a study carried out after the 1905 Revolution. The study revealed that the carpenters no longer '...regard themselves as future employers; they have become permanently hired laborers'.[4] Much the same trends were at work in every major city of Belorussia–Lithuania.

[1] Phillip Friedman, 'A sotsialer konflikt in lodz onhayb 19-tn y″h', *YIVO bleter*, II, No. 1–2 (November–December 1931), 145–9.

[2] Ia. Brafman, *Kniga kagala* (St Petersburg, 1875), II, 453–6; Halperin, 'Hevrot', 84 ff. See also Rabinowitsch, *Die Organizasionen*, 54–5. She notes that 'Even by 1850 a split occurred here [in Mogilev] between the masters and the journeyman [of the women's tailors' guild].' A similar event in Iaroslav is mentioned in Levitats, *The Jewish Community*, 234.

[3] 'K voprosu', 13; A. M. Ginsburg (Naumov, pseud.), 'Nachalnye shagi vitebskago rabochego dvizheniia', in Dimanshtein (ed.), *Revoliutsionnoe dvizhenie*, 101; Elie Raytshuk, 'Fun vaytn over', *Royte bleter*, 1.

[4] Iulii Martov, *Zapiski sotsialdemokrata* (Berlin, 1922), 187; A. I. Kastelianskii, 'Mebel'noe-stoliarno proizvodstvo v cherte evreiskoi osedlosti', *Stoliarno-mebel'noe proizvodstvo*, Vol. I of *Materialy i izsledovaniia o evreiskoi remeslennoi promyshlennosti* (Petrograd, 1915), 147.

If the workers' status underwent important alterations, so did that of the masters. During the nineteenth century more and more Jewish shops began to produce for stores rather than for individual orders, and the masters became far less independent, being subject to controls by the store owners, the 'magazinshchiks'. By the early twentieth century, for example, Jewish carpenter masters were largely dependent upon the furniture store owners for whom they produced. Speaking of the northwest region as a whole, the economist M. V. Dovnar-Zapolskii noted that while the artisan masters were considered independent within their own shops, this was largely not the case. If they exploited the labor of their journeymen and apprentices, they in turn were the object of exploitation.[1] This is suggested, too, by another authority who claims that the majority of Jewish artisan masters in the cities were independent in name only.[2]

While the masters were losing their independence, the employees found their own lot to be intolerable. Their condition was characterized by an ill-defined and extremely long working day. A journeyman was expected to work 'without limit', which usually meant from sunrise to sunset, while on Saturdays, after the Sabbath rest, and on Thursdays as well, his work extended into the early morning hours. In a petition to the Governor of Vilna Province in 1892 one worker complained that '...the work in the shop lasts from 7.00 a.m. to 11.00 p.m. or 12.00 p.m., and before holidays the employer makes us work all night.'[3] We know, too, that in Vitebsk the artisans seldom worked fourteen to fifteen hours a day; more often their day lasted seventeen to eighteen hours.[4] Similarly in Pinsk the average workday was

---

[1] Sh. Aynzaft, 'Der ekonomisher kamf fun di holtsarbeter bizn 1905-tn yor', *Visnshaftlekhe yorbikher* (1929), I, 93; A. V. Dovnar-Zapolskii, *Narodnoe khoziaistvo Belorussii, 1861–1914 gg.* (Minsk, 1926), 163–4.

[2] B. Brutskus, 'Ocherk ekonomicheskago polozheniia evreev v Rossii', *Ocherki po voprosam ekonomicheskoi deiatel'nosti evreev v Rossii* (St Petersburg, 1913), 27. A report from Minsk, published in *Voskhod*, XIX, No. 98 (17 December 1900), 14, states that: 'Almost all the crafts are now beginning to work predominantly for stores.'

[3] As quoted in Yefim Yeshurin (ed.), *Vilne, A zamlbukh gevidmet der shtot vilne* (New York, 1935), 133.

[4] 'Bor'ba vitebskikh rabochikh za luchshuiu zhizn', originally published as an appendix to *Rabochee delo*, No. 2–3 (August 1899), 1–16, and republished in Agursky (ed.), *Di sotsialistishe literatur*, 340–27; the quotation is from *ibid.*, 338.

sixteen to eighteen hours, and this was typical of all the cities in the northwest region prior to the advent of the mass strike movement.[1] Russian factory workers were much better off in this respect. Jewish craftsmen failed to profit from the labor legislation reluctantly promulgated by the Tsarist regime, and the eleven and one-half hour limit established in 1897 benefited only the factory worker. State-appointed factory inspectors rarely entered the dark, dingy shops where Jewish artisans were employed.

Wages were as meagre as the day was long. Piece work prevailed in many crafts, and weekly or monthly payments were often irregular. In Minsk journeymen scarcely averaged more than three rubles a week, though there was considerable fluctuation (some earned as much as eight rubles). In the workers' suburb of Kovno annual wages ranged between one hundred and three hundred rubles. While a good coat-tailor in Bialystok might earn as much as thirteen rubles a week, a fortune for any Russian worker, the average wages in that city were far lower.[2] Indeed, the very notion of weekly wages was meaningless, since almost all Jewish artisans had only seasonal employment. During the busy season they might do well, but if it was a short season (as

---

[1] *Tsu alle pinsker idishe arbayter un arbayterinen*, September 1903 (a proclamation of the Jewish Bund). For material on the length of the artisan's workday in other cities see *Der minsker arbeter*, No. 2 (January 1901), 1; *Der kampf*, No. 1 (September 1900), 1; *Der bialystoker arbeter*, No. 3 (December 1900), 7, 9; No. 4 (April 1901), 7; No. 6 (September 1901), 11, 12; No. 7 (January 1902), 10.

[2] *Der minsker arbeter*, No. 1 (December 1900), 4; No. 2 (January 1901), 6; No. 3 (June 1901), 8, 9, 10; Sam. Ianovskii, 'Opisanie odnogo mestechka', *Evreiskaia zhizn'*, No. 4 (April 1904), 146 (deals with both Jewish and Christian artisans, masters and journeymen); *Der bialystoker arbeter*, No. 3 (December 1900), 7; No. 4 (April 1901), 7; No. 6 (September 1901), 12; No. 7 (January 1902), 10. On Bialystok see also 'Der leben un kampf fun di idishe arbayter in russland un poylen (berikht fun di ortige komitetn fun bund tsum internatsionalen sotsialistishen kongress in pariz)', *Der idisher arbeter*, No. 10 (1900), 61–2. Added material on Jewish artisans' wages is available in *Sbornik*, I, 220 ff. Given extreme fluctuations in wages and frequent unemployment, one cannot meaningfully compare the wages of Jewish and non-Jewish workers. In the northwest provinces Christians were willing to work for lower wages than Jews, and during the course of the strike movement this proved to the advantage of employers. While the Jewish artisan's wages were higher, so were his expenses. Special preparations were necessary for the Sabbath and the Jewish holidays, and the religious school to which a worker sent his children was a considerable drain on his meagre income. Moreover, unlike the Christian worker the Jew had no village to fall back upon when the season ended and the prospects of work decreased. See E. Cherniovsky, *Der yidisher arbeter in vaysrusland bam baginen fun der yidisher arbeter-bavegung* (Minsk, 1932), 109 ff.; *Sbornik*, II, 167; Kastelianskii, 'Mebel'noe-stoliarno proizvodstvo', 121.

was true for the coat-tailors of Bialystok), the greater part of the year found them out of work or subject to the mercy of their employers. The complaint made by a group of workers in Minsk, 'From ten weeks of work we must live fifty-two weeks', was echoed by thousands of Jewish artisans who earned wages only part of the year.[1]

Low wages combined with long periods of unemployment forced most Jewish artisans to live in conditions of extreme poverty. A Lodz weaver who earned three to four rubles a week (when he worked) had an expense of three and one-half rubles per week for food, fuel, and laundry alone; a Bialystok carpenter, who earned as little as three rubles a week during the season and had to contend with frequent periods of unemployment, found he simply could not support himself on his miserable income.[2] In the middle of the nineteenth century the poorest worker in Vilna could not provide for himself and his family unless he earned 45 kopeks a day, but toward the end of the century thousands of workers were so poverty-stricken that even that sum seemed a fortune.[3]

According to Aaron Liebermann, one of the pioneers of the Jewish socialist movement, the majority of Jewish workers in the cities of Belorussia–Lithuania lived 'in the semi-darkness of cellars or similar hovels that had wet walls and floors, and were crammed together in an oppressive, stupefying atmosphere'.[4] An observer in Lodz described how he found ten people living in a

[1] *Der minsker arbeter*, No. 1 (December 1900), 1; carpenters in Vilna worked only nine months of the year, and a carpenter in Minsk complained that 'occasionally whole weeks go by with no work'. See *Der klassen-kampf*, No. 4 (April 1901), 4; Subbotin, *V cherte*, I, 37. Winter was usually the most difficult time for the artisan; see 'Der vinter', *Der minsker arbeter*, No. 1 (December 1900), 1 ff.; *Tsu alle vitebsker arbayter un arbayterinen*, 1901, and *Tsu alle grodner stoliares*, 1903 (?) (proclamations of the Jewish Bund). In this respect, too, factory workers had an advantage, as their job security was much greater.
[2] A typical Lodz weaver's budget is published in *Sbornik*, II, 162; on Bialystok see I. Khoroshch, 'Po promyshlennoi cherte osedlosti', *Voskhod*, xx, No. 7 (July 1901), 43; and No. 8 (August 1901), 52–3, for workers' budgets; see also Subbotin, *V cherte*, II, 30 ff.
[3] A. Korev (ed.) *Vilenskaia gubernaia*, Vol. III, of *Materialy dlia geografii i statistiki Rossii, sobrannye ofitserami general'nago shtaba* (St Petersburg, 1863), 392; Subbotin, *V cherte*, I, 86.
[4] 'Iz Belostoka', *Vpered*, No. 23 (15 December 1875), 723. Other accounts of Jewish workers' living conditions are to be found in Khoroshch, *Voskhod*, xx, No. 7 (July 1901), 43 ff. and similarly in Subbotin, *V cherte*, I, 37 ff., 91 ff., 139 ff. and II, 30 ff. Khoroshch found that 'Vilna artisans live rather cleanly and have pretentions to comfort'; similarly,

single room, forced to work and sleep in this limited area. 'There is no bed, one sleeps on the floor, winter and summer; the wretched creatures are dressed shabbily and their poverty is indescribable.'[1] In Ponevyezh (Kovno Province) several families are reported to have lived together in rooms where there was hardly any ventilation, while in Vilna 'When a worker's family had a room to itself, it was considered a luxury'.[2] Similarly in Minsk Province an observer noted that 'eight out of the ten families who earn their living by doing craft-work live in the most terrible poverty'. The Jewish press recounted the deplorable situation of the artisans in Vilna and Vitebsk where, it seems, people were 'simply dying of hunger'.[3]

Fortunately, the Jewish artisan had recourse to well-organized charitable institutions that helped to carry him through the long months of unemployment and to prepare him for the Jewish holidays.[4] But charity was obviously not the solution to chronic poverty, and most observers agreed that, for a variety of reasons, the Jewish artisan class was in a state of inexorable decline. For one thing, there were simply too many Jewish artisans. One economist pointed out that there were enough Jewish tailors 'to supply clothing for half the urban population of the Russian Empire'.[5] In every city of Belorussia–Lithuania the number of Jewish artisans was completely disproportionate to the total population.[6] Striking evidence of how numerous the Jewish artisan class was can be obtained by comparing the total with the

that the living quarters in Kovno were 'poor enough, but clean...' Nonetheless, he too stresses the frightful poverty he encountered in the major cities of the northwest region.

[1] Leonty Soloweitchik, *Un prolétariat méconnu, étude sur la situation sociale et économique des ouvriers juifs* (Brussels, 1898), 105.

[2] *Russkii evrei*, II, No. 31 (30 July 1880), 1214; Litvak, *Vos geven*, 121.

[3] I. Zelenskii (ed.), *Minskaia guberniia*, Vol. xv of *Materialy dlia geografii i statistiki Rossii, sobrannye ofitserami general'nago shtaba* (St Petersburg, 1864), 277; *Yudishes folks-blat*, No. 22 (3 June 1882), 338; *Nedel'naia khronika 'Voskhoda'*, v, No. 9 (2 March 1886), 259.

[4] See *Sbornik*, II, 221 ff. At the end of the century an estimated 18·8% of all Russian Jewish families celebrated the holiday of Passover with the aid of charity; the breakdown being higher for the Belorussian–Lithuanian provinces. In Vilna 37·7% of the Jewish population received charity.

[5] G. B. Sliozberg, *Pravovoe i ekonomicheskoe polozhenie evreev v Rossii* (St Petersburg, 1907), 17.

[6] *Nedel'naia khronika 'Voskhoda'*, VI, No. 40 (4 October 1887), 1101–2; *Razsvet*, I, No. 4 (4 October 1879), 1340.

number of artisans in provinces outside the Pale. Mogilev had over seven times as many tailors as neighbouring Smolensk; Vitebsk over four times as many as nearby Pskov.[1]

Moreover, poor workmanship by the Jewish artisans, their failure to mechanize and their continued use of primitive tools, made it difficult for them to compete either with the factories that were then emerging or with the handcraft industry of the peasants. The Jewish shops are described as being 'narrow, dirty, and dark' places with no ventilation, where workers labored in the damp, foul air.[2] Almost all the work was done by hand, and though some of the artisans were noted for their skills, the majority turned out cheap, crudely made products. In fact, one observer wrote that 'Jewish work' had become a synonym for bad work. In Vilna for example, with the exception of a few skilled tailors and engravers, the craftsmen produced grossly inferior work.[3]

Consequently, Jewish artisans were in constant danger of being ruined. The study of the Vilna carpenters, referred to above, concluded that competition from both the factory and the peasant would eventually doom the traditional artisan in that craft.[4] A similar dilemma confronted the locksmiths of Bialystok and the shoemakers of Vilna.[5] Although the backward state of industrial development in Belorussia–Lithuania had granted these artisans a certain respite, the future appeared very bleak. Realizing how desperate their economic situation was, many Jewish artisans felt there was no choice but to emigrate to Western Europe or the United States. Reports from Kovno and from Bobruisk in the 1890s spoke of Jewish workers 'emigrating in great numbers to America'.[6] Hence the artisan's dream of becoming an independent master had been replaced by a desire to start life anew in more congenial and hopeful surroundings.

[1] See the table in Margolis, *Geshikhte*, 42–3.

[2] *Der minsker arbeter*, No. 2 (January 1901), 6; *Der Klassen-kampf*, No. 5 (July 1901), 9.

[3] Korev (ed.), *Vilenskaia guberniia*, 411–12. For similar comments see *Sbornik*, I, 210 ff.; Kastelianskii, 'Mebel'noe-stoliarno proizvodstvo', 114 ff.; Khoroshch, *Voskhod*, xx, No. 6 (June 1901), 46.

[4] Kastelianskii, 'Mebel'noe-stoliarno proizvodstvo', 6 ff.

[5] Khoroshch, *Voskhod*, xx, No. 6 (June 1901), 46; *Der idisher arbeter*, No. 1[1896], 33; *Sbornik*, I, 246.

[6] *Voskhod*, xi, No. 7 (16 February 1892), 184; *ibid.*, No. 2 (13 January 1891), 52.

Emigration, however, was not the only solution proposed to combat the economic decline of the Jewish artisan class. Some publicists urged the Russian government to promote vocational education and credit societies; others demanded that Jewish artisans be allowed to settle in the interior of the Empire, where they might find new markets for their goods; another group advised artisans to establish new self-help associations, or to found artels.[1] Representatives of Jewish Marxism, on the other hand, advanced the idea that the problem could be solved by transforming the Jewish artisan class into a factory proletariat like that in the West. 'We are convinced', stated the Vilna socialist Gozhanskii in the early 1890s, 'that almost the entire class of artisans will eventually become factory workers.'[2] Thus inevitable economic development would halt the deterioration of the Jewish artisan class.

This was an attractive solution, especially to Marxists interested in organizing a labor movement. But for Jews to become factory workers factories would have to be built, and Jewish labor employed. As far as the first point is concerned, the provinces of Belorussia–Lithuania remained among the most backward in an Empire which was scarcely an industrial giant. As late as 1913, 45·3 per cent of all Belorussian laborers worked in establishments

---

[1] The leading adherent of the idea that the removal of the Pale would solve the problem of Jewish poverty was I. G. Orshanskii, *Evrei v Rossii*, 154 ff. The same view was advanced by Sliozberg, *Pravovoe i ekonomicheskoe polozhenie*, 123 ff., and by I. Bliokh, *Sravnenie material'nago byta i nravstvennago sostoianiia naseleniia v cherte osedlosti i vne eia* (St Petersburg, 1891), 304 ff. However, when a law passed in 1865 specifically permitted Jewish artisans to settle outside the Pale, only a small minority took advantage of the opportunity. Among the reasons for this surprisingly weak response was the fear that because of strict police supervision, the newly settled artisans were liable at any time to be sent back to their former homes. See I. G. Orshanskii, *Russkoe zakonodatel'stvo o evreiakh* (St Petersburg, 1877), 350 ff.; Sliozberg, *Pravovoe i ekonomicheskoe polozhenie*, 87 ff. Brutskus, 'Ocherk', estimates that during 1865–95 only 5% of all Jewish artisans left the Pale for the interior (33 ff.). An article in the Hebrew newspaper *Ha-Magid*, No. 49, 22 December 1869, suggested that special societies be created to help evacuate Jewish artisans from Russia, 'for after a large number of artisans are sent to other countries' competition will decrease. Wolf Mendlin, in his essays *Ba-me nevashaya, 4 ma'amarim be-she'elat ha-matsav ha-homri shel yehuday rossia* (St Petersburg, 1883), urged Jewish artisans to found self-help societies; while an article in *Voskhod*, xxi, No. 4 (24 January 1902), 16–18, suggested the use of artels. A similar position was taken by the author of an article in *Der yud*, No. 8 (April 1899), and in a series of articles entitled 'Tayere brider, bale melokhes un arbayters', which appeared in *Yudishes folksblat*, Nos. 31, 36, 38, 40–1, 43, 48, 49 (1882).

[2] Gozhanskii, 'A briv tsu di agitatorn', 627. Similar hopes were expressed in *Russkii evrei*, v, No. 35 (13 September 1883).

that employed fifty men or less, only 10 per cent in establishments hiring fifty to one hundred men. Further, the value of the yearly industrial production in the region was only six rubles per person; in Russia as a whole the average was thirty rubles.[1] Yet there were factories in the region, and more were being built. The key point is that those factory owners who prospered in Belorussia–Lithuania were extremely reluctant to hire Jews. Curiously, this held true not only for the Christian employers, who traditionally did not hire Jews, but for Jewish factory owners as well. The circumstances which prompted this attitude can best be illustrated by analyzing the situation in the one major industrial region of the northwest, the textile industry of Bialystok.

In the course of the nineteenth century, particularly during the Russo-Turkish war of 1877, Bialystok and its surrounding towns emerged as a textile center second in importance in western Russia only to Lodz, the 'Polish Manchester'. In both cities the industrial pioneers were foreigners, chiefly Germans, but Jewish capital and labor also played a significant role. According to one estimate, by the end of the nineteenth century, Jews owned 299 textile factories in and around Bialystok, and in Bialystok alone there were about 2,000–3,000 Jewish weavers.[2]

---

[1] I. I. Saladkov, *Sotsial'no-ekonomicheskoe polozhenie Belorusii do velikoi oktiabr'skoi sotsialisticheskoi revoliutsii* (Minsk, 1957), 17, 22. (The author includes the provinces of Vilna, Vitebsk, Minsk, Mogilev, and Grodno as parts of Belorussia.) See also Dovnar-Zapolskii, *Narodnoe khoziaistvo Belorussii*, 6. Detailed information on the factories of Belorussia–Lithuania in the early nineteenth century is available in *Belorussiia v epokhu feodalizma* (Minsk, 1961), III, 126 ff., 338 ff. For the situation at the end of the century see the tables in *Dokumenty i materialy po istorii Belorussii (1900–17 gg.)* (Minsk, 1953), III, 31 ff. For a comparison of Belorussia with other areas in the Empire, see also A. V. Pogozhev, *Uchet chislennosti i sostava rabochikh v Rossii* (St Petersburg, 1906), Table 4.

[2] On the rise of the Bialystok textile industry and the role played by Jews see A. S. Hershberg, *Pinkes bialystok* (New York, 1950), II, 11 ff.; A. Kotik, 'Proshloe i nastoiashchee belostotskoi evreiskoi tkatsoi promyshlennosti', *Teoreticheskie i prakticheskie voprosy evreiskoi zhizni*, No. 2–3 (St Petersburg, 1909), 118 ff.; Stanisław Kalabiński, 'Początki ruchu robotniczego w Białostockim okręgu przemysłowym w latach 1870–87', *Rocznik Białostocki* (Bialystok, 1961), II, 144 ff. On the number of Jewish-owned factories see *Sbornik*, II, 169, and 182, for the estimated number of weavers quoted above; according to 'Der leben un kampf', *Der idisher arbeter*, No. 10 (1900), 59, 3,000 Jewish workers were employed in one or another branch of the textile industry, and *Der bialystoker arbeter*, No. 3 (December 1900), 3, estimates the number of Jewish weavers in the city as 2,000. On the early history of Jewish weavers in the Belorussia–Lithuania area see A. Yuditsky, *Yidishe burzhvasie un yidisher proletariat in ershter helft XIX y"h* (n.d., n.p.), 48 ff.

The Polish socialist Feliks Kon, who visited Bialystok in the early 1880s, was amazed to find Jewish factory workers there. 'In Poland at that time there were Jewish artisans—journeymen,' he remarked, 'but Jewish proletarians were not heard of...Here in Bialystok there were hundreds of them in the textile factories...'[1] Other observers, too, were struck by this unusual Jewish working class. Subbotin compared the workers' living standards and wages with those in other cities and concluded that: 'With regard to the state of its Jewish population of 40,000, this city represents a kind of oasis, a bright spot in the gloomy setting of the Jewish Pale as a whole.'[2]

Nonetheless, by the late nineteenth century, it was clear that the future of the Jewish proletariat in Bialystok was no more promising than that of the artisan masses elsewhere in the Pale. The average Jewish weaver did not profit by the industrial revolution, which had made Bialystok a boom town, for he was not employed in the large, mechanized factories, but merely in the smaller factories and shops. Either that or he worked at home. The largest Jewish-owned factory that was willing to hire Jewish labor had only 67 looms. The great majority of Jewish weavers— 1,600—worked for middlemen who were known as 'loynketniks'; the latter received looms and raw materials from the factory owners and put the weavers to work in small shops. Particularly during the busy season, factory owners found this arrangement profitable, for the 'loynketnik' was able to exploit the workers far more than was possible in the factories.[3]

Working conditions in the average Jewish-owned weaving factory were deplorable. One observer commented: 'In a narrow room, old and young weavers labor at clumsy wooden looms. The faces of the older ones with their long, dirty, disheveled

[1] Kon, *Za piat'desiat let*, I, 58.

[2] Subbotin, *V cherte*, II, 64.

[3] The statistics are from 'Der leben un kampf', *Der idisher arbeter*, No. 10 (1900), 59. On the origins of the 'loynketnik' system see 'Tsu dem internatsionaln kongress fun veber un shpiner in berlin (der berikht fun bialystoker sotsialdemokratishn komitet fun dem algemaynen idishen arbayter-bund in russland un poylen)', *ibid.*, 23 ff.; the same institution prevailed in Lodz; see *Der frayhayts-glok*, No. 2 (April 1902), 1 ff.; Y. Sh. Herts, *Di geshikhte fun bund in lodz* (New York, 1958), 95 ff.; Ireneusz Ihnatowicz, *Przemysł łódzki w latach 1860–1900* (Warsaw-Wrocław-Cracow, 1965), 74–5.

beards, are exhausted, thin, completely pallid...Involuntarily, completely machine-like their heads and torsos move, keeping pace with the movements of the loom. So pass hours, days, years.' 'The factory buildings are small and there is no ventilation,' another report reads, '...there are always clouds of dust and the lighting is bad. Despite all the laws, medical facilities for the workers are in a very sad state.'[1] Conditions were even worse in the 'loynketnik' shops, where lower wages were paid for a working day that averaged from sixteen to eighteen hours, and where the absence of factory inspectors allowed the employers to treat their workers more arbitrarily than they might in the factories.[2]

By contrast, the larger, mechanized factories, where Jews were usually not employed, were light and clean if far from ideal, and the workers there impressed one observer as being far healthier and more robust than the Jewish factory hands.[3] Unable to find work in the mechanized factories, which were rapidly making the methods of hand weaving obsolete, the Jewish weaver in Bialystok was in a sorry plight. By the end of the century, it was obvious that hand looms were no longer profitable; yet, as a socialist journal commented: 'Here in Bialystok only Christians work at the mechanized factories. Jews have no entry there...we do only hand weaving.'[4] Similarly, there were no Jewish spinners in the city because by the 1890s spinning had become completely mechanized.

Why were Jews not employed at the mechanized factories? Why was it the case that, almost invariably, the transition from

[1] Khoroshch, *Voskhod*, xx, No. 3 (March 1901), 55; the factory he describes typically employed ten weavers and six girl assistants; 'Tsu dem internatsionaln kongress', 23.
[2] During the Russo-Turkish War, the boom years in the textile industry, a factory weaver earned as much as 15–20 rubles a week; in the early 1880s he could still earn 11 rubles a week. By 1900 wages in the factories had dropped to 6–8 rubles a week, and, in the 'loynketnik' shops, 4–6 rubles. During the frequent crises wages dropped as much as 100%. See *ibid.*, 24 ff.; Subbotin, *V cherte evreiskoi osedlosti*, II, 61; 'Der leben un kampf', *Der idisher arbeter*, No. 10 (1900), 60; *Di arbayter shtime*, No. 1 (23 July 1897), 1; *Der bialystoker arbeter*, No. 1 (April 1899), 33; P. An-man, pseud. (Pavel Rozental), 'Bialystoker period in lebn fun ts. k. fun bund 1900–2', *Royter pinkes* (1921), I, 46. For a comparative scale of wages for Jewish and Russian weavers see Cherniovsky, *Der yidisher arbeter*, 109.
[3] Khoroshch, *Voskhod*, xx, No. 3 (March 1901), 64; see also Subbotin, *V cherte*, II, 61.
[4] 'Der dampf-shtul un der idisher arbeter', *Der bialystoker arbeter*, No. 5 (May 1901), 3.

hand to power looms entailed a shift in the ethnic composition of the work force?[1]

The explanation that is most often given for this phenomenon involves the problem of the 'Sabbath rest'. Since the Jewish worker generally refused to work on Saturday and the Christian took his day off on Sunday, were both to work together in a mechanized factory, the power looms would remain idle two days out of the week. This being unprofitable, factory owners felt it was out of the question to hire both ethnic groups. 'Everyone knows', reads a report in a Jewish journal, 'how difficult it is for a Jewish weaver to be hired by a Jewish factory owner...he is immediately asked: "And what about Saturday?" He stands there like a dead one and goes away miserable.'[2] The socialist press declared unequivocally that this was the main reason why Jews were not hired in the big industrialized textile factories.[3]

Yet there is some doubt whether the 'Sabbath rest' was that decisive an issue. Khoroshch, for example, states that 'Many weavers told me that if they were hired in the mechanized factories they would work on Saturday'.[4] Moreover, Jewish factory-owners must have realized there was an obvious solution: to hire only Jewish workers and close the plants on Saturday. This solution was adopted in Pinsk (an unusual city in that its Jewish proletariat was employed in the mechanized factories); however, the absence of a sizeable contingent of Christian workers

[1] *Ibid.* See also *Der fraynd*, No. 138 (24 June 1903), 4; Kotik, 'Proshloe', 121; A. Ziskind, 'Fun bialystoker arbeterleben; veber oif mekhanishe shtulen', *Fragen fun leben zamlbukh*, No. 2–3 (St Petersburg, 1912), 113. For a contemporary's description of this process see Mordechai Fogorelsky, 'Zikhroynes fun a bialystoker "esesovets"', *Bialystoker shtime*, XXI, No. 207 (June 1941).

[2] *Der fraynd*, No. 138 (24 June 1903).

[3] 'Der leben un kampf', *Der idisher arbeter*, No. 10 (1900), 59; see also *Sbornik*, II, 185. *Nedel'naia khronika 'Voskhoda'*, V, No. 34 (24 August 1886), 913, comments that the 'religiousness of the Jewish masses, which does not permit them to work on Saturday', largely explains why Jewish weavers were unable to work in the mechanized factories. The 'Sabbath rest' was a problem not only in Bialystok, but in other cities as well—especially in Lodz. There, according to one observer, Jews were not hired because they 'want to work only on Sunday and not on Saturday; the factory owners themselves regard Sunday as the rest day'. S. R. Landau, *Unter jüdischen Proletariern* (Vienna, 1898), 76.

[4] Khoroshch, *Voskhod*, XX, No. 4 (April 1901), 148. For evidence that some Jewish weavers in Bialystok did work on Saturdays, see *Sbornik*, II, 181.

in that city may well have prompted this decision.[1] Indeed, what seems to have been crucial was not the issue of the 'Sabbath rest', but that, for other reasons, employers preferred to hire non-Jews. Among these was the Jews' lack of training in technical skills, which led many factory owners to believe Jewish weavers would not be able to operate the mechanized looms.[2] The socialists in Bialystok concluded that unless there were qualified Jewish masters to supervise work in the modern factories, the Jews had little chance of being hired as power-loom weavers. Another reason was that the non-Jewish (mostly Polish) workers in Bialystok, who regarded employment in the mechanized factories as their monopoly, resisted any attempt on the part of Jewish workmen to encroach upon their 'rights'. Fierce battles broke out between Jewish and Polish workers when in 1903 a factory owner decided to retain some Jewish workers after the transition from hand to power looms.[3] It also appears that Jewish industrialists refused to hire Jews because they felt that proper employer-employee relationships were impossible when both were of the Jewish faith.[4] The following selection from the memoirs of Yitskhak Nisenboim confirms this point. Present at a series of discussions aimed at persuading Jewish factory owners to hire their co-religionists, the author recalls that:

They refused, citing various excuses, both economic and political. The talks got nowhere. One of the 'Jewish' excuses especially annoyed me. 'I have contact with the non-Jewish worker only in my factory,' one owner said, 'when he leaves the factory I have nothing more to do with him and he has nothing to do with me. I don't know what goes on in his home, and it doesn't occur to him to invite me to a family celebration. But it is different with a Jewish worker. If his wife gives birth to a son he invites me to be the child's godfather, and how can I refuse to do such a good deed? And if I am the child's godfather, I am

---

[1] See B. Hofman (ed.), *Toyzent yor pinsk* (New York, 1941), 90 ff.; Khoroshch, *Voskhod*, xx, No. 10 (October 1901), 25 ff. In Horodok, a small town adjacent to Bialystok, Jews and Christians were employed together in mechanized factories; Koroshch, *Voskhod*, xx, No. 8 (August 1901), 37 ff., mentions only that the problems of 'Sabbath rest' were causing the Horodok factory owners considerable trouble.
[2] *Sbornik*, II, 187.
[3] 'Der dampf-shtul', *Der bialystoker arbeter*, No. 5 (May 1901), 6. Fogorelsky, *Zikhroynes*.
[4] Kotik, 'Proshloe', 121.

obliged to take an interest in him. If the worker comes in late, he has an excuse; the child—my child is sick, his wife—the mother of my child, is sick, and so on. Why should I have such troubles?'[1]

Finally, and this is perhaps the most important reason, most employers preferred Christian to Jewish workers because the former proved to be more reliable. The Jewish strike movement in the Pale will be discussed in a later chapter; for the present we will note merely that the movement struck terror in the hearts of the employers, who reacted in a predictable way. In Smorgon, for instance, a Jewish factory owner explained his policy of hiring Christians rather than Jews as follows: 'The Jews are good workers, but they are capable of organizing revolts...against the employer, the regime, and the Tsar himself.' Probably for much the same reason a Jewish factory owner in Dvinsk circulated an announcement to the effect that 'Christian workers are needed at Mister Lur'e's factory...'[2] Socialist and non-socialist observers alike agreed that the Bialystok employers' fear of the Jewish workers' revolutionary potential led them to prefer the relative (though by no means absolute) stability of the non-Jewish labor force.[3]

Given these circumstances, the future of the Jewish weavers in Bialystok seemed pretty bleak by the end of the century. This was summed up in a remark made to Khoroshch by an acquaintance: 'A few years will pass and there won't be any more Jewish weavers in Bialystok.' Much the same despair was voiced by another

[1] Nisenboim, *Alay heldi* (Warsaw, 1929), 130–1. Leschinsky, in his interesting study *Der idisher arbeter (in rusland)* (Vilna, 1906), argues that above all the factory owner wanted a homogeneous work force, and for this reason preferred not to hire both Jewish and Christian workers; see especially 96 ff.

[2] Iv. Peskovoi, 'V smorgoni (vospomaniia rabochego proshlom)', *Krasnaia letopis'*, No. 8 (1923), 81; *Nedel'naia khronika 'Voskhoda'*, xviii, No. 30 (25 July 1899), 925.

[3] Khoroshch, *Voskhod*, xx, No. 4 (April 1901), 151; Kotik, 'Proshloe', 121; 'Der dampf-shtul', *Der bialystoker arbeter*, No. 5 (May 1901), 7. The owners, who were accused of reprehensible behavior toward their fellow Jews, the workers, claimed that Russian law prohibited opening the factories on Sunday. There is no evidence, however, that this law was ever implemented. See Landau, *Unter jüdischen Proletariern*, 41 ff., who comments that, in Czestochowa, '...the factory inspectors are humane men who interpret the law mildly'; see also comments in the Zionist publication *Der jüdischer Arbeiter*, No. 1 (1 August 1898), 9. It is interesting to note that in Lodz Zionists constructed a special mechanized factory for Jewish weavers; see *Di arbayter shtime*, No. 22 (March 1901), 8 ff.

observer who predicted that, in the near future, people would say: 'Ah, you see! Bialystok, a Jewish city, Jewish factory owners, but not a single Jewish worker!'[1] As was true for the Jewish artisan, the only viable alternative for the weavers appeared to be emigration; according to a report from Bialystok many of them did precisely that.[2]

Jewish workers in the other major cities as well (Pinsk being the one exception) were not accepted in the large factories; either the Jewish capitalists proved unable or unwilling to modernize and enlarge their plants, or, if they did, were loath to employ Jewish labor. Almost invariably, the larger and more modernized the factory, the fewer the number of Jewish workers employed.[3] This was also true of the more industrialized areas of southern Russia, where Jews failed to gain a foothold in the large factories and remained, as in Belorussia–Lithuania, a proletariat of small shops and unmechanized plants.[4]

If Jewish workers were excluded from the mechanized factories, they did enter certain new industries in Belorussia–Lithuania, and new types of Jewish workers took their place alongside the traditional craftsmen. In the 1880s, for example, hundreds of young Jewish women were drawn into hosiery manufacture, which was concentrated in Vilna Province. These women worked mainly at home, and soon came under the control of middlemen ('Commissioners') who supplied them with raw materials and the machines. At first wages were extremely high but inevitably, with the influx of workers, the wage rate was reduced to that of the typical artisan.[5]

---

[1] Khoroshch, *Voskhod*, xx, No. 7 (July 1901), 33; *Der fraynd*, No. 138 (24 June 1903).
[2] *Sbornik*, II, 189.   [3] Leschinsky, *Der idisher arbeter*, 31.
[4] In general, Jewish factory owners lagged behind their Christian counterparts in modernization. This is illustrated by a list of major factories in Minsk Province in the 1860s: the mechanized factories were all owned by Christians; Jewish-owned firms invariably were smaller and, from the standpoint of technology, extremely primitive. See Zelenskii (ed.), *Minskaia Gubernaia*, 235 ff. Of course, there were exceptions: Israel Poznansky, who owned one of the largest textile plants in Lodz, was a tycoon in industry, but he did not employ Jews. See *Der jüdischer Arbeiter*, No. 1 (1 August 1898), 9; 'Pis'mo rabochago Tsibul'skago', in *Otchet I. I. Ianzhula po izsledovaniiu fabrichnozavodskoi promyshlennosti v Tsarstve Polskom* (St Petersburg, 1888), 135–6; Ihnatowicz, *Przemysł Łódzki*, 182.
[5] See *Sbornik*, I, 243 ff.; *Nedel'naia khronika 'Voskhoda'*, IV, No. 50 (15 December 1885), 1374 ff.; 'Evreiskiia chulochnitsy', in *Voskhod*, xx, No. 38 (14 June 1901), 5–7; M. R.,

Toward the end of the century a number of Jewish-owned tanneries, some of which employed as many as fifty men, were established in Belorussia–Lithuania. Smorgon, a small city in Vilna Province, had twenty-two tanneries and a contingent of 600 tanners, 400 of whom were Jews. These workers formed a kind of intermediate category, certainly one that combined the disadvantages of both the artisan and the factory worker: like the latter, the tanners were not able to rise above their status as wage-earners, while their working conditions and techniques were as primitive as those that characterized the artisans' shops. Although they were paid somewhat higher wages than the artisans, this was offset by the occupational hazards in their field. According to one source, a tanner had a life expectancy of forty years and many of them became invalids after ten or fifteen years.[1]

The rise of the tanning industry was paralleled by that of bristle-making; the latter industry, which developed in small towns within the provinces of Vitebsk, Grodno, Mogilev, and Suvalki, was monopolized by Jews. While the bristle-making plants, too, were relatively large, conditions were extremely primitive, and the work hazardous. In Belorussia–Lithuania there were over 500 Jewish bristle-workers; along with the tanners, they were destined to play an extraordinary role in the labor movement.[2]

The only factories of any size to employ Jewish labor were those which produced cigarettes and matches. Located in almost

'Chulochno-viazal'nyi promysel' v gorode Vil'ne', *Voskhod*, XXI, No. 46 (14 November 1902), 4–7. Litvak, *Vos Geven*, 57 ff., also discusses the stocking-makers of Vilna.

[1] On the rise of the tanning industry in Belorussia–Lithuania, see Cherniovsky, *Der yidisher arbeter*, 32 ff. *Sbornik*, II, 102, lists a total of 2,403 Jewish tanners. Jewish-owned tanneries employed both Jewish and Christian labor, the former working in the less dangerous 'dry' division, the latter in the 'wet' division. This mixed labor force, as we shall see, created serious problems for the labor organizers. For descriptions of the tanners' working conditions see 'Di lage fun di oshmianer un smargoner arbayter un zayr shtrayt', *Der idisher arbeter*, No. 2–3 (February 1897), 28–32; and No. 4–5 (November 1897), 32 ff.; Khoroshch, *Voskhod*, XX, No. 8 (August 1901), 46 ff.; Abraham Ain, 'Swislocz: Portrait of a Jewish Community in Eastern Europe', *YIVO Annual of Social Science*, IV (1949), 101 ff.; *Voskhod*, XIX, No. 66 (21 August 1900), 11.

[2] On the number of bristle workers see *Sbornik*, II, 109; on working conditions and methods of production see Ben-Uziel, 'In baginen fun der bershter-arbet ba yidn in rusland', *Virtshaft un leben*, I, No. 1 (July 1928), 54 ff.; *Mezrich zamlbukh* (Buenos Aires, 1952), 163 ff., 219 ff.; *Der idisher arbeter*, No. 1 [1896], 41–55. The best source on the conditions of the bristle-workers is the organ of their union, *Der veker*, published during 1898–1903.

every major city in Belorsussia–Lithuania, these factories were owned mostly by Jews and staffed almost entirely by Jewish labor. Shereshevsky's cigarette factory in Grodno, the second largest in the Empire, employed more than a thousand workers, and if the other factories were not as large, they managed to dwarf the rest of the establishments where Jewish labor was employed.[1]

In many respects these cigarette factories, which were non-mechanized, resembled enormous workshops; hand work of inferior technique was performed by a labor force that consisted mostly of women and children. Six-year-old boys were among the employees at the local cigarette factory in Borisov, while ten-year-old girls could be found working in a Mozir plant.[2] Wages were paid for piece work and were considerably lower than those received by the average artisan. Women and children were considered fair game for the most shocking exploitation. A report from Minsk describes the deplorable conditions at several of the local cigarette-wrapper factories where the majority of the workers were young children: 'For the most difficult and debilitating work the young laborer receives thirty to fifty kopeks a week... The unfortunate child-laborers are thoroughly exhausted by their work at the...factories, where they remain from sixteen to eighteen hours at a stretch.'[3] The older girls did not fare much better; they averaged only two rubles a week for their work and suffered from various lung diseases caused by the constant inhalation of nicotine. Shmaryahu Levin, the well-known Zionist, was moved to pity when he saw these '...half-

---

[1] Shereshevsky's plant was founded in 1862; by 1881 it employed 100 workers, by 1885, 885, and by the turn of the century, more than 1,000. See Yuditsky, *Yidishe burzhvasie*, 79; *Vilenskii fabrichnyi okrug-otchet za 1885 g. fabrichnago inspektora okruga G. I. Gorodorka* (St Petersburg, 1886), 561; *Sbornik*, II, 77. Among the other large factories were Janovsky's cigarette factory in Bialystok (370 employees) and Edelshtein's cigarette factory in Vilna (over 200 employees). In Dvinsk Zaks' match factory employed 800 workers (Berman, *In loif fun yorn*, 3). In sum (*Sbornik*, II, 75) there were 37 Jewish-owned cigarette factories in Belorussia–Lithuania which employed a total of 3,055 workers.

[2] *Sbornik*, II, 77, states that 70% of all employees in Jewish-owned cigarette factories in the Pale were women and children. On Borisov and Mozir (Minsk Province) see *Posledniia izvestiia*, No. 162 (13 January 1904); No. 186 (9 July 1904).

[3] Quoted from a report in *Minskii golos* in Saladkov, *Sotsial'no-ekonomicheskoe polozhenie*, 26. See also the description in *Vilenskii fabrichnyi*, 55.

grown girls who poured out evenings from the factory of Shereshevsky, their lungs filled with tobacco dust'.[1]

The cigarette and match factory workers comprised the only real 'factory proletariat' among the Jewish population of Belorussia–Lithuania: three thousand employees, however, scarcely represented the formidable power envisioned by the Marxists when they predicted the transformation of the Russian Jewish working class into a factory proletariat. In fact, the Jewish proletariat remained a proletariat of small shops and declining fortunes. Like most proletariats in the late nineteenth century, the Jewish working class was poverty-stricken, diseased, and slumridden. Naturally, this provided an incentive to fight for better economic conditions; yet unlike other proletariats, the Jewish working class had no chance to enter the large, modern factories, where meaningful concessions might be won from reluctant, but realistic, employers. Hence, while the conditions of their life might encourage the Jewish workers to fight, their gains were likely to be limited by social and economic factors over which they themselves had scarcely any control.

[1] Shmaryahu Levin, *The Arena*, trans. Maurice Samuel (New York, 1932), 168. See also Gozhanskii, 'Erinerungen fun a papirosn makherke', written in the 1890s in Vilna and published in *Unzer tsayt*, No. 7 (July 1928), 89–95; No. 8–9 (September–October 1928), 110–26; No. 10 (December 1928), 85–92. See especially No. 10, 87 ff. Other descriptions are available in *Der idisher arbeter*, No. 4–5 (November 1897), 23 ff.; *Di arbayter shtime*, No. 28 (August 1902), 8; and No. 16 (March 1900), 5; Landau, *Unter jüdischen Proletariern*, 56 ff. The rape of the sixteen-year-old girl by a master at a cigarette factory in Dvinsk is described in *Posledniia izvestiia*, No. 82 (21 August 1902).

CHAPTER 2

The Socialists Confront the Workers

> Like a faithful mother, knowledge will guide us peacefully over the sea of tears and pain to the land of life.
>
> A Vilna worker, 1892

The Jewish community of late nineteenth century Russia was no stranger to class conflict. Long before the period of organized revolt, Jewish workers had petitioned and even rioted against what they considered to be arbitrary and discriminatory rule by the 'kahal', the community's administrative organ. In 1843, for example, the artisans of Dubrovno declared that they were being 'illegally oppressed and ruined' by the 'kahal's' taxation system. After 1827, when the 'kahal' had been given the unwanted responsibility of selecting recruits for the Tsar's army, bitter complaints were raised among the Jewish workers that the poor were being drafted instead of the rich. 'It's a good deed to hand over the simple people,' a folksong of the period went, 'shoemakers, tailors are good-for-nothings.' Riots broke out in several towns, and petitions inveighed against the practice of recruiting one-half of the men from among artisans when, according to the latter's estimate, one-fifth would have been a just proportion.[1]

Hunger riots also were not infrequent. In 1886, more than two hundred poverty-stricken artisans in Vitebsk threatened violence unless they were given work or assistance from charity. 'Even if

---

[1] The petition is published in Margolis, *Geshikhte*, 341 ff.; see 347 ff. for a similar petition from Minsk. The folksong is published in Saul M. Ginsburg and P. S. Marek, *Evreiskiia narodnyia pesni v Rossii* (St Petersburg, 1901), 51–2. See also 42 ff. Yet another petition, from Dubno, is published in Margolis, *Yidishe folksmasn in kamf kegn zayre unterdriker* (Moscow, 1940), 119 ff. On the social crisis engendered within Russian Jewry by the so-called 'Rekrutshchina', during which young Jewish boys were drafted into the army and often forced to forsake their faith, *ibid.*, 56 ff., 119 ff.; A. I. Paperna, 'Iz nikolaevskoi epokhi, vospominaniia', *Perezhitoe*, II (1910), 44; Margolis, *Geshikhte*, 326 ff.

you arrest us', they said, 'we won't lose anything; then at least we will be in warm rooms and be given bread, which we lack now.'[1]

It is likely that there were more disputes between employers and workers than the limited source material reveals. We know of a few early strikes in Vilna, the first in a cigarette factory in 1871, and of scattered strike activity in other cities.[2] It is clear, however, that Bialystok was the chief center of agitation during the 'prehistory' of the Jewish labor movement. Being the most industrialized city in Belorussia–Lithuania, Bialystok had a labor force consisting of thousands of Germans, Poles and Jews who were among the first in Russia to conduct major strikes. 'In those quiet, still times,' a socialist journal boasted, 'when Jewish workers throughout Russia were sound asleep, dreaming of the Messiah and the world to come, we Bialystok workers were already waging economic battles, beating up the industrialists, breaking looms, striking, struggling.'[3] As early as 1882 Jewish weavers staged a strike which was exceptionally well organized for that period. Supported by funds collected both by other Jewish workers and by German weavers, the workers not only achieved their end, but, according to one expert, theirs was the first strike in Russia 'that demonstrated the existence of a trade union organization among the workers'.[4]

---

[1] *Nedel'naia khronika 'Voskhoda'*, XI, No. 9 (2 March 1886), 259–60. In 1890, workers in Horoditsh threatened reprisals unless aid was forthcoming, saying 'they would be compelled to take by force the goods of those upon whom fortune has bestowed wealth'. (Margolis, *Yidishe folksmasn*, 85.) For other examples, *ibid.*, 80 ff., and *Yudishes folks-blat*, No. 10 (5 March 1886), 153.

[2] On the Vilna strike of 1871 see E. A. Korol'chuk, *Rabochee dvizhenie semidesiatykh godov* (Moscow, 1934), 42–3. Another strike at the same factory that occurred four years later is described by Liebermann in *Vpered*, No. 23 (15 December 1875), 726. On the early strike movement in general see Menes, 'Di yidishe arbeter-bavegung in rusland fun onhayb 70er bizn sof 90er yorn', *Historishe shriftn*, III, 9 ff.; Herts *et al.*, *Di geshikhte fun bund* (New York, 1960), I, 63 ff.

[3] *Der bialystoker arbayter*, No. 1 (April 1899), 16. For an example of Jewish weavers destroying their looms see *Der bund*, No. 5 (October 1904), 20, which describes the breaking of looms in Zdunska-Wola, a town near Lodz.

[4] Quoted from S. N. Prokopovich, *K rabochemu voprosu v Rossii* (St Petersburg, 1905), in V. Sviatlovskii, *Professional'noe dvizhenie v Rossii* (St Petersburg, 1907), 12. For descriptions of the strike, *ibid.*; Kalabiński, 'Początki', 166 ff. (from a correspondence in *Robotnik*, No. 4 [1883]); *Nedel'naia khronika 'Voskhoda'*, II, No. 2 (16 January 1883), 35–6. For material on an earlier unsuccessful strike of Jewish weavers in nearby Ruzhany see *Razsvet*, No. 4 (4 October 1879), 1939.

The socialists confront the workers

Several years later Bialystok witnessed the first struggle between the weavers and their arch-enemies, the 'loynketniks'. One writer termed it a 'real revolution', and went on to describe the workers' remarkable solidarity: 'Jew or Christian, each of the weavers contributes two rubles a week, even more if necessary, to support those who are unemployed; they (the latter) are given 3–4 rubles a week...'[1]

It is not clear what role, if any, the socialist intellectuals played during the early years of the Bialystok movement; we know only that the city was the scene of socialist agitation in the 1870s and that by the early 1880s socialist propaganda had already begun to take hold among the Jewish weavers.[2] It may well be that the excellent organization the weavers achieved was their own doing, not the result of supervision from above. Nevertheless, the early Jewish strike movement was sporadic, and failed to develop either permanent organizational features or long-range goals. An organized labor movement (and the word 'organized' should be emphasized) developed only when Jewish socialists from among the intelligentsia had established contact with the proletariat.

The importance of the Jewish intelligentsia for the development of Russian Jewish political movements has already been noted. And it is scarcely surprising that many of these intellectuals should have been attracted to radical ideologies. A Russian Jew with a gymnasium certificate, or even a university degree, could not hope for a career in Russian academic or bureaucratic circles. Nor was it easy for him to enter other professions. A career in radical politics was open, however, and many Jews made this their opportunity. Moreover, if these intellectuals were no longer able to identify with the old Jewish culture, nor free to become assimilated into Russian life, they could at least identify with 'the people', the peasantry or the proletariat. And, obviously, Russian anti-semitism only heightened their desire to seek the total overthrow of the regime, and to substitute for it a society of justice and equality.[3] Thus a substantial number of Jews were active in various

[1] *Yudishes folks-blat*, No. 29 (16 July 1887), 466–7. See also Kalabiński, 'Początki', 186 ff.
[2] *Ibid.*, 164 ff., 172 ff.; Kon, *Za piet'desiat let*, I, 58.
[3] On the Russian Jewish radical intelligentsia see Mishkinsky, *Yesodot leumiim be-hithavutah shel tenuat ha-poalim ha-yehudit be-rusiah (mi-rashitah ve-ad 1901)*, unpublished Ph.D. dis-

phases of the Russian revolutionary movement: the 'going to the people' of the 1870s; the Social Revolutionary (SR) Party which continued the Russian Populist tradition in the twentieth century; above all, the Marxist movement, with its many converts among the Russian radicals in the 1880s and 1890s. And in Belorussia–Lithuania Jewish radical intellectuals were the medium through which the unorganized labor movement of Jewish workers in that region was transformed into a highly organized struggle.[1]

The generation of Jewish intellectuals which, in the 1880s and 1890s, undertook to spread socialist ideas among the workers of the Pale, presented no united ideological front. This was a period of transition in the history of Russian socialism, and in Belorussia–Lithuania, as elsewhere, some radicals remained faithful to the ideas of Populism while others converted to Plekhanov's version of Marxism. Eventually, the majority embraced the new creed, but when they first approached the workers it was with considerable ideological confusion.[2]

From the workers' standpoint this hardly mattered. Beginning with the 1870s, and continuing through the 1880s and 1890s, Jewish socialists of various tendencies—Marxists, Populists, and those who fit neither category—began to propagandize among the Jewish artisans. It is extremely important to note that these socialists were not interested in organizing a mass labor

sertation, The Hebrew University of Jerusalem, 1965; and Jonathan Frankel, *Socialism and Jewish Nationalism in Russia, 1892–1907*, unpublished Ph.D. dissertation, Cambridge University, 1961. Some excellent biographies of Russian and Polish Jewish revolutionaries are available; see Isaac Deutscher, *The Prophet Armed: Trotsky, 1879–1921* (London, 1954); Z. A. B. Zeman and W. B. Scharlau, *The Merchant of Revolution, The Life of Alexander Israel Helphand (Parvus), 1867–1924* (London, 1965); J. P. Nettl, *Rosa Luxemburg*, 2 vols. (London, 1966); Israel Getzler, *Martov* (Cambridge, 1967).

[1] For a thorough study of Jewish participation in the early Russian radical movement see Cherikover, 'Yidn revolutsionern in rusland in di 60er un 70er yorn', *Historishe shriftn*, III, 60–172.

[2] The socialists of Minsk and Vilna, for example, the two cities with the largest concentration of socialist intellectuals, were divided into the two camps of Populism and Marxism. See T. M. Kopel'zon, 'Evreiskoe rabochee dvizhenie kontsa 80-kh i nachala 90-kh godov', in Dimanshtein (ed.), *Revoliutsionnoe dvizhenie*, 68–9; Zhenie Hurvich, 'Di ershte propagandistishe krayzl', *Royte bleter*, 1 ff. The ideological eclecticism of the typical Jewish socialist in the 1880s can be seen from the career of Reuban Amsterdam, an activist from Vitebsk, who began as an advocate of the 'Enlightenment' movement, passed through several phases of Zionism, and finally became a non-Zionist Marxist. See Litvak, *Vos geven*, 105.

movement. Nothing, in fact, was further from their minds. Rather, they proposed to implement their program through the 'kruzhok', the circle, an institution that was to characterize the movement of the 1880s and 1890s, as it did in the Russian interior. The early circles, notably those in Vilna during the 1870s, were composed mainly of students; later, however, increasing numbers of intellectuals began to approach the local workers, forming circles of workers and intellectuals in the major cities of Belorussia–Lithuania. Naturally the Marxists were especially eager to influence members of the proletariat, but the Populists were hardly less active, and in Vilna it was they who took the initiative in founding circles of spat-makers, locksmiths, printers, and hosiery workers.[1]

The purpose of the circle, according to one of the Minsk socialists, was 'to create a worker-intelligentsia, which in the future would be able independently to carry on more extensive propaganda among the workers'. Gozhanskii, whose views on the future of the Jewish artisan class we have already cited, formulated his goals as follows: 'Small groups of class-conscious worker-revolutionaries must be founded, and when the revolutionary movement begins, these small groups are to become leaders.'[2] The goal, then, was to create a worker elite, and the job of that

---

[1] See L. Aksel'rod-Ortodoks, 'Iz moikh vospominanii', *Katorga i ssylka*, No. 2 (63), (1930), 32. On the circles in the 1870s see Nahum A. Bukhbinder, 'Iz istorii evreiskago sotsialisticheskago dvizheniia v 70-kh gg.', in V. Nevskii (ed.), *Istoriko-revoliutsionnyi sbornik* (1924), II, 37 ff. The Vilna circle headed by Aaron Liebermann in the mid-1870s is described by Cherikover, 'Der onhayb fun der yidisher sotsialistishe bavegung', *Historishe shriftn*, I, 470–532, the early history of the Minsk movement by Isak Gurvich, 'Pervye evreiskie rabochie kruzhki', *Byloe*, No. 6 (June 1907), 65 ff. See also Frumkin, 'Iz istorii revoliutsionnago dvizheniia sredi evreev v 1870-kh godakh', *Evreiskaia starina*, IV, No. 2 (April–June 1911), 221–48, and No. 4 (October–December 1911), 513–40. On the origins of the circles in other important cities of Belorussia-Lithuania see the following: Baynish Mikhalevich, *Zikhroynes fun a yudishen sotsialist* (Warsaw, 1921), I, 4 ff.; Il'ia Vilenskii, 'Sotsial-demokr. rabota v Vitebske v 90-kh godakh', *K dvadtsatpiatiletiiu pervogo s'ezda partii* (Moscow-Leningrad, 1923), 149 ff.; 'Gomel'skoe rabochee', in Agursky (ed.), *Di sotsialistishe literatur*, 365 ff.; and 'Der leben un kampf', *Der idisher arbeter*, No. 11 (1901), 45–7; Mendel Daytsh, 'Vegn mayn revolutsionere arbet', *Royte bleter*, 1; H. Shkliar, 'Onhayb fun der yidisher arbeterbavegung in kovne', *Lite*, II (Tel Aviv, 1965), 183 ff.; Aba Lev, 'Pervye shagi evreiskogo rabochego dvizheniia v g. Grodno', in Dimanshtein (ed.), *Revoliutsionnoe dvizhenie*, 264 ff.

[2] E. A. Gurvich, 'Evreiskoe rabochee', 38; Gozhanskii, 'Evreiskoe rabochee dvizhenie nachala 90-kh godov', in Dimanshtein (ed.), *Revolutsionnoe dvizhenie*, 83.

elite would be to lead the future struggle. It is important to stress here that by the term 'revolutionary movement' Gozhanskii and his colleagues had in mind a distinctly Russian movement. Though Belorussia–Lithuania was open to both Polish and Russian cultural influences, the local Jewish intelligentsia was attracted chiefly to the latter, and the radicals regarded themselves as the bearers both of Russian culture and of the Russian revolutionary tradition. 'Convinced and enthusiastic cosmopolitans' was how one participant in the Vilna movement described its leaders, but they were cosmopolitans who spoke Russian and who prized the rich heritage of Russian literature. Not without reason were they labeled 'russifiers' by the irate Polish socialists who were similarly eager to propagandize among the local working population.[1]

Certainly, none of these Jewish intellectuals was interested in founding a specifically Jewish movement. Yet, the circles they led were attended almost exclusively by Jewish workers. While this can be explained in part by the predominance of Jewish workers in the cities of Belorussia–Lithuania, it was also true that 'Russian reality' played a role. The fact is that in Russia Jews and non-Jews had difficulty in communicating, even on the subject of socialism. 'It is not clear to many', Gozhanskii acknowledged:

Why we began to work among Jewish laborers. Weren't there other workers in Vilna? Certainly, there were artisans...among the Poles, Lithuanians, and Belorussians. Why were we shut up in our own world? That, comrades, is impossible to understand if one fails to recall the nature of the Jewish ghetto. The nationalities were separated by an impenetrable wall; each lived its own life, and had no contact with the other.

[1] The quotation is from Aksel'rod-Ortodoks, 'Iz moikh vospominanii', 37. Kopel'zon, 'Evreiskoe rabochee', 71, adds that 'Our goal was the formation of cadres for the Russian revolutionary movement...' Speaking for the Vilna Jewish socialists, Martov notes that 'We gravitated toward St Petersburg and Moscow, they [i.e., the Polish socialists] toward Warsaw'. Martov, *Zapiski sotsialdemokrata*, 210. Jews, it should be noted, usually inclined toward the dominant culture; hence their attraction to German throughout the Hapsburg Empire. On the accusations of the Poles see Kopel'zon, 'Evreiskoe rabochee', 73; Joseph Pilsudski, then a leader of the Polish Socialist Party, informed Kopel'zon that 'You Jewish socialists are russifiers, you must transform your Russian orientation into a Polish orientation, teach Polish, agitate and propagandize largely in Polish'.

In Minsk, we are told, 'the conditions of life at that time were such that there was almost no access to the non-Jewish workers'. Similarly in Vitebsk it was impossible for the Jewish revolutionaries to establish contact with Russian workers.[1] Martov also remarks that 'Our movement worked exclusively among the Jewish proletariat...',[2] but he gives as the major reason the fact that Jews preferred the Russian culture offered in their circles, while the Polish workers were attracted to their own language and culture which were taught in circles led by Polish socialists. Yet in Minsk, where the non-Jewish working class was not predominantly Polish-oriented, Christian workers still failed to enter the circles led by Jews. There were some instances of Jewish intellectuals working among Christian workers, and vice versa, but they were comparatively rare. A sense of 'estrangement' Jewish leaders felt—much like that Vladimir Medem experienced when he sought to spread the gospel of socialism among Christian workers in Minsk—was surely a major factor.[3] This is well illustrated by the experience of Sholem Levin, a Jewish socialist in Minsk. Employed at a Christian-owned bindery (one of the rare instances in which a Jew was employed by Christians), Levin attempted to agitate among his Christian fellow-workers. 'Very often', he relates:

Someone would send along a bottle of 'monopolke' (whiskey). They would pour it into tea glasses and drink it down like a glass of water. I had to drink along with them, otherwise I would not have been a 'good brother'. I hoped that by becoming their 'good brother' I would be able to make them class conscious. In the end neither of us achieved anything. They could not make me a drunkard, and I could not make them class conscious.[4]

The Jewish socialists thus found themselves presiding over an all-Jewish movement; yet their attitude toward the Jewish proletariat was far from positive. 'In no sense did the initial founders

[1] Gozhanskii, 'Evreiskoe rabochee', 89; E. A. Gurvich, 'Evreiskoe rabochee', 35–6; Ginzburg, 'Nachalnye shagi', 107.
[2] Martov, *Zapiski sotsialdemokrata*, 210–11.
[3] See Vladimir Medem, *Fun mayn leben* (New York, 1923), I, 195.
[4] Sholem Levin, *Untererdishe kemfer* (New York, 1946), 151.

of the worker-circles in Vilna', the titular head of the Vilna movement recalls in his memoirs, 'carry on extensive work among the Jewish masses; they wished merely to create a few more developed workers, to make them class conscious socialists, to prepare them for agitation in Russia, in the industrial centers, among the Russian working class.'[1] To the socialist leaders the word 'proletariat' meant an industrial proletariat like that which had already developed in England and Germany, and which was in the process of development in the Russian interior. They simply could not believe in the revolutionary potential of a region that had few factories and no great concentration of workers. The socialists of that time, especially those who were under the influence of Marxism, saw no possibility of a conscious class struggle among the workers of small shops.[2] The future of the revolution lay in the industrial centers of the Empire. As one activist put it, 'our eyes were turned toward the Russian workers, toward the great factories'. 'There was no reason to think', stated Gozhanskii, 'that these masses (of Jewish artisans) were capable of revolutionary work.'[3] Indeed, Feliks Kon did not consider the thousands of Jewish artisans he knew in Poland as proletarians, and noted that in the two years he had resided in Warsaw he 'didn't meet a single Jewish worker'.[4]

If the masses had no revolutionary potential, individual artisans might nonetheless be transformed into revolutionary activists. This transformation was to be achieved through an intensive educational campaign. The workers, whose native language was Yiddish, were to be taught Russian in special circles devoted to 'gramota' (reading and writing). This emphasis on Russian was inevitable, given the orientation of the leaders, and it was also made necessary by the dearth of secular literature in Yiddish. Once the workers had attained a satisfactory knowledge of Russian, they were introduced to Russian literature, the basic

[1] Arkady Kremer, 'Mit 35 yor tsurik', *Arkady, Zamlbukh tsum andenk fun Arkady Kremer* (New York, 1942), 395.
[2] Jacob Peskin, 'Di "grupe yidishe sotsial-demokratn in rusland" un Arkady Kremer', *Historishe shriftn*, III, 549; Kremer, 'Mit 35 yor tsurik', 395.
[3] Levin, *Untererdishe kemfer*, 140; Gozhanskii, 'Evreiskoe rabochee', 82.
[4] Feliks Kon, 'Moi pervye vstrechi s evreiskimi rabochimi', in Dimanshtein (ed.), *Revolutsionnoe dvizhenie*, 25.

writings of the leading political scientists and economists, and the mysteries of the natural sciences. Turgenev and Korolenko were among the authors read by workers who participated in the Gomel circles, while in Vilna and Minsk the works of Mill, Darwin and Marx were studied.[1]

The workers also attended lectures on a wide variety of subjects. Leon Bernshtein taught his worker-pupils in Vilna 'how the world was created, the sun and the earth, the seas and volcanoes'; he also lectured on a subject as comprehensive as 'The life of peoples', beginning with a study of primitive tribes and ending with 'the English, their Parliament and trade unions'. The topics discussed in another circle ranged from the formation of planets and of primitive society to that of classes and the state, the history of slavery, capitalism, and scientific socialism.[2] Somewhat closer to home was a lecture Kremer gave in a Vilna circle on the co-operative movement in Belgium; on the other hand Lev Jogiches, also an important leader in the city, thought it necessary not only to lecture on anatomy, but to illustrate his lecture by bringing a skeleton to the circle.[3]

This is not to imply that the propaganda work of the circles was entirely abstract, that it had no relevance to the life of the proletariat. The workers also discussed problems of more immediate interest, such as wages and the length of the working day.[4] Nonetheless, the circles were primarily educational institutions which offered 'courses' (in one instance, courses on three different levels at once) and maintained their own libraries. For the socialists believed that by reading Turgenev, studying Darwin, and contemplating skeletons workers would develop a sense of

[1] Kopel'zon, 'Evreiskoe rabochee', 71. Avram Gordon, *In friling fun vilner yidisher arbeter-bavegung* (Vilna, 1926), 20, notes that the workers in Vilna read Turgenev, Shelgunov, Korolenko, Nekrasov and Bellamy, while Leon Bernshtein, *Ershte shprotsungen* (Buenos Aires, 1956), 66, points out that the 'circle workers' eagerly attended the Vilna theater. See also Levin, *Untererdishe kemfer*, 104, 107; I. Gurvich, *Byloe*, No. 6 (June 1907), 72; Martov, *Zapiski sotsialdemokrata*, 228; Hillel Kats Blum, *Zikhroynes fun a bundist* (New York, 1946), 134. On Gomel see *Iskra*, No. 40 (14 May 1903), 6.

[2] Bernshtein, *Ershte shprotsungen*, 64; Kopel'zon, 'Evreiskoe rabochee', 72.

[3] Isar Kahan, 'Bay Aleksandern in krayzl', *Arkady, Zamlbukh*, 146; Kopel'zon, 'Evreiskoe rabochee', 72. Nor was the study of chemistry overlooked. See Anna Rozental, 'Bletlekh fun a lebens-geshikhte', *Historishe shriftn*, III, 416 ff.

[4] See, for example, 'Voprosy (zaniatiia v vilenskikh s.d. rabochikh kruzhkakh)', in Agursky (ed.), *Di sotsialistishe literatur*, 392–1.

'class consciousness'—that is, an awareness of the forces operating in nature and society. They were thus following both the Populist tradition (particularly that of Lavrov) and the guidelines of Plekhanov's version of Marxism. After all, had the latter not maintained in his famous brochure, 'Our Disagreements', that the socialists' job was to lead the workers to a degree of consciousness 'without which a serious struggle against capitalism is impossible'? Clearly this required a vigorous campaign of propaganda through which the workers could be enlightened.[1]

It was no accident, therefore, that Gozhanskii was commonly known as 'Teacher', or that the early Jewish socialists in general were called 'philosophers'. The intellectuals believed their task was primarily pedagogic; hence they regarded the artisans who attended the circles as their pupils. And they were eager pupils indeed. It is a commonplace that Russian Jewry was notable for its desire and respect, even reverence, for education. Khoroshch describes a poverty-stricken furniture maker in Bialystok whose 'desire for education was so great that, despite the difficult sacrifice it meant, despite his inability to support himself on his miserable, unsteady income, he spent one-fourth to one-fifth of it on education'.[2] 'Education' in this case meant traditional Jewish education, like that pursued by pious artisans in their traditional guilds. By the turn of the century, however, at least some workers had begun to feel a need for a new sort of education; one artisan, for example, told Khoroshch that he longed 'to read a scientific book, a journal'.[3] Exactly how widespread this feeling was is difficult to determine, but the very success of the circle movement proved that Khoroshch's informant was not alone. For it was precisely the circle which offered the workers 'scientific books'. The reading of such books required a knowledge of Russian, and this too was offered by the 'kruzhok'. The 'Haskalah' ('Enlightenment') movement, referred to earlier, made it possible for many Russian Jews to pursue secular studies. This movement, however, was

[1] Georgii Plekhanov, 'Nashi raznoglasiia', in David Riazanov (ed.), *Sochineniia* (Moscow–Petrograd, 1923), II, 336 and 331 ff. This brochure, which was avidly read by the Jewish socialists of Belorussia–Lithuania, converted many of them to the Plekhanov interpretation of Marxism.

[2] Khoroshch, *Voskhod*, xx, No. 7 (July 1901), 43.   [3] *Ibid.*

largely a middle class affair, an opportunity for the children of merchants and Rabbis, not of artisans. In a very real sense the 'kruzhok', since it performed much the same function for the artisans, represented a working class 'Haskalah'. And the circle workers exhibited the same intense desire for secular knowledge as had their 'bourgeois' co-religionists earlier in the century.[1]

What kinds of workers were attracted to the circles? It is interesting to note that members of the small Jewish 'worker aristocracy' were especially prevalent. Printers, for example, were well represented. One writer describes these craftsmen as the 'intellectuals' among the workers, 'the chief contingent among our more advanced workers'.[2] Also much in evidence were engravers, jewellers, binders, and watchmakers. Both Avrom Gordon and Moise Lur'e, who were active in the 'opposition' movements of the 1890s, were engravers, as was one of the leaders of the Kovno movement.[3] Although other groups of artisans, particularly tailors, were active in the circles, factory workers were rarely to be found there. In the words of a socialist leader in Vilna, 'We would capture with joy each new male or female worker if he or she came from a factory'.[4] Thus the most oppressed of the Jewish workers were the least attracted to the new movement.

Once in the circle, the Jewish artisan came to regard his

---

[1] See Litvak, *Vos geven*, 148 ff., whom I have followed in comparing the 'Haskalah' with the circle movement.

[2] E. A. Gurvich, 'Evreiskoe rabochee', 33, 39. See also Kopel'zon, 'Evreiskoe rabochee', 73, and I. Gurvich, *Byloe*, No. 6 (June 1907) 67. Shkliar, 'Onhayb', 192, notes that 'The printers were the most intelligent of the workers'. In 1894 the leader of the Gomel circle was a printer; see Aleksandr Notkin, 'Otryvki vospominanii o pervom sotsial-demokraticheskom kruzhke v Gomele v 1894 godu', *K dvadtsatpiatiletiiu*, 160. This phenomenon was not limited to the Jewish labor movement. On the remarkable role played by printers in the labor movements of Europe and America see Seymour Lipset, Martin Trow, and James Coleman, *Union Democracy* (New York, 1962), 26 ff.

[3] On Gordon and Lur'e see below, Chapter 3. On the engraver Klebnikov see Shkliar, 'Onhayb', 184; engravers were also among the pioneers of the labor movement in the little town of Bielsk, near Bialystok. See Berl Shtern, *Zikhroynes fun shturmishe yorn (Bielsk, 1898–1907)* (New York, 1954), 26 ff. On the participation of watchmakers and jewellers see Levin, *Untererdishe kemfer*, 136, and Martov, *Zapiski sotsialdemokrata*, 193. Moise 'der Aynbinder' ('the Binder') is the subject of an excellent sketch in Bernshtein, *Ershte shprotsungen*, 129 ff., and binders also played a notable role in the Vitebsk movement. See Vilenskii, 'Pionery', 149.

[4] John Mill, *Pionern un boyer* (New York, 1946), I, 69. According to Kopel'zon, 'Evreiskoe rabochee', 80, 'The tailors in Vilna were the most cultured among the Jewish masses...'

socialist 'teacher' with much the same reverence his ancestors had felt for learned Rabbis. 'I remember as if it were today', one of them writes, 'with what a remarkable feeling of fear and awe I and other students sat on a wooden bench near a large brick oven that was hardly warm. Opposite us, at a table, sat a young man of twenty-seven or twenty-eight...' The young man was Arkady Kremer, perhaps the most important figure in the Vilna circle movement. The same writer goes on to say that after a lecture from Kremer he returned home as if 'a new soul had entered me'.[1] Another circle member says of her teacher: 'His knowledge was unlimited. I believed that, were there only a few more like him, one could already begin the revolution.'[2]

It is hardly surprising, then, that the circle workers would begin to pattern their lives on those of the socialist intellectuals. The typical 'enlightened' Jewish worker, we are told, went about dressed 'in a Russian black shirt, carrying a Russian book under his arm and with Russian on his lips'.[3] With secular knowledge suddenly made available to them, a demonstrable change took place in the workers' values: they no longer identified with the culture from which they had come, but attempted to enter the world of the intelligentsia. Many, like Jashka 'the Vitebskite', active in the Dvinsk movement, affected a knowledge of Russian which was usually far from perfect. Jashka spoke a mixture of Russian and Yiddish which 'was a sign of education, of enlightenment. One would insert between two phrases the Russian words "tak chto" (so that), "takim obrazam" (in this way), and similar expressions which had nothing to do with what one wished to say. That, however, was Jashka's language!'[4]

Many workers concluded from their exposure to secular education that such knowledge was the answer to all their

---

[1] Kahan, 'Bay Aleksandern', 145.

[2] Miriam Raskin, *Tsen yor lebn* (New York, 1927), 30.

[3] Mikhalevich, *Zikhroynes*, II, 32.

[4] Berman, *In loif fun yorn*, 107. Compare the remarks of Gerald Brenan, *The Spanish Labyrinth* (Cambridge, 1962), 174, on the Spanish worker-anarchists: 'Like other uneducated people who have suddenly had their eyes opened to the possibilities of knowledge, he spoke in an inflated style, using long incomprehensible words.' Aksel'rod-Ortodoks, 'Iz moikh vospominanii', 37, notes that 'Russian-Yiddish' was the language employed in the Vilna circles of the 1880s.

problems. The comment by the Vilna worker which we have used as an epigraph for this chapter expressed an attitude shared by the majority of circle workers. Their eagerness to read and study was expressed in their desire 'to accumulate more and more knowledge'.[1] Of a certain Moses 'the Binder', a member of the Vilna movement, we are told that he would:

Read everything he could get his hands on. Yet in the course of time he developed a feeling for good books. Among the books in the bindery he would read only those which enriched him spiritually, which satisfied his need to learn. He loved literature, and was especially interested in the classics. His favorites were works of the great satirist Saltykov-Shchedrin, and those of Turgenev and Tolstoy, Zola and Dickens.[2]

With his love for the printed word, Moses 'the Binder' was typical of the worker to whom the circle period brought enlightenment. Obviously, he and his fellow circle members in Vilna, Minsk, and other major cities throughout Belorussia–Lithuania constituted a worker elite, easily distinguishable from the thousands of Jewish artisans and factory workers untouched by the circle movement. Only those who were talented, ambitious, and intellectually curious came to the circles; and while they were emulating their intellectual teachers the masses continued to work sixteen hours a day and pray together with their masters in the artisans' synagogues. The socialists had intended to create an elite, but an elite which would devote itself to the revolutionary movement. This policy, for reasons which we shall shortly discuss, was a failure.

The era of the circles in the Russian Jewish labor movement, which is also known as the period of propaganda, was marked not only by the teaching of chemistry, anatomy, and the classics to a small group of enthusiastic workers; it was also characterized by the first co-operative attempts by the intellectuals and workers at labor organization and preparation for strikes.

We have already noted that the circle leaders took a dim view of the revolutionary potential of the Jewish masses; in fact, they

[1] Bernshtein, *Ershte shprotsungen*, 43.
[2] *Ibid.*, 132.

knew little about the circumstances in which the masses lived. 'I had no idea of the actual working conditions', acknowledged a leader of the Vitebsk movement, and Gozhanskii observed that by and large socialist leaders were completely ignorant of the workers' lives.[1] Nonetheless, during the 1880s some intellectuals did attempt to organize strikes, or at least to support the workers in their struggle for better working conditions. Several of the strikes seem to have occurred spontaneously. In Minsk, for example, a number of locksmiths went on strike in 1887 for a twelve-hour day; when their demands were refused they left their employers, and persuaded journeymen and apprentices in other shops to quit work. This strike, which was typical of thousands that were soon to break out over the entire northwest region, does not appear to have been instigated by the intellectuals, although there is some evidence that a few of the workers involved were veterans of the circle movement of the 1870s.[2] In the same year the Vilna stocking-makers struck for higher wages; and a year later Lev Jogiches, whose activity in the circles we have already described, led a strike of thirty Vilna printers.[3]

The stocking-makers' movement of the 1880s is particularly interesting, for it indicates that at least some socialist intellectuals were interested in 'trade-union' activities during that early period. The young girls were especially good subjects, since many came from 'bourgeois' families and, judging by contemporary standards, were fairly well educated. 'They knew some Russian', a contemporary wrote, and 'were accustomed to reading books; they were somewhat advanced, an intellectual could talk to them.'[4] Jogiches, the Populist Notkin, and Kremer all made attempts to organize them, as did several other, lesser known

[1] Ginzburg, 'Nachalnye shagi', 106; Gozhanskii, 'Evreiskoe rabochee', 82.

[2] For further information on this strike see the interesting collection of official Russian documents in 'Der ershter shtrayk in minsk', *Royte bleter*, 25–8. E. A. Gurvich claims that some of the strikers had belonged to Rabinovich's Minsk circle of 1875 ('Evreiskoe rabochee', 41). A spontaneous strike staged by printers in Minsk is described by I. Gurvich, *Byloe*, No. 6 (June 1907), 73.

[3] Subbotin (*V cherte*, I, 79) called the strike an 'interesting phenomenon'. On the printer's strike, see Kopel'zon, 'Evreiskoe rabochee', 71. The author says that 'Among us the strike movement had already begun in 1888', but he adds, 'I am speaking of the strike movement led by our organization' (70).

[4] Litvak, *Vos geven*, 59.

figures. Michael Halperin, whose activities anticipated those of the 'agitators' of the late 1890s, talked to the stocking-makers about their working conditions, explained to them how they were being exploited, and concluded that they 'must organize and together demand higher wages'.[1]

It was perhaps under the supervision of the socialists that the stocking-makers organized what may well have been the first 'kassa', or self-help fund, in Vilna. During 1888–9 other 'kassy' were formed by printers, tailors, carpenters, locksmiths, and cigarette-makers, and in Minsk similar organizations were established.[2] Although the early 'kassy' were not specifically designed to aid members during strikes, this proved to be one of their functions; for the most part, however, they appear to have operated as general self-help societies.[3]

Unfortunately, little is known about these early 'kassy'; those 'Statutes' which have been preserved derive from a later period, and they will be examined in another chapter. The origins of the 'kassy', however, pose a special problem which it would be well to consider here. The question of whether the new, trade union type of organization was an outgrowth of the medieval guild has been the subject of considerable discussion and controversy. It is particularly relevant to the Jewish labor movement in Russia, for there the old guild system continued to flourish while the 'kassy' were being established. We have already noted that while the guilds had continued to exist, master journeyman unity had occasionally broken down. This process was greatly accelerated

[1] Quoted from Yehudah Appel, *Be-tokh rashit ha-tehiah* (Tel Aviv, 1936), in Shmuel Eisenshtadt, *Perakim be-toldot tenuat ha-poalim ha-yehudit* (Palestine, n.d., n.p.), I, 80. For material on the role of other intellectuals in the stocking-makers' trade, see Kopel'zon, 'Evreiskoe rabochee', 65; Menes, *Historishe shriftn*, III, 30.
[2] About seventy Vilna stocking-makers paid twenty kopeks each per month to their 'kassa' when preparing for a strike (Litvak, *Vos geven*, 59). On the other 'kassy' see Kopel'zon, 'Evreiskoe rabochee', 73; E. A. Gurvich, 'Evreiskoe rabochee', 50–1. The Vilna women tailors' 'kassa' held its tenth anniversary celebration in 1899, the only such organization in existence for ten consecutive years. See *Di arbayter shtime*, No. 14 (1899), 13. Whether the 'kassy' were organized by the workers themselves, or by the intellectuals, is a moot point. Gordon (*In friling*, 13) implies that they were founded by the workers, with no outside help.
[3] Frumkin, 'Ocherki', *Evreiskaia starina*, VI, No. 1 (January–March 1913), 118 ff., discusses and quotes from a Vilna 'kassa' statute from the later 1880s, which, as far as I know, has not been published. The other statutes he uses are from the 1890s.

toward the end of the nineteenth century. A special study of the guild system in Mogilev reveals that the numerous artisan societies were in various stages of development. Like the shoemakers' guild, some of the organizations still united masters and journeymen in one society, whereas others (the table-makers' guild, for example) had already split along class lines, the journeymen symbolizing their independence through the purchase of a special Torah scroll.[1]

Similar changes were apparent in other cities and towns. In Lodz, in 1901, some of the weavers refused to remain in the same guild as their masters, while in Zhitomir, two years later, rather than spend money on a new Torah scroll, members of a furniture-makers' guild preferred to join the revolutionary organization.[2] However, a note of caution should be interjected. The splitting up of a guild into two new societies by no means implied the creation of a workers' organization that was dedicated to the use of the strike and other weapons. Frequently all it meant was a continuation of the old guild traditions within a new framework. For example, the guild of women tailors in Mogilev split as early as 1850, but during the next fifty years the journeymen workers continued to attend to their religious and social needs as before, the only difference being that they no longer met with their masters.[3] This journeymen's guild scarcely resembled the Minsk and Vilna 'kassy' even in the early stages of their development. Having come under the wing of the socialist intelligentsia, the members of the 'kassy' lived in a world entirely different from that of the Mogilev tailors, who were surrounded by the trappings of tradition. And although both the guild and the 'kassa' shared identical aims—namely, to improve their members' lot, economically and socially—it is untenable to claim, as some historians do, that the latter was a direct outgrowth of the former.[4]

---

[1] Rabinowitsch, *Die Organisationen*, 47–55. This valuable study is the only one we possess on the structure and evolution of the artisan guilds in the late nineteenth century.

[2] *Der frayhayts-glok*, No. 1 (September 1901), 15; *Posledniia izvestiia*, No. 104 (4 January 1903). [3] Rabinowitsch, *Die Organisationen*, 54 ff.

[4] This mistaken opinion is held by Sviatlovskii, *Professional'noe*, 21 ff., and Vladimir Akimov, pseud. (Makhnovets), *Materialy dlia kharakteristiki razvitiia rossiikoi sotsialde-mokraticheskoi rabochei partii* (Geneva, 1904), 11.

The socialists confront the workers

Thus, when guild members joined 'kassy', as occurred in Zhitomir, they were announcing their departure from the traditional way of life. In Vitebsk one of the leaders of the revolutionary movement was a member of the dyers' guild, but by committing himself to the new ideology this man was rejecting and rebelling against the old. Commenting on the existence in that city of both guilds and 'kassy', a contemporary pointed out that it became more and more difficult to reconcile the differences between guilds and the revolutionary organizations.[1] The guild and the 'kassa' (or the circle) could only regard each other with mutual suspicion and enmity.

The same holds true of the relationship between self-help societies of Jewish factory workers and the new 'kassy'. The factory workers, whose roots scarcely went back more than a generation, did not possess guilds, but they did occasionally form mutual funds. Sometimes these organizations were founded on the initiative of the factory owner; this was the case at Zaks' match factory in Dvinsk, and in Zhitomir, where a factory owner organized a fund 'for the help of members in time of need'; similarly at the Shereshevsky factory in Grodno the owner contributed 150 rubles a year to a self-help and sick fund for his employees.[2] In other cases it was the workers who, motivated by a desire to secure themselves against frequent crises and unemployment, formed their own societies.[3] These societies, however, did not evolve into 'kassy', and it may be safely assumed that the Vilna cigarette-makers' 'kassa' of the late 1880s existed independently of the self-help fund on which other employees of the Edelshtein factory relied.

In a less tangible way, however, the guilds (and the far less important self-help funds in the factories) may have contributed to the rise of the organized Jewish labor movement. The fact that the artisan guilds continued to exist during the nineteenth century extended to the Jewish working class a feeling for, and an under-

[1] Ginzburg, 'Nachalnye shagi', 101–2.
[2] Menes, *Historishe shriftn*, III, 52; *Di arbayter shtime*, No. 16 (1900), 5; *Russkii evrei*, VI, No. 13 (29 March 1884), 10–11; *Vilenskii fabrichny*, 89.
[3] *Nedel'naia khronika 'Voskhoda'*, I, No. 49 (4 December 1882), 1343; and II, No. 9 (6 March 1883), 222.

standing of, organization which was lacking among the non-Jewish workers. This type of contribution is very difficult to assess: surely very few 'kassy' members were aware that their organization owed anything to the guilds whose principal tenets they had rejected. As one activist from Vitebsk wrote, 'I was close to the locksmith and carpenter organizations, and I do not recall that there was any discussion of religious societies'.[1] Nonetheless, one cannot dismiss the fact that organization was an integral part of the Jewish artisan's heritage, that he therefore was more amenable to organizational discipline than the non-Jewish worker in Russia. This is certainly one possible explanation—though by no means the only one—for the remarkable organizational achievements of the Jewish labor movement. Hence, while the traditional 'hevrah' and the radical 'kassa' were clearly in opposition, representing as they did two entirely different worlds, the heritage of the former may well have facilitated the latter's development.[2]

The period of the 1880s and early 1890s, when the socialists first established contact with the workers, was dominated by the circles and the creation of an enlightened elite. Much less important at the time, but vitally important for the future, were the embryonic trade union activities engaged in by limited numbers of workers and intellectuals. In the subsequent phase the emphases were reversed; organization and strikes came to the fore, while further attempts to 'enlighten' the workers in circles were removed from the center of the stage.

[1] Comments made by Mezivetskii in Dimanshtein (ed.), *Revoliutsionnoe dvizhenie*, 127.
[2] The point that trade unions did not develop out of guilds was made by Sidney and Beatrice Webb in their *History of Trade Unionism* (London, 1920); see Chapter 1. See also Lujo Brentano, 'On the History and Development of Guilds', in Toulin Smith (ed.), *English Guilds* (London, 1870), clxv ff.

CHAPTER 3

The New Policy of Agitation

In the streets, to the masses.

Title of a popular song, Vilna, in the 1890s

The purpose of the circle movement was to create small cadres of enlightened, progressive workers who would be dedicated to the idea of revolution and willing to devote their lives to bring about a new order of society. As the years passed, however, it became increasingly clear that the 'pupils' in these circles were developing ideas and attitudes inimical to those of their teachers. Not only were the circle members cut off from the workers who had not been exposed to socialist propaganda, but they were rapidly acquiring a 'condescending, contemptuous attitude' toward the masses whom they felt were unworthy of 'the teachings of socialism'.[1] This attitude of condescension was due in part to the circle workers' distaste for Yiddish, an attitude they shared with the intellectuals. Many of the circle members regarded their own language as a disgraceful kind of jargon,[2] and regarded those who spoke it as uncultured. Much to their chagrin the socialist leaders discovered that many of the circle members had no desire to become selfless revolutionaries, but were bent on acquiring the knowledge they would need to pursue 'intellectual' careers. As Martov noted, for some of them the circles were only 'a means of acquiring knowledge, a personal escape from the gloom in which the working masses lived'.[3] Of course there were exceptions like Liza 'the Tailor', a graduate of one of the Vilna circles, who went on to become a leader in the labor movement in Kovno.[4] But far too many workers regarded the circle as a school, not as a school of socialism, and while they respected their

---

[1] E. A. Gurvich, 'Evreiskoe rabochee', 43.
[2] See Levin, *Untererdishe kemfer*, 111.
[3] Martov, *Zapiski sotsialdemokrata*, 227.
[4] Shkliar, 'Onhayb', 183; Bernshtein, *Ershte shprotsungen*, 77 ff.

teachers' knowledge, they often disregarded the revolutionary message the latter sought to bring.

Given this attitude, defections were inevitable. It was a common practice for circle workers to leave the movement and become 'externs', that is, candidates for high school equivalency examinations who hoped eventually to enter a university. 'Sometimes our most capable students', Martov noted, 'prepared to take exams as "externs" and to become intellectuals.'[1] Others hoped to leave the provincial backwaters for the great centers of learning such as St Petersburg; and while they intended to take part in the labor movement of such centers, they were mainly interested in the cultural opportunities the cities offered. Thus Maks Nodel, one of Martov's pupils in a Vilna circle, dreamed of going to St Petersburg where he would join the labor movement and student groups, and become acquainted with:

The writers and literary men whose works he had read…Deep in his heart was the hope that, with the aid of the intelligentsia in St Petersburg, he would be able to complete his education, which had been interrupted when he left school. He entertained the prospect of becoming not just an 'intellectual' worker but a full-fledged intellectual, with an excellent education and a new, and better profession.[2]

A defection of a somewhat different order also proved troublesome to the leaders: in the late 1880s the majority of workers in Minsk who had been exposed to propaganda began to emigrate to America, thereby threatening the movement with total collapse. One of the activists in Minsk had the feeling that 'In fact we were only preparing socialist workers for America'.[3] Even worse, in the eyes of the socialists, was the tendency other

---

[1] Martov, *Zapiski sotsialdemokrata*, 223; see also Mikhalevich, *Zikhroynes*, I, 32; Kopel'zon, 'Evreiskoe rabochee', 78. Another participant in the Vilna movement remarks that some of the workers desired 'to acquire knowledge and a higher rank on the social ladder'. See Pati, pseud. (Srednitskaia), 'Zikhroynes vegn Arkadin', *Arkady, Zamlbukh*, 52. Gozhanskii ('Evreiskoe rabochee', 83) notes that when some workers had obtained a certain amount of training in Russian and other subjects they went on to enter such professions as dentistry, etc.

[2] Bernshtein, *Ershte shprotsungen*, 68–9. Nodel did in fact leave Vilna for St Petersburg and was arrested there. He later emigrated to London, where he became a dentist.

[3] E. A. Gurvich, 'Evreiskoe rabochee', 46; I. Gurvich, *Byloe*, No. 6 (June 1907), 75.

workers showed to leave the movement and become self-employed 'bosses'.[1]

By the early 1890s the circle movement was clearly at an impasse: it had managed to lift a small number of intelligent workers out of their class, but the latter had failed to manifest the revolutionary zeal expected of them. The socialists gradually recognized the impasse for what it was, and this recognition led them to adopt a new approach that was calculated to produce revolutionaries, not would-be intellectuals and degree candidates.[2] In Vilna, the capital of Russian Jewish socialism, disillusionment with the circle movement led the leadership to extend both the range and focus of their attack and to appeal to the economic interests of the Jewish masses.

Various influences led the socialists to adopt this new position. One such influence was the very success of the early strikes and the first 'kassy' that had emerged during the propaganda era. 'The experience of the first strikes', one socialist leader commented, 'proved that if one only talks to the masses about an issue that is of interest to them...they listen carefully.'[3] Another was the example of the Polish labor movement. As early as the 1880s Polish socialists had begun mass agitation among the workers; in 1889 the 'Union of Polish Workers' was founded, an organization which stressed decisive action by the masses against their employers. The Vilna socialists, who were within close enough range to study the new tactics, were much impressed. According to one Jewish activist, the 'Union' brought to their attention new approaches to be tried both among the artisans and the factory hands. Martov was even more explicit and claimed that the Polish organization was a 'direct influence' on the decision of Kremer and the other leaders to shift to mass agitation.[4] And

[1] Gozhanskii, 'Evreiskoe rabochee', 84; see also Chapter 1, p. 9.
[2] Kopel'zon, 'Evreiskoe rabochee', 78. See also Pati, 'Zikhroynes', 52; Martov, *Zapiski sotsialdemokrata*, 224; Bernshtein, *Ershte shprotsungen*, 43. See also comments in Vladimir Kossovsky, 'Zubatov "likvidirt dem bund"', *Arkady, Zamlbukh*, 180.
[3] Mikhalevich, 'Erev "bund"', *Royter pinkes*, I, 34. See also Kossovsky, 'Zubatov', 180.
[4] Martov, 'Razvitie krupnoi promyshlennosti i rabochee dvizhenie do 1892 g.', *Istoriia Rossii v XIX veke* (St Petersburg, n.d.), 157; see also Tsoglin (Taras) in Dimanshtein (ed.), *Revoliutsionnoe dvizhenie*, 77; Kopel'zon, 'Evreiskoe rabochee', 74. On the 'Union of Polish Workers (Związek Robotników Polskich)' see Res, pseud. (Feliks Perl),

Gozhanskii mentions two Polish socialists in Vilna who explicitly denounced the circle program as fruitless.[1]

The attitude of Georgii Plekhanov, the leading exponent of Russian Marxism, also influenced the Vilna leaders in their search for new methods. Writing on the Russian famine of 1891, Plekhanov maintained that workers need not be fully class conscious before they can participate in the struggle for a better world, that 'people who have not yet become socialists have already worked for the good of socialism, and that is due to agitation'. Class consciousness, he added, was not instilled through the propaganda techniques of small circles, but through active participation in a massive campaign for better economic conditions. 'History is not made in the circles, but among the masses', and 'if the Russian socialists wish to play an active role in the coming Russian revolution they must become agitators'.[2]

Fortified by Plekhanov's article,[3] the Polish example, and early success at home, the Vilna socialists determined to take up a new role—that of labor leaders whose chief concern was to improve the conditions of the proletariat. Their first target was the most serious problem affecting the Jewish worker: an ill-defined and interminably long working day. The problem of the workday was brought home to the socialists even in their circle activities; since most of the participants were obliged to work until late at night, their studies suffered. The result, as Kremer noted, was that

Dzieje ruchu socjalistycznego w zaborze rosyjskim do powstania PPS (Warsaw, 1958), 334 ff.

[1] Gozhanskii, 'Evreiskoe rabochee', 84. The Polish socialists were A. Domaszewicz and Stanislaw Trusiewicz, the former one of the founders of the Lithuanian Social Democratic Party, the latter a leader of the SDKPiL (Social Democracy of the Kingdom of Poland and Lithuania). On Domaszewicz's role in Vilna see Mill, *Pionern un boyer*, I, 36. The influence of the Polish movement on the Jewish socialists is analyzed in Mishkinsky, *Yesodot*, Chapter 5. On the pioneering role of the Polish labor movement in the Russian Empire, see Perl (*Dzieje ruchu*, 71) who explains this by the fact that the Polish workers, particularly those in Warsaw, were the bearers of a strong revolutionary tradition, having participated in the revolts against Russian rule. See also Stepniak, pseud. (S. Kravchinskii), *The Russian Storm Cloud* (London, 1886), 144; M. K. Dziewanowski, *The Communist Party of Poland* (Cambridge, Mass., 1959), 8.

[2] Plekhanov, 'O zadachakh sotsialistov v bor'be s golodom v Rossii', in Riazanov (ed.), *Sochineniia*, III, 386, 413, 414. The article appeared in 1892.

[3] 'For us', Gozhanskii remarked ('Evreiskoe rabochee', 83), 'this brochure was very convincing.' Peskin ('Di "grupe"', 550) commented: 'Plekhanov's brochure had a great influence, not only on the Russian socialists, but on the Jews as well.'

'the job of enlightening the workers could be carried on only on Friday evenings and on Saturday... Education, the circles, had already become a matter of life or death to a great number of the better workers, and a reduction in the working day—a necessity.'[1] By making this problem the focus of their attack the socialists simultaneously hoped to extend their contact to the masses and make the traditional circle program more effective.

The main question now became how to approach the mass of workers outside the circle movement. Gozhanskii had this to say about the socialists' first contact with the workers at Edelshtein's tobacco factory.

When they heard words and ideas which they had never heard before; when they were summoned to something new; when they began to see some sort of movement around them, their first response was: 'nothing will come of this, everything you say is useless, because everything depends on fate. We poor people were born that way, and so we shall die, and nothing will improve our situation.'[2]

Gozhanskii, seeking to allay their fears, came up with an 'idea of genius' that was eventually to transform the entire course of the Jewish socialist movement. 'Quite by accident', he relates, 'I discovered an old law Catherine II had issued in 1789, the first statute of which states that artisans are to work only twelve hours, with a half-hour break for breakfast and a one and one-half hour break for dinner.' The law (which dates from 1785, not 1789) had apparently come to the attention of a city official, who unintentionally made his discovery known to the socialists.[3]

---

[1] Kremer, 'Mit 35 yor tsurik', 396.

[2] Gozhanskii, 'Evreiskoe rabochee', 85–6. Subbotin encountered the same attitude among the workers in Vilna. Describing the workers of that city, he commented: 'these poor people [are] thoroughly fatalistic; to questions concerning their affairs they respond, "as God wills", "as God grants", etc.' (*V cherte*, I, 94).

[3] According to the account in Akimov, *Materialy*, 9, the Mayor of Vilna mentioned this law in one of his public statements. Martov, too, gives the same account ('Razvitie', 158); see also Frumkin, 'Ocherki', *Evreiskaia starina*, VI, No. 1 (January–March 1913), 113 ff., who believes that mention was first made of the law in a dispute between the artisans and the local Artisans' Bureau. It was Martov (*Zapiski sotsialdemokrata*, 193) who termed Gozhanskii's discovery an 'idea of genius'. The law itself, which was issued as a clause in Catherine's 'Charter on the Towns', 21 April 1785, was published in *Polnoe sobranie zakonov Rossiiskoi Imperii s 1649 goda*, XXII, 1784–8 (St Petersburg, 1830), 378, and republished in *Ustav remeslennyi, izdanie 1879 goda* (St Petersburg, 1879), 28.

Once armed with the law, the socialists found the masses responsive to their agitation. Realizing that they had a legal right to protest, the artisans were willing to enter the fight for a shorter day. 'If there is a law to work twelve hours', they said, 'why should we work sixteen?' This, Gozhanskii concluded, 'was the basis upon which contact with workers was established'.[1]

It should be emphasized that the first major appeal to the masses by the Jewish socialists had a legal basis, that it suggested lawful means, in a country where strikes were forbidden, whereby workers might demand economic improvements. The Vilna socialists thus sought to rouse the masses by promising that seemingly illegal protests enjoyed official sanction. The idea of appealing to the authorities was not new to the workers; it was, in fact, a device traditionally employed. In 1889, for example, only a few years before the new policy was adopted in Vilna, shop assistants in Minsk addressed a petition to the Governor of the Province demanding that stores be closed at 9.00 p.m. rather than at midnight.[2] When in 1892[3] Jewish artisans learned that the workday was regulated by law, they immediately bombarded the authorities wtih requests that the law be enforced. Martov says that petitions were sent 'to the Artisans' Bureau, the City Hall, the police chief, the Governor, and the factory inspector'.[4] One such petition by a Vilna worker reads as follows:

According to the law of 1879 (*sic*), the working day in the artisans' shops is limited to twelve hours. Thirteen years have passed since then, and neither I nor my comrades, the other workers, have felt the

---

It reads as follows: 'The working day of artisans is from 6.00 a.m. to 6.00 p.m., including half an hour for breakfast and one and one-half hours for dinner and rest.'

[1] Gozhanskii, 'Evreiskoe rabochee', 87.

[2] Ch. (Cherikover?), 'Di lage fun di minsker handel-ongeshtelte in di 80-ker yorn', *Tsaytshrift*, IV (1930), 133–4.

[3] There is some confusion as to the exact date. Frumkin, 'Ocherki', 113, claims the law was discovered in 1893, as do several other sources. However, the law is mentioned in one of the speeches given by Jewish workers in Vilna on May Day, 1892, published in *Pervoe maia 1892 goda, Chetyre rechi evreiskikh rabochikh* (Geneva, 1893), 3. One of the speakers stated that 'Workers, instead of laboring twelve hours a day, as stipulated by law, work fifteen and seventeen hours a day'. Moreover, the petition by a Jewish worker in Vilna in 1892 quoted above (Chapter 1, p. 11) specifically mentions the statute of 1785. Martov ('Razvitie') agrees that the law was discovered in 1892.

[4] Martov, *Zapiski sotsialdemokrata*, 194. See also Kremer, 'Mit 35 yor tsurik', 396–7; Peskin, 'Di "grupe"', 552 ff.; Frumkin, 'Ocherki', 113.

beneficial impact of this law on our lives...We appeal to Your Excellency with a humble request for help. Only Your Excellency has the power to quell the inhuman bestiality of the employer; only you can improve our difficult and unfortunate situation.[1]

It was with appeals such as these, wholly within the traditional framework, that the socialist movement on a mass scale began in Vilna. The socialists were content to use such traditional means because, in their view, once the authorities failed to help the workers the latter would resort to illegal acts. This assumption was, in fact, correct.

The 1785 statute proved effective as a lever with the masses in many cities of Belorussia–Lithuania. In Minsk, where the movement took a similar course to that in Vilna, workers sent several collective petitions to the local Governor in 1894 demanding that a twelve hour day be instituted by the police.[2] The statute was invoked in Brest–Litovsk, Mogilev, Bialystok and Vitebsk: in Dvinsk workers first exhibited signs of unrest after rumors spread that such a law did in fact exist. Moreover, the socialists continued to appeal to the masses on the basis of this law years after the labor movement had begun. Workers in Vilna were still being exhorted as late as 1897 to demand the twelve hour day as stipulated in the old statute.[3]

The origins of the Jewish mass strike movement are thus intimately linked to the idea of legalism, the same type of legalism that was later to haunt the socialists in the guise of police socialism. For the time being, however, the socialists had realized their

---

[1] *Vilne, A zamlbukh*, 133, 134. The worker mistakenly gives the date as 1879.

[2] 'Iz Minska', *Rabotnik*, No. 3–4 (1897), 61. On the origins of the Minsk mass movement see also Bukhbinder, 'Evreiskoe rabochee dvizhenie v Minske, 1895–1905 gg.', *Krasnaia letopis'*, No. 5 (1923), 122 ff.; Levin, *Untererdishe kemfer*, 97 ff.; 'Der leben un kampf', *Der idisher arbeter*, No. 10 (1900), 67 ff.; Lev, 'Di yidishe arbeter-bavegung in minsk bizn yor 1900', *Visnshaftlekhe yorbikher*, I, 112.

[3] *Tsu alle vilner arbayter un arbayterinen*, Vilna, 12 November 1897. For its application in other cities see: *Ko vsem rabochim i rabotnitsam*, Mogilev, 1903; *Der idisher arbeter*, No. 4–5 (November 1897); Mikhalevich, *Zikhroynes*, I, 22; comments of Mezivetskii in Dimanshtein (ed.), *Revoliutsionnoe dvizhenie*, 128; Berman, *In loif fun yorn*, 79. In Gomel in 1894, upon the suggestion of the intellectuals, workers sent a petition to the authorities demanding a fourteen-hour day though no mention of the law was made. See 'Gomel'skoe rabochee dvizhenie', in Agursky (ed.), *Di sotsialistishe literatur*, 362. The law was also utilized by the Lithuanian Social Democrats; see 'Litovskoe rabochee dvizhenie', *Rabotnik*, No. 5–6 (1899), 3.

objectives; once the mass appeals began, the movement quickly got out of hand, and while the authorities were willing initially to aid the workers, many officials eventually came to side with the employers in labor disputes. In Vilna, for example, tailors sent petitions to the factory inspector in 1893 demanding a twelve-hour day; although the latter did not object to their demands, the owners were alarmed and began to fire the 'rebels'. As a result, the workers abandoned all pretense of legality, called a general strike, and added to their original petition new demands that were not covered by law. According to one source, many of the workers were arrested.[1] This, of course, was precisely what the socialists were counting on to further unrest among the masses. In Minsk workers had become so impatient that even before a formal answer arrived from the Governor, several strikes broke out. As the number of strikes increased in that city, the attitude of the authorities hardened.[2] Clearly, the statute of the eighteenth century monarch proved a most effective battle cry, unleashing the pent-up hostilities workers had long been harboring toward their employers. Once this happened the workers' impatience could not be controlled; the traditional practice of writing petitions was largely discarded in favor of more direct action.

'The struggle for a "legal" workday', Kremer notes, '...opened our eyes.'[3] Indeed, the wave of strikes that broke out in Vilna following Gozhanskii's discovery made final the decision to break with the past and initiate an altogether different tactical course. In 1893 there was an outburst of strikes that culminated in the general tailors' strike mentioned above—'an event of the first order',[4] as one of the socialists described it—which precluded a return to the traditional circle movement. Once the socialists

---

[1] 'Materialy dlia kharakteristiki rabochego dvizheniia nashego goroda Vil'ny za poslednie 4–5 let (sobrany v 1895 g.)', in Agursky (ed.), *Di sotsialistishe literatur*, 416 ff. See also Aleksander Malinowski (ed.), *Materiały do historii PPS i ruchu rewolucyjnego w zaborze rosyjskim od r. 1893–1904* (Warsaw, 1907), I, 50. (The printed volume was not available to me, my source being a typescript copy in the Bund Archives, New York City.) According to Elie Raytshuk (*Royte bleter*, 1), 'When the strike broke out, many workers who had been informed on by the employers were arrested'.

[2] 'Iz Minska', *Rabotnik*, 61–2; Levin, *Untererdishe kemfer*, 98, reports that 'The police quickly took the employers' side and began to persecute workers who had demanded a shorter working day'.

[3] Kremer, 'Mit 35 yor tsurik', 397.   [4] Mill, *Pionern un boyer*, I, 151.

had seen the masses in action, they were determined to harness this power to serve the revolution.

The new program of 'agitation' formulated in Vilna during 1893–4 was based on the idea that the masses could be imbued with a sense of class consciousness through participation in the struggle for economic improvements. In practice what this meant was that the circle as a 'school of socialism' would be supplemented, though not replaced, by mass organization and a mass strike movement. Since all of the workers desired better standards of living the movement would easily attract them; inevitably, these workers would realize that the economic and political struggle were inseparable, that an imposing alliance existed between their immediate enemy, the employer, and their distant and yet unrecognized enemy, the Tsar. 'From economics to politics'—this was the slogan of the new movement, which appealed not to the 'aristocracy' of the circles but to the uneducated masses who obviously were not going to devote their free time to reading Darwin. Thus it could concentrate not on the Maks Nodels and the Moses 'the Binders', but on the nameless thousands whose concern was low wages, not reading lists, and whose leaders would be agitators, not teachers.[1]

The program of agitation formulated in Vilna was the greatest single contribution the Jewish Marxists of Belorussia–Lithuania made to the general Russian social democratic movement. Its tenets were carried by activists from the northwest region to the interior; in St Petersburg, as in the cities of the Pale, its acceptance signaled the end of the circle period.[2] In Belorussia–Lithuania it was applied successfully wherever the circle movement had taken root, although outside of Vilna and Minsk the evolution of the movement was telescoped far more rapidly. Thus in Gomel (where the first circle had been established in 1893) the strike movement began in 1894, while in Vitebsk, after only a few

[1] The two major texts of the 'agitation' program are Arkady Kremer's *Ob agitatsii*, written in 1893 and first published in Geneva in 1896, and Gozhanskii's 'A briv tsu di agitatorn', also written in 1893 and published in *Historishe shriftn*, III, 626–48.

[2] See Richard Pipes, *Social Democracy and the St Petersburg Labor Movement, 1885–97* (Cambridge, Mass., 1963), 60 ff.; J. H. L. Keep, *The Rise of Social Democracy in Russia* (Oxford, 1963), 45 ff.

years of circle propaganda, the socialists decided 'to move from the stage of theoretical preparation to the practical implementation of our ideas'.[1] In Grodno the first strike wave occurred in 1897, two years after the first circles were founded, whereas in Kovno an agitation program was carried on simultaneously with circle propaganda.[2] Furthermore, the institution of the 'kassy', which had originated in the two centers of the movement, took root in the other major cities and became the organizational backbone of the new campaign.

Despite local differences, once it became organized the Jewish labor movement everywhere within the Pale was clearly the result of an alliance between the workers and the socialists who had forged the new tactics of agitation. Prior to this alliance, as we have seen, workers had been capable of sporadic strike activity and some degree of organization, but they lacked any real direction until the intellectuals entered the labor movement. A report from Grodno, for example, commented: 'Among us the labor movement began in 1897 with the help of several newly-arrived workers. An important role was also played by a group of intellectuals. The workers and the intellectuals both went over to mass agitation.'[3] Often it was the 'propagandized' workers who initiated the new tactics. This was true in Vitebsk, where, we are told, 'The newly-arrived workers in our circles, together with the older, more class-conscious workers, began to organize workers of various crafts'. In Gomel, too, a sufficient number of circle graduates were active in the movement to be crucially important in the transition from propaganda to agitation. An analysis of the labor movement in Gomel claims that owing to the circles there a worker-intelligentsia was born 'which stood on a higher level than the masses, which was well acquainted with

---

[1] Vilenskii, 'Pionery', 149; see also Avram der Tate, pseud. (Leib Blekhman), 'Zikhroynes fun der sotsialistisher un arbeter-bavegung', in Gregory Aronson *et al.* (eds.), *Vitebsk amol* (New York, 1956), 275 ff. On Gomel see 'Der leben un kampf', *Der idisher arbeter*, No. 11 (1901), 45–7, and 'Gomel'skoe rabochee', in Agursky (ed.), *Di sotsialistishe literatur*, 362 ff.

[2] On Grodno see 'Der leben un kampf', *Der idisher arbeter*, No. 10 (1900), 65 ff.; 'Di arbayter bavegung in grodno', *Di letste pasirungen*, No. 14 (12 July 1905), 3; Lev, 'Pervye shagi', in Dimanshtein (ed.), *Revoliutsionnoe dvizhenie*, 264 ff. On Kovno, see Shkliar, 'Onhayb', 183 ff.

[3] 'Der leben un kampf', *Der idisher arbeter*, No. 10 (1900), 65.

the misery of the workers' situation; thus appeared the first agitators who influenced the masses'.[1]

Even in Bialystok, where the labor movement was well under way even before the new approach had been formulated in Vilna, an organized movement did not emerge until emissaries from the 'capital' arrived to spread the new doctrine. Five months after Gozhanskii's arrival in Bialystok in 1895, 'kassy' were set up and the movement organized along the lines of the Vilna model. 'Never had we met with such success', Gozhanskii reported. 'In a short time we had managed to bring the city to its knees.' Four years later, when Pavel Rozental arrived to take charge of the local organization in Bialystok, it was hardly distinguishable from the organization in Vilna.[2] Thus one can safely assume that were it not for the intervention of the Vilna socialists, the Jewish labor movement in Bialystok would have continued on its desultory, unorganized course.

The organized Jewish labor movement, then, came about as a result of the intellectuals' decision to promote a mass movement. We must now consider the attitude of the other element in the circle movement, namely the 'pupils'. Some of these, as we have seen, were willing to accept the new tactics. And at an 1892 May Day celebration in Vilna, one worker asserted: 'We must struggle against our most immediate enemies, namely our employers whom we come into conflict with every day. We must unite, form workers' councils and "kassy", and hold strikes.' This view, however, was not shared by all the speakers, some of whom continued to stress the overriding importance of 'science', the hall-mark of the circle movement.[3] This difference of opinion led to the emergence in Vilna of a group opposing the new program.

[1] Avram der Tate, *Zikhroynes*, 282; 'Gomel'skoe rabochee', in Agursky (ed.), *Di sotsialistishe literatur*, 362.
[2] Gozhanskii, 'Evreiskoe rabochee', 90; An-man, 'Bialystoker period', 46–7. See also Mill, *Pionern un boyer*, I, 72, who mentions several leaders in Vilna who undertook to 'colonize' Bialystok during 1894–6.
[3] *Pervoe maia 1892 goda*; the quotation is from 3; the conflicting views are cited on 11–12. Interestingly enough, a third worker mentions with approval the struggle for a shorter workday because workers will then have more leisure time 'to read a good book' (p. 16).

Opposition was certainly predictable. Understandably, some of the circle workers regarded the new program of the intellectuals as a threat to what had become the vested interests of those who came to the circles not to improve their economic situation but their minds, who had no desire to organize strikes and found 'kassy', but who wished to study Russian and to read Marx. They shared their teachers' initial attitudes toward the artisan masses. Much to their chagrin they discovered that their teachers' attitudes were changing, and they realized that any commitment to a labor movement dominated by strikes would mean a death blow to the old order.

The leader of the Vilna opposition was Avram Gordon, an engraver and a member of the Jewish artisan elite that had supplied the circles with so many of their recruits. An autodidact of considerable learning, typical of his group in his passion for knowledge, Gordon was well able to express the indignation his comrades felt at this 'betrayal' by the intellectuals. In his polemics against the Vilna socialists, which reached a peak in 1893,[1] he reiterated the basic premise of the circle movement. 'Only when the masses become more enlightened', he insisted, 'will it be possible to strike out against the old traditions, against fanaticism, privileges, and oppression.' The masses had to 'develop' before they could participate actively in a labor movement; this could only be accomplished through education in the circles.[2]

Gordon's statements clearly show the influence of the Russian Populist Lavrov, who also believed that 'Knowledge is the fundamental power of the revolution which is underway and the force essential to carry it out'.[3] Like Lavrov, Gordon maintained that the intelligentsia alone could transmit this knowledge to the workers. The socialists, he thought, had understood this

---

[1] According to a list prepared by Gordon, his first political talks date from 1890. In 1892 he gave a speech at the May Day celebration entitled 'On the Shameful Leadership of the Intellectuals'. The opposition movement as such crystallized in Vilna in 1893. See 'Tsu der geshikhte fun der "arbeter opozitsie"', *Yedies fun yidishn visenshaftlekhn institut*, No. 4–5 (April–May 1937), 7 ff.

[2] Avram Gordon, *In friling*, 28. This collection of speeches, which Gordon reconstructed from memory many years later, is our major source of information on his 'opposition' movement.

[3] As quoted in Franco Venturi, *Roots of Revolution*, trans. by Francis Haskell (New York, 1960), 458.

when '...they performed their cultural work with a hot and holy fire which the movement had encountered only once in its history, in its early youth'.[1] But once the intellectuals abandoned the circles for agitation, they had begun to worship false gods; moreover their dedication to the program represented a deliberate and wholesale betrayal of the circle movement. 'They (the intellectuals) suggest to the workers a switch from propaganda to agitation. What does this mean? It means that the intellectuals will know Marx, Plekhanov, etc., they will be completely educated. And we workers? We won't know anything, because only agitation will be carried on among us.'[2]

As Gordon saw it, the intellectuals had adopted the new campaign in order to keep the dependent workers ignorant and helpless, and he offered examples from history to prove that the intelligentsia as a class had been highly treacherous to the proletariat. Adopting some of the ideas of Proudhon, whose writings he knew, and a tone similar to that of the Polish-born anarchist Machajski, Gordon launched into a bitter attack against the pernicious influence of the intellectuals. 'They believe only in their own theories,' he wrote, 'commit the greatest errors, drag the workers after them blindly, and cause the greatest disasters.'[3] In short, Gordon believed that the intellectuals wanted a monopoly on knowledge, that most precious of commodities; and with secular schools beyond the reach of the workers of the Pale, the one avenue of knowledge available to them was rapidly being closed.

Gordon's views were shared by a good many other workers, who constituted an opposition that by 1893 had split the Vilna movement in half. On one side were the intellectuals who provided the theoretical formulations for the agitation program; on the other, the enraged circle workers. Martov notes that in the debates between the advocates of agitation and those of the opposition group, the latter were usually successful. 'Our workers', he added, 'especially the women, avidly followed his

[1] Avram Gordon, *In friling*, 12.
[2] As quoted by Gozhanskii, 'Evreiskoe rabochee', 85.
[3] Avram Gordon, *In friling*, 45. Gordon cited both the French Revolution of 1789 and the revolutions of 1848 as evidence of the intelligentsia's malice towards the working class.

[Gordon's] indictments. He succeeded, among other things, in winning victories over us in several "kassy" meetings.'[1] Nor was the opposition confined to Vilna. In Minsk, too, an opposition movement appeared, headed by Abraham Liesin, who was later to become a well-known Yiddish poet. Like the opposition group in Vilna, workers in Minsk who protested the use of agitation believed that 'The work...must be carried on in depth, among a few workers, rather than extensively, among the masses...As many education circles as possible must be founded; one first has to learn Russian, for only then can the workers be given the fundamentals of theoretical socialism.'[2] Opposition groups emerged also in Gomel and Brest–Litovsk.[3] A movement known as the 'Group of Worker Revolutionaries', headed by the engraver Moise Lur'e, was active in Bialystok in 1897; hostile to the new program of the intellectuals, the 'Group' emphasized the workers' need for education, a stand that was taken by an association in Grodno which likewise resisted the tactics of agitation.[4]

[1] Martov, *Zapiski sotsialdemokrata*, 230. Bernshtein, *Ershte shprotsungen*, 157, writes that 'Workers went over to the opposition thanks to Avram's appeal to their desire for knowledge'. See also *Rukopis' T. Kopel'zona, 1907, ob oppozitsii 1893 g.* (The Bund Archives, New York City); David Zaslavsky (F. P., pseud.), 'Di oppozitsie fun 1893 yor', *Di hofnung*, No. 14 (25 September 1907), 4. It is interesting to find that, among the oppositionists, such 'elite' craftsmen as engravers and jewellers were heavily represented. One of Gordon's chief lieutenants was Abraham 'the Jeweller', and Gordon's first speech in Vilna was delivered at a meeting of the jewellers' 'kassa'.

[2] Levin, *Untererdishe kemfer*, 102. See also Frumkin, 'Ocherki', *Evreiskaia starina*, VI, No. 1 (January–March 1913), 259 ff.; Lev, 'Di yidishe arbeter', 113; Khanke Kopelovich, 'Der onhayb fun kamf', *Royte bleter*, 4; M. Ivensky, 'A. Valt (Liesin), der onfirer fun der ershter idisher national-sotsialistisher bevegung', *Di tsukunft*, XXIV, No. 4 (April 1919), 205–8; Sh. Rabinovich, 'A. Valt (Liesin) un zayn kamf gegen kosmopolitizm, "ekonomizm" un broshurizm', *ibid.*, 208–11. A second group of oppositionists in Minsk, led by Yefim Halperin, seems to have had more in common with Gordon than did the poet. The Minsk opposition broke out in 1895.

[3] Bukhbinder, 'Evreiskoe rabochee dvizhenie v Gomele, 1890–1905 gg.', *Krasnaia letopis'*, No. 2–3 (1922), 42; Mikhalevich, *Zikhroynes*, I, 21.

[4] An-man, 'Bialystoker period', 52. For additional material on the Grodno group, about which there is conflicting evidence, see Lev, 'Pervye shagi', 268–73; Akimov, 'Stroiteli budushchago', *Obrazovanie*, XVI, No. 4 (April 1907), 115; Bronisław Szuszkiewicz, 'Organizacja grodzieńska P.P.S. w latach 1898–1910', *Niepodległość*, XVI, No. 3 (44) (November–December 1937), 513 ff. On the Bialystok 'Group' see B. Eidel'man, 'K istorii vozniknoveniia Rossiskoi sots.-dem. rabochei partii', *Proletarskaia revoliutsiia*, No. 1 (1921), 35; S. Gel'man, 'Pervaia podpol'naia tipografiia gruppy "Rabochee znamia"', *Katorga i ssylka*, No. 6 (27) (1926), 46; Mikhalevich, *Zikhroynes*, I, 44. On Lur'e particularly see David Gershanovich, 'O Moise Vladimiroviche Lur'e', *K dvadtsatpiatiletiiu*, 166–74; Kazimierz Pietkiewicz, 'Mojżiesz Łurje i "Raboczeje

Gordon's opposition in Vilna was based on more than a general feeling of betrayal and anger at having lost the privileges derived from association with the circle. He and his followers were indignant at certain specific proposals by the agitators, among them the decision to use Yiddish as the language of agitation. Most believed this to be utterly impractical. 'If, in general, much in our plan was psychologically indigestible to our workers', Martov wrote, 'the idea of carrying on all, or almost all, of the propaganda in Yiddish provoked immediate rebellion.'[1] Indeed, the Russian orientation which the workers had adopted in the circles proved a major obstacle to their acceptance of the new program.

The oppositionists were most effective in their criticism of the idea that agitation could in fact improve the condition of the masses. In a speech entitled 'Our Hand-workers and the Labor Movement', delivered in 1891, Gordon discussed the general decline of Jewish crafts that had come with industrialization. 'The machine and the factory', he stated, 'are bound to undermine the position of the hand-workers more and more. Difficult as their situation has been up to now, it will become even more serious because of this.'[2] Strikes may be a valuable weapon for an industrialized factory proletariat, Gordon argued, but not for the artisans who were doomed to extinction. In Minsk Liesin ridiculed the program of agitation, calling it a struggle of 'pauper against pauper'. 'In Western Europe and in the great Russian factory centers', he contended, 'workers struggle against

znamia"', *Niepodległość*, VI (1932), 26 ff. Both the Grodno and Bialystok groups were associated with the St Petersburg 'Workers' Flag', and it seems likely that the Grodno group had some contacts with the PPS (Polish Socialist Party). Neither was directly inspired by Gordon's 'opposition' but they had many ideas in common. Mill, *Pionern un boyer*, I, 105, argues that after the Vilna group dispersed some of its members joined the 'Workers' Flag', while according to Blum, *Zikhroynes*, 38, Gordon and Lur'e were in direct contact. At one time Lur'e planned to set up a printing press in Bialystok where Gordon could issue proclamations. For evidence of a similar opposition group in Kovno see Shkliar, 'Onhayb', 207 ff.

[1] Martov, *Zapiski sotsialdemokrata*, 230. Not all the adherents of the Vilna 'opposition' felt this way. Gordon opposed the opening of a Yiddish section in the illegal library of the organization, but another 'opposition' member, Alter 'the Spat-Maker', agreed to the proposal on the grounds that education, no matter what language employed, was beneficial to the workers. See Litvak, *Vos geven*, 99–100.

[2] Avram Gordon, *In friling*, 35.

capitalists who are very wealthy, while in our Jewish towns and cities the workers struggle against paupers like themselves.'[1] In 1893 members of the 'opposition' in Vilna intervened during a strike and tried to persuade the participants that such a form of protest was futile. As a report from that period noted: 'They negated the significance of the strike "kassy", considering them entirely pointless institutions.'[2] As Gordon saw it, the intellectuals were guilty of 'scholasticism', of 'dogmatism', of lumping together all workers without distinction, be they factory workers in St Petersburg or tailors in Vilna. Interestingly enough, the same argument was used by leading Zionists such as Leschinsky and Ber Borokhov in their polemics against the Bund.[3]

In their attempt to refute this charge, both Kremer and Gozhanskii conceded that, given the peculiar nature of the Jewish proletariat, the socialists were operating under severe handicaps. Kremer admitted that since many Jewish artisans might in time become employers who could operate independently within their own shops, 'a worker regards his situation as temporary and agrees to put up with a certain amount of sacrifice'. Gozhanskii even questioned whether one could hope to improve the living conditions of the Jewish artisan masses when, as he said, 'Some masters are so poverty-stricken that an increase in wages will force them to close down the shops'.[4]

Nonetheless, when they adopted the tactics of agitation the socialists were forced to reconsider the negative attitude they had formerly had toward the revolutionary potential of the Jewish working class. This reconsideration led both Kremer and Gozhanskii to the paradoxical conclusion that the very nature of the Jewish working class might foster rather than impede the labor movement. Thus Kremer claimed that artisans 'are more cultured,

[1] Ivensky, 'A. Valt', 207.
[2] *Materialy*, Agursky, 415–17. In fact, the intervention was successful. The striking workers were convinced of the futility of their 'kassa' and it soon collapsed.
[3] Leschinsky's *Der idisher arbeter* (*in rusland*) has already been discussed. In his preface, he says that the purpose of his book is to prove that the Bund was wrong in claiming that the Jewish proletariat could be compared to that of industrialized countries or even to the Russian working class. This was the purpose, too, of Borokhov's study of the Jewish strike movement which is cited below.
[4] *Ob agitatsii*, 24; Gozhanskii, 'A briv', 633. See also Chapter 1, p. 9.

more developed' than factory workers. Moreover, by virtue of their greater mobility they are more willing to strike than are factory workers.[1] Gozhanskii noted that shop owners would find it more difficult to replace striking artisans since the latter were skilled, whereas factory hands were more easily replaced. Furthermore, an artisan could always work at home if he were not hired in another shop, while a factory worker was dependent upon a job in the factory for his livelihood. Lastly, since the artisan had behind him a long tradition of organization, and a genuine feeling of solidarity for the workers in his particular craft, he was considered an apt subject for the new campaign of agitation.[2]

Such arguments, signaling a complete about-face in the attitudes of the leaders, contained a considerable amount of truth. The artisans did, in fact, strike in great numbers, and revealed a talent for organization which far surpassed that of any labor force in the Empire. But the basic premise of the opposition groups, namely that the Jewish artisan class was doomed to extinction and that the class struggle would be one of 'pauper against pauper', was not refuted. The Marxists could only hope that eventually the Jewish artisan class would be absorbed into the factories. For, if this did not occur, the initial victories of the agitation tactics might not endure.

The various opposition groups which sprang up during the transition from propaganda to agitation were short-lived, as the new approach won thousands of adherents among the economically dissatisfied artisan masses. Once the circle workers had to rely on their own resources, they found them very thin indeed; abandoned by their former teachers, overwhelmed by the masses who had no sympathy for their views, they had little opportunity to maneuver or to grow.[3] Nonetheless some of their ideas persisted. Although Mill claims that by 1894 Vilna had 'no memory' of Gordon's group, as late as 1901 two workers could still be found propagating his views in that city.[4] In Minsk, after the

---

[1] *Ob agitatsii*, 24.   [2] Gozhanskii, 'A briv', 640 ff.

[3] See Mill, *Pionern un boyer*, I, 104-5; Bernshtein, *Ershte shprotsungen*, 159; Zaslavsky, 'Di oppozitsie'.

[4] One of these workers was an engraver. See H. Botvinik, 'Di vilner may-demonstratsie in 1902 yor', in *Hirsh Lekert, tsum 20-tn yortog fun zayn kepung* (Moscow, 1922), 26-7.

first opposition group led by Liesin had been squelched by the strike movement, a new group emerged with similar attacks against the proponents of agitation; as late as 1900 the issue of the circles versus mass agitation was still being debated.[1] Throughout the history of the Russian Jewish labor movement pro-'kruzhok' sentiments and resentment at the 'betrayal' of the intellectuals were never entirely absent.

It is important to note that the transition from propaganda to agitation did more than shift the emphasis from the circle to more dynamic means of protest such as the strike. By stressing the role of the masses, whose language it was obliged to adopt, the new movement set out on the road toward an affirmation of Jewish nationalism. Moreover, the decision to appeal to the masses produced a new kind of leadership.

The circle intellectuals remained major figures in the movement's higher echelons, but they were not suited to lead the masses in their economic struggle. For one thing, they were frequently ignorant of Yiddish; for another, as we shall see, the movement's need for secrecy often isolated them from the rank-and-file. The new 'agitators', as they were known, were often drawn from the 'half-intelligentsia', so-called because its members had not completed their education and had no diplomas. Such 'half-intellectuals', often recruited from the local Yeshivas, did not possess the educational attainments of a Martov. But their knowledge of the language and life of the masses better qualified them to become labor leaders.[2]

[1] Bukhbinder, *Krasnaia letopis'*, No. 5 (1923), 131 f.; Medem, *Fun mayn leben*, I, 200.
[2] See comments in Peskin, 'Di "grupe"', 551–2, and Kopel'zon, 'Evreiskoe rabochee', 74. According to Ginzburg, 'Nachalnye shagi', 102, 'The majority were from the petty-bourgeoisie which at that time had no access to the upper or middle schools, but which all the same had a great desire for education, read a good deal, and were highly intelligent'.

CHAPTER 4

The New Organization

> No worker alone is in a position to carry on a struggle
> against his employer...none of us through his own
> strength is able to attain a shorter workday and higher
> wages for his hard labor. Therefore we all unite, in order
> to stand together and to support each other.
>
> From a 'kassa' statute of Vilna tailors, 1896

The transition from propaganda to agitation brought with it new
forms of organization that either replaced or supplemented the
traditional circles. In the larger centers a hierarchical scheme of
organization was commonly used. On the lowest level were the
trade union organizations, the heirs of the early 'kassy' that had
formed during the 1880s and 1890s. Comprised of the maximum
number of workers they could recruit from a given craft, the
trade unions were variously known as 'skhodkes' (assemblies),
'fakh ferzamlungen' or 'fakh komisies' (craft assemblies or craft
commissions), 'ferayns' (unions), or simply 'kassy'. The
members would elect representatives to an all-craft council, called
the 'agitation "skhodke"', 'agitation assembly', or 'central
commission'. Supervising the movement from above was the
local 'committee' or, as it was termed in Minsk, the 'razborke'.
These committees, which existed in the major cities, consisted
of both elected and appointed members.[1]

---

[1] On local organization see 'Ustav rabochei organizatsii', in Moise Rafes, *Ocherki po
istorii 'bunda'* (Moscow, 1923), 315–26 (Vilna); Levin, *Untererdishe kemfer*, 100–1, and
Medem, *Fun mayn leben*, I, 198 ff. (Minsk); 'Konstruktsiia partiinoi organizatsii
"Bunda"', in Rafes, *Ocherki*, 326–8 (Kovno); An-man, 'Bialystoker period', 46 ff.
(Bialystok); 'Ustav professional'nago soiuza', in Bukhbinder, *Krasnaia letopis'*, No. 2–3
(1922), 100–2, and 'Gomel'skoe rabochee', in Agursky (ed.), *Di sotsialistishe literatur*,
360 (Gomel); 'Di arbeter bavegung in grodne', *Di letste pasirungen*, No. 14 (12 July 1905);
Mikhalevich, *Zikhroynes*, I, 22 (Brest–Litovsk); Aronson, 'Tsu der geshikhte fun der
sotsialistisher un arbeter bavegung', in *Vitebsk amol*, 302 (Vitebsk). In smaller towns the
organizational pattern was less complex, frequently consisting only of workers'
assemblies and an assembly of representatives; see, for example, Shtern, *Zikhroynes*, 23
(on Bielsk, a town near Bialystok). In Dvinsk the pattern of organization was somewhat

Class struggle in the Pale

In 1897 many of the local committees united to form the social democratic party known as the Bund, which claimed to speak for the Jewish proletariat in the Pale of Settlement and represented it in the international socialist movement. The party provided the organizational framework within which the labor movement operated.[1]

The backbone of the new organization, created as a result of the transition to agitation, was the 'kassa'. The 'kassy' of the circle period were merely self-help funds—they now became full-fledged underground trade unions, dedicated to the economic struggle. Their aim was 'to unite the workers to struggle for a better life and to supply the means needed to implement this struggle'.[2] The first sentence of a similar statute from Vitebsk in 1898 reads as follows: 'Our "kassa" has as its purpose the unification of the workers of our craft in one general union for the struggle with our bosses, in order to improve our economic situation.'[3] Members were expected to pay weekly or monthly dues, and in return were given financial support during strikes. As if to emphasize the difference between the new 'kassy' and the old, one statute stipulated that dues were to be used only for strikes; special collections were authorized for members who were either temporarily unemployed or in difficult financial straits.[4] In Gomel the members of a 'kassa' were obliged to pay as much dues as they could afford, but this meant 'no less than 10 kopeks a month'.[5] In some instances members were also required to pay

different; rather than uniting in assemblies of their own crafts, the workers were organized in groups which embraced several crafts. See Avram der Tate, *Bleter fun mayn yugent, Zikhroynes fun a bundist* (New York, 1959), 220. This seems to have been the case, too, during the early years of the Kovno movement; see Shkliar, 'Onhayb', 188 ff.

[1] The history of the Bund is treated in this work only when its policies directly affected the labor movement. For standard histories see: Herts *et al., Di geshikhte fun bund* I, II (New York, 1960, 1962), III (New York, 1966); Bukhbinder, *Istoriia evreiskogo rabochego dvizheniia v Rossii* (Leningrad, 1925); Rafes, *Ocherki*. See also Henry Tobias, *The Origins and Evolution of the Jewish Bund until 1901*, unpublished Ph.D. dissertation, Stanford University, 1957; Mishkinsky, *Yesodot*; and Frankel, *Socialism*; Henry Shukman, *The Relations between the Jewish Bund and the RSDRP*, unpublished Ph.D. dissertation, Oxford Univerity, 1960.

[2] 'Ustav rabochei organizatsii', in Rafes, *Ocherki*, 315.

[3] Quoted by Lur'e, in Dimanshtein (ed.), *Revoliutsionnoe dvizhenie*, 116.

[4] 'Der statut fun der kasse un baylage vegn der noytikayt ayntsuordnen biblioteken (algemayne yesoydes, vilne 1894)', published in *Unzer tsayt*, No. 2 (5 February 1928), 89.

[5] See 'Ustav professional'nago soiuza', Bukhbinder, *Krasnaia letopis'* No. 2–3, 101.

entrance fees which, in a Vilna cigarette makers' 'kassa', amounted to as much as 25 kopeks.[1] Members were admitted only after careful checks had been made to ascertain their responsibility. One statute stated that 'only honorable men are accepted into the "kassa"; men who will not refuse to go on strike if the majority of the "kassa" members find it necessary; who do not talk too much; who are not hypocrites; who will not talk about what is discussed at the "kassa" assemblies, and who understand what is said to them.' To qualify for admission to another 'kassa' candidates were required to understand 'the conflicting interests of workers and capitalists, the need for unity, and the aims of the "kassa"'; and at a special meeting they had to prove that they grasped every point in the statute.[2] Special precautions were taken to insure that only workers were admitted, a necessary provision if one recalls the nature of the Jewish artisan class. 'In no instance can an employer be a member of the "kassa"', one set of rules reads, and it goes on to say that those workers who feel otherwise are making a 'great mistake'. Another statute, too, insisted that 'Employers cannot become members of the "kassa"'.[3] Members who became independent masters were immediately ousted from the 'kassa'. In Kovno when the carpenters' organization was found to consist of both employers and employees, it was disbanded by the leadership.[4]

'Kassa' members elected various officials, such as treasurers, 'representatives', 'elders', library heads, etc. It devolved upon the leaders of the 'kassa', who were usually termed 'representatives', to make vital decisions such as when to hold a strike. The statutes defined their role as follows: 'When a strike in a work-

[1] See the statute attached to Gozhanskii's 'Erinerungen fun a papirosn makherke', *Unzer tsayt*, No. 8–9 (September–October 1928), 122.

[2] 'Ustav vilenskoi kassy bor'by', in Agursky (ed.), *Di sotsialistishe literatur*, 389; the statute is also published in *Unzer tsayt*, No. 3–4 (March–April 1928), 119–24, and apparently dates from 1896. The workers involved were tailors. The second quotation is from 'Erinerungen', *Unzer tsayt*, No. 8–9 (September–October 1928), 125. In Vilna members were elected at general meetings of the 'kassa' (Agursky (ed.), *Di sotsialistishe literatur*, 389).

[3] 'Der statut', *Unzer tsayt*, No. 2 (5 February 1928), 90; 'Ustav professional'nago soiuza', Bukhbinder, *Krasnaia letopis'*, No. 2–3 (1922), 101.

[4] See Shkliar, 'Onhayb', 190. Such clauses, of course, illustrate the point already made regarding the rather thin line separating employer and employee.

shop is necessary, every member must report this to his represent-ative...' 'Every representative must meet with the members no less than once a week, and report to them on everything con-cerning their craft and the movement as a whole.' 'The represent-atives of the "kassa" must be skillful in speaking to the members and must understand whatever is going on in the craft.'[1] In the Vilna 'kassa' a foreman ('starshina') and a 'controller' were elected, the latter openly and the former in secret. The controller was responsible for the financial operations of the 'kassa', while the members were 'forbidden to do anything without the per-mission of their foreman and were obliged to carry out all the tasks he gave them'.[2] At the 'kassa' meetings, which were held regularly, all matters of interest to the particular craft were discussed and debated.[3]

Upon occasion special 'kassa' celebrations were held, usually to commemorate the founding of the organization. These events were often attended by representatives of other 'kassy', who brought greetings from their own organizations and shared in the exuberant spirit which invariably pervaded these celebrations. The following description of the fifth anniversary celebration of the Bialystok woodworkers' 'kassa' in 1901 is indicative of the atmosphere that typified these gatherings:

The place where the gathering was held was decorated with two red flags and pictures of Karl Marx and Ferdinand Lassalle. On the flags was written: 'Workers of all countries, unite'; 'Unity and struggle are the strength of the worker, long live the fifth anniversary.' A member opened the celebration with a speech in which he explained the

---

1 'Ustav professional'nago soiuza', Bukhbinder, *Krasnaia letopis'*, No. 2–3 (1922), 101; 'Ustav vilenskoi kassy bor'by', in Agursky (ed.), *Di sotsialistishe literatur*, 388. On the functions of the elected officers see especially 'Ustav rabochei organizatsii', in Rafes, *Ocherki*, 316 ff.

2 Rafes, *Ocherki*, 317. According to 'Der statut', *Unzer tsayt*, No. 2 (5 February 1928), 92–3, a committee of three to seven men ruled the 'kassa'; members of the committee were elected indirectly for a period of one or two years.

3 Akimov, *Materialy*, 24. He comments: 'The skhodka ["kassa"] deliberates and con-siders questions relating to its craft', while in Minsk members of the 'kassy' 'would meet secretly every week and discuss everything concerning their craft' (Levin, *Untererdishe kemfer*, 100). At such meetings workers were 'forbidden to talk all at once. When one person speaks all the others must be quiet, so as to hear what he says.' ('Erinerungen', *Unzer tsayt*, No. 8–9 [September–October 1928], 126.)

importance of the holiday and briefly noted the progress that had been made by the carpenters' craft during the last five years. Another person spoke about the woodworkers' craft, and praised our brothers who have fallen in the struggle. Everyone had a good time until late at night and, singing revolutionary songs, everyone was inspired with the thought of taking a firm stand for our ideas.[1]

These occasions had a distinct didactic purpose. At a carpenters' celebration in Gomel speeches were given on the need to shorten the working day, on economic and political action, and on the history of the carpenters' movement in that city; in Kovno tailors, who assembled to celebrate the fourth anniversary of their 'kassa', heard a speech on 'Social Democracy and the Trade Union movement'. While the 'kassa' celebrations were also used to raise funds,[2] their main function was to instill in the workers a feeling of dedication to the movement. Characterized by a show of brotherhood and solidarity, the gatherings proved to the workers that they were not alone in the struggle for justice, and thus helped to fortify them and make them more willing to risk the dangers of membership in an illegal organization.[3]

It is difficult to ascertain how many workers the 'kassy' attracted because there were considerable fluctuations in membership. A successful strike might swell the membership of a 'kassa', whereas a failure might destroy the entire organization. In the early years of the movement, when the strikes were most successful, membership was correspondingly high. For example, in Vilna, where the mass movement had originated, there were twenty-seven craft organizations in 1895 having a total of 962 members, approximately 30 per cent of the workers in those crafts; in 1899 there were 1,304 dues-paying members of the

---

[1] *Der bialystoker arbeter*, No. 4 (April 1901), 8.

[2] See *Der kampf*, No. 1 (September 1900), 16; *Posledniia izvestiia*, No. 99 (28 November 1902); and No. 94 (13 November 1902). At the tailors' meeting in Kovno (No. 99) more than five rubles were collected for workers who had been arrested, and three for political agitation. The cigarette-makers' 'kassa' in Vilna ('Erinerungen', *Unzer tsayt*, No. 8–9 [September–October 1928], 123) was authorized to hold dances to raise funds.

[3] Thus during a celebration of the carpenters' 'kassa' in Gomel, which attracted 300 men, 'everyone swore to carry on the bitter struggle to the end'. See Levin, 'Di ershte yorn fun der revolutsie', *Royte bleter*, 7.

'kassy', or 24 per cent of the total number.[1] These same proportions held true for Minsk, where in 1895–6 100 per cent of all the bristle workers, 75 per cent of all the binders, and 40 per cent of all the locksmiths were organized—a total of 800 organized workers.[2] According to one estimate, prior to 1900 20 per cent of all the Jewish workers in Bialystok and almost 40 per cent of those in Gomel were organized.[3] The decline of the strike movement, however, caused a decrease in the 'kassy' membership, and shortly before the first Russian revolution a well-informed observer estimated that only 2,000 workers were enrolled in 'kassy' throughout the Pale of Settlement. On the other hand, a significantly greater number of workers were still influenced by the 'kassy', a fact which must be taken into account in any attempt to evaluate the impact these institutions had on the Jewish working masses.[4]

The leaders of the craft 'kassy', generally known as 'agitators', replaced the circle intellectuals as the decisive figures of the new movement. In his 'Letter to the Agitators', Gozhanskii wrote that an agitator:

Must have many acquaintances among the workers of the craft in which he wishes to agitate; his relations with them must be such that he will be aware of the slightest details affecting a worker's life in the craft...he must know and understand what improvement the workers particularly desire; he must be acquainted with the economic nature of the craft in order to know what can and cannot be achieved.[5]

As leaders of the economic struggle, the agitators constantly had to recruit members, plan strikes, and attend meetings. About one agitator in Vilna we are told:

The movement took up so much time that he was forced to cut down on sleep. He had to go to a meeting of his craft organization, and to

---

[1] 'Materialy', Agursky (ed.), *Di sotsialistishe literatur*, 420; 'Der leben un kampf', *Der idisher arbeter*, No. 11 (1901), 41 ff. These statistics were published by the movement itself, and there is an obvious danger that they might be exaggerated.

[2] 'Der leben un kampf', *Der idisher arbeter*, No. 10 (1900), 69 (Table).

[3] See the figures in *Di geshikhte fun der idisher arbayter bevegung in rusland un poylen* (Geneva, 1900), 40–1. The following figures are given in round numbers: Dvinsk, 400 organized workers; Bialystok, 1,000; Gomel, 360; Minsk, nearly 1,000.

[4] Akimov, *Materialy*, 25. He maintains that 30,000 Jewish workers were under the influence of the local organizations.   [5] Gozhanskii, 'A briv', 365.

participate in a discussion on the strikes that were to be declared in other crafts where he was the agitator. He also had to go to a meeting the agitators were having with the intellectuals. Apart from this he took part in many circles, in some as a teacher, in others as a pupil.[1]

Like the intellectual leaders of the circles, the agitators became figures of veneration, charismatic leaders to the masses whom they promised a better life. 'Yashka was a passionate agitator', a contemporary from Dvinsk reported:

With his ardent nature he won over all those to whom he spoke. I, too, was captivated by his inspired words (literally 'hot breath') despite the fact that I understood nothing of what he said to me. I was agitated and stunned by the very fact that Yashka had taken me under his wing and had spoken to me.[2]

The agitators conducted their campaign in special streets known as 'birzhes', which became focal points of activity in the local movement. Here workers and agitators met to discuss the problems of the day, and confer with the 'representatives'; this was the place, too, where 'kassy' members would pay their dues, where legal and illegal literature was distributed, and where important meetings were arranged. Within the comparative safety afforded by these special streets workers would often walk arm in arm dressed in the latest 'proletarian' fashions, as they denounced the members of the 'bourgeoisie' who, as in Minsk, might just happen to be walking on the other side of the street. When a 'birzhe' was overrun with police spies, it was simply moved to another location. In Vitebsk, where the police made a concerted effort to eliminate the meeting place on Zemkovskii Street, 'The struggle was waged in the open; the police threatened the workers with the use of force, but the workers went from one sidewalk to another, went to another street and met there, and returned to the first street. The police finally gave up.'[3] In a country where freedom of assembly and speech was denied, the

[1] Bernshtein, *Ershte shprotsungen*, 65. The description is of Maks Nodel who, we have seen, eventually left Vilna for St Petersburg, where he hoped to become an 'intellectual'.
[2] Berman, *In loif fun yorn*, 107. The man who wrote these comments failed to understand because the agitator spoke a peculiar mixture of 'Yiddish-Russian'.
[3] See Ginzburg, 'Nachalnye shagi', 111.

'birzhes' were vitally important, and despite frequent police raids they were regularly used as arenas for agitation. Without them it is doubtful whether the mass movement would have survived.[1]

The agitators of a particular city held periodic assemblies where problems affecting the entire labor movement in that locality would be aired. These assemblies frequently took control of the 'kassy's' financial affairs and determined whether strikes should be declared. The powers of the agitation assemblies and the local committees differed from place to place. In Vilna the central commission (the equivalent of the agitation assembly) had a free hand in practical matters, while problems of theory and tactics were dealt with exclusively by the Committee. On the other hand, in Gomel the agitation assembly was not allowed to make final decisions on strikes. 'Without the permission of the Committee', the statutes maintained, 'workers do not have the right to hold a strike.'[2] Such an extreme degree of centralization, however, seems incongruous, and it is probable that strikes were usually called by the 'kassy' representatives, with the higher echelons being informed only when the strikes were of major scope.

The local Committee was regarded as the 'ministerial cabinet of the city organization'. Its members were likely to be intellectuals who were usually far removed from the actual class struggle. In part, this aloofness from the masses was due to the conspiratorial nature of the movement. In Gomel, for example, the statute of the 'kassa' stipulated that, 'Each member is to know only his own representative, to whom he pays (his dues), but not the other representatives...only the representatives, and not the masses, are to know the treasurer...'[3] In Bialystok 'kassy' members were unaware that an agitation assembly existed; the latter organization, in turn, was equally unaware of the existence of the local Committee. In Minsk, Vladimir Medem,

[1] Berman, *In loif fun yorn*, 105 ff.; see also Bernshtein, *Ershte shprotsungen*, 33–5; Levin, *Untererdishe kemfer*, 134–5; Medem, *Fun mayn leben*, I, 208–9. The use of special streets for meeting places was often supplemented, as in Lodz, by the cafés; see *Flug-bletel* (Lodz), No. 2 (July 1902).
[2] 'Ustav professional'nago soiuza', Bukhbinder, *Krasnaia letopis'*, No. 2–3 (1922), 101; 'Ustav rabochei organizatsii', in Rafes, *Ocherki*, 324.
[3] 'Ustav professional'nago soiuza', Bukhbinder, *Krasnaia letopis'*, No. 2–3 (1922), 102.

a member of the Committee, was expressly forbidden to take part in mass agitation, while in Riga one writer commented: 'None of the workers...knew our (the intellectuals') real names and addresses.'[1] The only link between the agitation assembly and the Committee was provided by a 'farmitler' or middleman, whose duty in Vilna, at least, was 'to convey all the demands of the central commission to the Committee, and the decision of the Committee to the central commission'.[2]

Members of the local Committees served the movement in various ways: they wrote articles, published proclamations, addressed meetings, and maintained connexions with labor leaders in other cities. Since they regularly attended meetings of the Bund, they helped to shape the ideology of the Party and to determine its relations with other socialist parties in the Empire. All of which is not to say that the Committee was composed strictly of intellectuals, or even 'half-intellectuals'. In Bialystok in the late 1890s all three members of the Committee were workers, while in Minsk the Committee was half-worker, half-intellectual.[3] Whatever their background the important point is that all Committee members were Marxist-oriented party members. As such, they conceived their task to be the eventual conversion of the 'economic' struggle against the employers into a political struggle against the regime itself. Such attitudes created the potential for diagreements with some 'kassy' members, who were chiefly interested in raising their economic standards. The

[1] Raphael Abramovich, *In tsvay revolutsies* (New York, 1944), I, 64; An-man, 'Bialystoker period', 47; Medem, *Fun mayn leben*, I, 208; Martov, *Zapiski sotsialdemokrata*, 175, notes that 'Members of the organization were never called by their real names...' Jacob Peskin, the leader of the Dvinsk movement, was recognized only by a few active workers as he strolled through the local 'birzhe'; see Berman, *In loif fun yorn*, 181.

[2] 'Ustav rabochei organizatsii', in Rafes, *Ocherki*, 324. See also Medem, *Fun mayn leben*, I, 200; Levin, *Untererdishe kemfer*, 147. It should also be noted that it was their ignorance of Yiddish, and not only the need to keep their identities secret, that made it virtually impossible for the intellectuals to take an active part in practical labor agitation. Among the Vilna leaders who initiated the transition from propaganda to agitation only two people, Gozhanskii and Kremer's wife, Pati, knew Yiddish well.

[3] An-man, 'Bialystoker period', 47; Medem, *Fun mayn leben*, I, 208. On the question of the proportion of intellectuals to non-intellectuals in the higher echelons of the movement ('intellectual' meaning educated) see Henry Tobias and Charles E. Woodhouse, 'Primordial Ties and Political Process in Pre-Revolutionary Russia: the Case of the Jewish Bund', *Comparative Studies in Society and History*, VIII, No. 3 (April 1966), 331–60.

conflict between economic and political aims was to have a considerable impact upon the Jewish labor movement.[1]

The various local movements in the provinces of Belorussia–Lithuania were co-ordinated by the Central Committee of the Bund and the party's 'Foreign Commitee', which operated abroad. Workers' 'kassy' were generally organized to deal with a specific locality and were not in contact with 'kassy' in other cities. However, there were several notable exceptions to this, the most remarkable being the union of the bristle workers, the so-called 'Bershter-Bund'.

Writing of these workers, Medem called them 'the cream of the crop ("di smetene") in our movement'.[2] Since many of them worked in small towns on the Prussian border, they were especially valuable as smugglers, both of illegal literature and of revolutionaries.[3] As Levin comments, 'In some small towns there was a large number of organized workers, especially bristle workers. With their help it was possible finally to institute a well-organized apparatus whereby illegal literature was smuggled in from abroad.'[4] As a group they were considered extremely intelligent, the most 'developed' as one socialist called them. In Minsk they enjoyed the highest literacy rate of any single proletarian group, and a study conducted by the Jewish Colonization Association found that 'In many respects the bristle workers are more cultivated than their colleagues in other industries...'[5] This is explained by the fact that a large percentage of them came from middle class families (i.e. families of shopkeepers, merchants, and the like); several bristle workers who later became leaders of the movement were sons of fairly well-to-do families. A feuilleton in the socialist press describes one such worker as 'half bristle

[1] See below, Chapter 7.
[2] Medem, *Fun mayn leben*, I, 213.
[3] *Ibid.*; Bernshtein, *Ershte shprotsungen*, 105.
[4] Levin, *Untererdishe kemfer*, 108.
[5] *Sbornik*, II, 110; the first quotation is from Mikhalevich, *Zikhroynes*, II, 8, who adds that 'The bristle workers represented a great social force in the little factory towns and made their influence felt on life there'. On the literacy rate of the bristle workers see 'K voprosu o polozhenii evreev remeslennikov', *Nedel'naia khronika 'Voskhoda'*, XX, No. 39 (21 June 1901), 19. For a description of a highly cultured bristle worker whose favorite authors were Lermontov and Pushkin, see Avraham Liesin, 'Di amolike opozitsie in minsk', in his *Zikhroynes un bilder* (New York, 1954), 288–9.

worker and half Yeshiva student'.[1] Like the Vilna stocking makers, and like the 'labor aristocracy' of the circles, the bristle workers proved highly susceptible to the appeals of the movement.

As early as 1890 the bristle workers held strikes, and in 1891 they founded 'kassy' in Vilna and other cities.[2] In 1895 delegates from these 'kassy' met in Vilna, where they issued a brochure stressing the interdependence of all bristle workers.[3] The result of this and similar meetings was the establishment in 1898 of the 'Jewish Bristle-Workers' Union in Poland and Lithuania'; the Union elected a Central Committee and began to issue a special publication, *The Awakener*. At its founding Congress, which apparently took place in Kovno, the Union could already boast of a number of achievements: 'The number of organized workers in cities where organizations exist amounts to 60 per cent... Practically everywhere the length of the working day is 12–13 hours.'[4]

Thus was born 'the only example in Russia...of an organization in different towns and cities of workers in a single trade'.[5] In order to explain why the bristle workers were able to pioneer in the history of Russian trade unionism reference must be made to the nature of the industry itself. Generally speaking, the pro-

[1] 'A kholom erev yom tov-dem ershten may', *Der veker*, No. 4 (May 1900), 3–4. For a list of bristle workers of middle class origin who were notable as activists see Cherniovsky, *Der yidisher arbeter*, 134. In an attempt to explain why so many middle class youths entered this industry, this source notes that there was a slight possibility that the bristle workers might eventually become wealthy 'industrialists', a possibility that was unheard of for other artisans. Bristle making, it should be added, required more skill than did crafts in most other workshops. See *Sbornik*, II, 108 ff.

[2] Malinowski, *Materiały*, 252; 'Materialy', Agursky (ed.), *Di sotsialistishe literatur*, 412–707. See also S. Dubnov-Erlich, *Garber-bund un bershter-bund*, trans., L. Hodes (from Polish) (Warsaw, 1937), 181 ff.

[3] On the conference see Ben-Uziel, 'In baginen fun der bershter-arbet ba yidn in rusland', *Virtshaft un lebn*, I, No. 1 (July 1928), 57 ff. According to Ben-Uziel, it was decided at that time to dispatch two agitators to Suvalki Province, and especially to Vilkovishki (Wilkowiszki), the capital of bristle production in that province. For a summary of the above-mentioned brochure see Agursky (ed.), *Di sotsialistishe literatur*, 409–7.

[4] 'K evreiskim rabochim-shchetochnikam', a Russian translation of the manifesto issued in 1898 and published in *Listok 'rabotnika'*, No. 9–10 (November 1898), 13. On the founding Congress see Bernshtein, *Ershte shprotsungen*, 101 ff. At a previous meeting, held in 1897, delegates to the Congress reported that both the wages and the cultural level of the bristle workers had risen considerably; see Ben-Uziel, *Virtshaft un lebn*, I, No. 1 (July 1928), 58.

[5] *Rabochee delo*, No. 4–5 (September–December 1899), 112.

duction of bristles was very well organized, especially in comparison to that of, say, shoes or dresses. Bristle factory owners purchased raw materials abroad, in Leipzig, and sold the finished products at distant markets in Russia and abroad. Unlike the masters of the artisan shops, they acted in unison, instituting co-operative buying and selling arrangements and maintaining similar conditions in their establishments. For their part the bristle workers were accustomed to travel from one city or town to the next to find new openings for work. If the industry brought the owners into close contact, it also forged a far more homogeneous work force than that which existed in other crafts. According to the Union proclamation, the opportunity to meet workers in other cities led the workers to realize that their interests were identical and thus promoted a feeling of 'craft solidarity'.[1]

At the same time, the very mobility of the bristle workers increased the prospect of strike-breaking. As the brochure issued at the 1895 conference explained, 'every time it is necessary to begin a struggle we are frightened by the thought that we will be replaced by (other) workers, to whom our conditions will appear excellent'. Hence the need for absolutely uniform conditions. 'If the same arrangements will prevail there as here (i.e. a 12-hour day), our employers will lose the desire to invite them, and they themselves will not answer their (the employers') call.'[2]

As one Russian socialist journal summed it up: 'It is undoubtedly only the special conditions of bristle production... the identical foreign market and the frequent traveling back and forth of the workers, which make possible the formation of such a union under our barbaric, despotic police regime.'[3] Paradoxically, the most immediate cause for the formation of the Union was the threat to workers from an association of factory owners. 'The employers too were not asleep', we read in the manifesto of 1898.

[1] 'K evreiskim', *Listok 'rabotnika'*, No. 9–10 (November 1898), 12.
[2] Quoted in 'Materialy', Agursky (ed.), *Di sotsialistishe literatur*, 408.
[3] *Rabochee delo*, No. 9 (May 1901), 99. The Union itself drew precisely the same conclusion; see *Der veker*, No. 11 (March 1902), 5.

The bristle factory owners could not but be aware of the existence of worker unions, and in order to fight them decided to create their own union, a sort of 'syndicate'. The owners agreed not to hire in their factories workers who had been fired by one or another member of the 'syndicate', and they resolved to help each other in times of strikes.[1]

In banding together the owners had essentially defeated their own purpose, for the syndicate inevitably prompted the workers to unite.

The chief function of the Bristle-Workers' Union was 'to carry out more successfully the struggle for the improvement of (our) conditions',[2] and it had the support of dedicated cadres of worker-agitators, who brought the idea of the class struggle from the large industrial centers such as Vilna to the small towns in which the bristle industry was concentrated. Thus Avram 'The bristle worker', we are told, travelled 'from city to city on missions for the movement,...one night (he) would sleep here, another there among the bristle workers, at an inn, or in a cheap hotel'.[3] Similarly Alter 'The bristle worker', who was originally from Vilna, 'went off to Ponevyezh in order to begin the struggle for better working conditions in the local bristle factories'.[4] Those intellectuals who were associated with the Union, which was reputed to be a strictly proletarian organization, helped edit the official journal that was published during 1898–1903.

[1] 'K evreiskim', *Listok 'rabotnika'*, No. 9–10 (November 1898), 13; see also Dubnov-Erlich, *Garber-bund*, 198. The manifesto states that 'The bristle workers were forced to counter the organization of the employers with their own powerful organization...' A syndicate of employers of 1905 is described in *Di letste pasirungen*, No. 23 (18 October 1905), 4. The employers created a self-help fund, worked out agreements on production and established a black list. The syndicate consisted of 17 of the wealthiest bristle factory owners. On the relationship between the owners' syndicate and the workers' union see also Bernshtein, *Ershte shprotsungen*, 91; he notes that 'employers...founded an association even before the bristle workers organized a union...'

[2] 'K evreiskim', *Listok 'rabotnika'*, No. 9–10 (November 1898), 13.

[3] Bernshtein, *Ershte shprotsungen*, 91, 93; like many other leaders in his craft, Avram was fairly well educated. On his role in the bristle makers' movement see also Medem, *Fun mayn leben*, I, 213.

[4] Mill, *Pionern un boyer*, I, 72–3. For a description of another agitator who travelled from city to city, see Joseph Grinberg (Ishayke der Vilner Bershter), 'Erinerungen vegen bershter-bund', *Der veker*, VI, No. 309 (15 October 1927), 19–21; No. 310 (22 October 1927). At the age of fifteen Grinberg went from Vilna to Vilkovishki to spread the 'new word', as he puts it.

In 1900 the Union claimed a membership of 800 workers. By this time its organizational structure was fairly sophisticated: Poland and Lithuania had been divided into districts, each with its own strike 'kassa' and its own 'center', while the Central Committee supplied the local organizations with funds and illegal literature and was responsible for maintaining close ties among them.[1] It should be noted that the Union neither confined itself to Poland and Lithuania nor to bristle workers alone. Agitators were sent, for example, to Volynia (in the Ukraine) to organize the workers there, and the Union hoped eventually to establish an all-Russian organization. It also took the lead in organizing workers of other crafts in the smaller towns.[2] Special care was taken to eliminate the possibility of long, costly and unsuccessful strikes: 'The center must see to it that the number of strikes in a district not exceed the help available from the "kassy" and the other bristle workers in that district.' The Union laws further stipulated that strikes could be held only after local groups had consulted with the district Committee.[3] When in 1902 the strike movement had reached its natural limitations, the Union resolved that 'in regions where the Bristle-Workers' Union has already attained many economic improvements, only those strikes may be held which are initiated by the factory owners' attempt to take back what (we) have already won'.[4]

Like any trade union, the Bristle-Workers' Union sought to eliminate specific abuses from which its members suffered. It attacked the practice of paying middlemen by the piece, and suggested that workers co-operate with them only if weekly

[1] On the number of organized workers see *Rabochee delo*, No. 8 (November 1900), 66. On the organization of the Union see 'Soiuz shchetinshchikov v zhandarmskom osveshchenii', a police report made on the request of Zubatov and published in Rafes, *Ocherki*, 333; 'Unzer 8-ter tsuzamenfahr', *Der veker*, No. 3 (January 1900), 1. By the eleventh conference of the union, held in 1902, a special 'Polish Committee' was in existence which comprised the local organizations in Suvalki Province; see the minutes in *Der veker*, No. 12 (March 1903), 2. By 1905 the 'Committee of the Polish District of the Bristle-Workers' Union' had eleven different groups for a total of 150 members; see 'Di tetigkayt fun komitet far'n poylishen rayon fun dem yudishen bershter-bund (April–September)', in *Di letste pasirungen*, No. 23 (18 October 1905), 3–4.

[2] *Der veker*, No. 3 (January 1900), 5; Rafes, *Ocherki*, 333.

[3] 'Vegen shtrayken', *Der veker*, No. 3 (January 1900), 4; *ibid.*, 1.

[4] *Di arbayter shtime*, No. 30 (October 1902), 17. The union also chastized its members for striking too often; see 'Di bershter zind', *Der veker*, No. 10 (August 1901), 6–8.

wages were paid.[1] It opposed child labor (that is, using apprentices who were under fifteen years of age), demanded better medical facilities, denounced the practice of overtime work, and attempted to satisfy the cultural needs of its members.[2] The bristle-makers' organization also took a political stand. A police agent at the time noted in his report that initially the Union had been concerned only with 'trade union gains',[3] yet in 1898 it declared its allegiance to the Bund and to Social Democracy. In line with the Party's insistence on political action, the Union declared in 1902 that it was 'in fact...a political organization, which fights not only individual capitalists but the regime and the present order'. Indeed, at the Union's tenth conference all legal activities (such as legal libraries) were specifically condemned, and members who engaged in such activities were expelled.[4] Within the Union, as in the Jewish labor movement as a whole, the economic and the political struggles, at least in the opinion of the leaders, were thought to be inseparable.

The rise of the Bristle-Workers' Union was paralleled by that of a similar organization of Jewish tanners. In 1898 the first tanners' conference convened, and delegates emphasized the similarities between their industry and that of the bristle producers. Here too the degree of organization and interrelation of the various factories was in sharp contrast to the anarchical condition of the artisan shops. As a result the manifesto of the Union stated that:

[1] Thus the ninth conference declared that 'We must help the middlemen in their struggle when they demand booklets with a specified weekly wage...but not when they demand a higher price per pud [a certain quantity of raw material]'. ('Unzer 9-ten tsuzamenfahr', *Der veker*, No. 6 [July 1900].) If the middlemen were paid by the piece, the workers could be compelled under the sweat shop system to work longer hours.

[2] On overtime work see the resolution of the fourteenth conference of the Polish District of the Union, published in *Posledniia izvestiia*, No. 193 (9 August 1904), 5. The conference resolved that 'the organized workers make clear to the broad masses...the evil of overtime work, against which a struggle is necessary even if several workers themselves request it'. The Union also instructed its members in health measures; e.g., methods they could use to keep their blood circulating during work; see *Der veker*, No. 3 (January 1900), 6.

[3] Rafes, *Ocherki*, 334. The document is not dated.

[4] 'Unzer 10-ter tsuzamenfahr', *Der veker*, No. 8–9 (March 1902), 1, 2. This step was most likely taken under the influence of Zubatovism, or police socialism, which made a special effort to gain adherents from among the bristle makers. See below, Chapter 7.

One will not be able to win improvements of any kind in one area when conditions in another place remain unchanged. It is clear, then, that in order to succeed in our struggle we must know exactly what the conditions and the state of the tanneries are in various places... we must work out requirements that hold for all places, and for this a union is necessary.[1]

There were several exact parallels. 'The cities and towns of the tanning industry are closely connected... after working for a short time in one place, a tanner goes off to another, and this can be very harmful to our struggle because the employers may use the newly-arrived workers during a strike.' Moreover, in the tanning, as in the bristle industry, the employers had organized early in an effort to thwart the strike movement.[2] Nonetheless, there was one important difference. Almost all the bristle workers in the Pale were Jews, which contributed to their exceptional solidarity, whereas the tanning industry hired both Jewish and non-Jewish workers. The relationship between Jewish and non-Jewish workers in the labor movement will be discussed in a later chapter; for the present suffice it to say that the heterogeneous nature of the proletariat in the tanning industry created serious obstacles which ultimately delayed the establishment of the Tanners' Union until January, 1902.[3] Avram der Tate notes the difficulties encountered in organizing the Christian tanners, and the subsequent dilemma faced by leaders of the Jewish tanners. 'We could not found a "tanners' union" of Jews only, omitting Christians, not taking them into consideration. They played an important role in the leather industry, but there was no one to organize them.'[4] The Union's answer to the problem, though hardly adequate, was to establish a federation: the Jewish workers were affiliated with the Bund, the Poles with the Social

---

[1] 'Der manifest fun algemaynem sotsial-demokratishen federativn garber-bund', published in Dubnov-Erlich, *Garber-bund* (section trans. by Kh. Sh. Kazdan), 150–1. See also Avram der Tate, *Bleter*, 101. There is some confusion as to where the first conference was held. Avram der Tate, one of the leaders of the Tanners' Union, claims it was in Vilna, while Y. Mindel, 'A historishe yubilii', *Der Homer*, No. 4 (June 1926), 46, says it was held in Bialystok. According to Herts *et al.*, *Di geshikhte*, I, 228, two conferences took place in 1898, the first in Bialystok and the second in Vilna.

[2] 'Der manifest', in Dubnov-Erlich, *Garber-bund*, 151.

[3] See Avram der Tate, *Bleter*, 101 ff.

[4] *Ibid.*, 102.

Democratic Party of the Kingdom of Poland and Lithuania (the SDKPiL).[1]

The organizational structure, activity, and political orientation of the Tanners' Union were much like those of the bristle workers, but its multi-national character probably rendered it less powerful.[2] It failed to publish a journal during the period under consideration, and it held conferences less frequently than did the Bristle-Workers' Union. After the second conference of the federated union in 1902, a combination of arrests and unsuccessful strikes led to a general decline. A year later the Bristle-Workers' Union also suffered a severe blow when the last member of its Central Committee was arrested; subsequently, it too proved to be less effective.[3]

One other group of Jewish workers, the shop assistants, tried to organize along the same lines as the tanners and bristle workers. It appears that, at first, the attitude of these shop assistants toward the labor movement was negative; despite the fact that their working conditions were as bad, if not worse, than those of most artisans, many of them refused to regard themselves as 'laborers'.[4] According to the socialists, 'the shop assistants considered themselves the aristocracy of the working people and had no desire to support the (other) workers in their struggle against the exploiters and the regime'. Kopel'zon notes that 'In those days (the 1880s) the shop assistants still dreamed of setting up their own stores, although they were unable to...'[5] In time, however, this attitude

---

[1] 'Der manifest', in Dubnov-Erlich, *Garber-bund*, 153–4, 158. Russian workers were also urged to join; see *Iskra*, No. 19 (1 April 1902), where the 'Manifesto' is published along with an appeal to Russian tanners to adhere to the Union. A declaration of the Russian Social Democratic Labor Party entitled 'K kozhevenikam', and published in *Posledniia izvestiia*, No. 50 (1 January 1902), states, 'We must unite with the tanners of other cities, and form a trade union with them.' *Posledniia izvestiia*, No. 76 (3 July 1902), mentions a proclamation issued by the 'Head Committee' of the Russian section of the federated tanners' union, evidence that such a section existed, if only on paper.

[2] 'As a trade union organization the tanners' union is independent, but as a socialist organ it is a part of the general Jewish workers' union' (the Bund); quoted from the 1901 conference of Jewish tanners in Dubnov-Erlich, *Garber-bund*, 52–3.

[3] *Ibid.*, 67, 222. A brief description of the activities of both the bristle-makers' and the tanners' unions is available in Iulii Gessen (ed.), *Khrestomatiia po istorii rabochego klassa i professional'nogo dvizheniia v Rossii* (Leningrad, 1925), I, 60 ff.

[4] See 'Der fakh prikaztshikes', in *Der minsker arbayter*, No. 4 (November 1901), 9–10; *Tsu alle mohilever prikaztshikes un prikaztshises*, December 1903.

[5] *K vitebskim prikazchikam i prikazchitsam*, *n.d.*; 'Evreiskoe rabochee', 42. The highest wages received by the Vilna shop assistants were five rubles a week, but this was

79

gave way to more militant sentiments: they ceased to look down upon the workers as 'rebels' and joined the struggle.[1] In Berdichev, according to a report, the shop assistants abandoned their 'petty-bourgeois, middle-class ideals and...devoted themselves to the proletarian struggle'.[2]

The shop assistants maintained a network of legal self-help societies, and this organizational experience doubtless stood them in good stead when they joined the labor movement.[3] In Vitebsk their revolutionary 'kassa' was the best organized in the city, while in Vilna a celebration of the fifth anniversary of their union ('soiuz') in 1902 was attended by 200 shop assistants, who sang revolutionary songs, displayed a red flag, and listened to a speech entitled 'Why do we need political freedom?'[4]

Efforts to organize a shop assistants' Union on an inter-city basis were initiated in Vilna. In 1900 a special co-operative kitchen was opened by the shop assistants' organization, the proceeds of which were used to finance agitation work among shop assistants in other cities. In 1901 the leader of the Vilna shop assistants, Kalmon Krapivnikov, held a meeting in Dvinsk which was to lay the foundation for the Union. However, the venture was unsuccessful; the kitchen was closed in 1901 and Krapivnikov

considered rare; see *Nedel'naia khronika 'Voskhoda'*, VI, No. 50 (15 December 1885), 1375. For other material on the conditions of shop assistants in the Pale see *Der bund*, No. 6 (May 1905), 15; *Posledniia izvestiia*, No. 53 (24 January 1902); and No. 89 (10 October 1902). Shop assistants in Berdichev earned only 1.50–2 rubles a week.

[1] *K vitebskim prikazchikam i prikazchitsam*, n.d.; *Der bund*, No. 6 (May 1905), 15; *Posledniia izvestiia*, No. 89 (10 October 1902), 2.

[2] *Posledniia izvestiia*, No. 170 (25 February 1904). See also two proclamations published in Bukhbinder, *Krasnaia letopis'*, No. 5 (1923), 155–7 (entitled 'Brat'ia i sestry prikazchiki'). The Bund attempted to draw the 'petty-bourgeoisie' (and especially the shop assistants) into the movement by predicting they would inevitably decline into the working class. See especially 'Di klaynburzhvazie un der proletariat', *Flug-bletter, herois-gegeben fun kovner sotsial-demokratishen komitet fun bund*, No. 2 (February 1904), 1.

[3] On the existence of Jewish 'Shop Assistants' Societies' in Bialystok, Vilna, and Lodz, see *Nedel'naia khronika 'Voskhoda'*, VIII, No. 3 (22 January 1889), 69; XVIII, No. 49 (14 November 1899), 1547; and XIX, No. 17 (2 March 1900), 17–18. See also Menes, *Historishe shriftn*, III, 49. Russian shop assistants also had their own legal societies; see V. Grinevich, *Professional'noe dvizhenie rabochikh v Rossii* (Moscow, 1922), 8 ff.

[4] See the description in *Posledniia izvestiia*, No. 87 (25 September 1902), 1, and No. 170 (25 February 1904), for an account of a similar celebration in Berdichev where speeches were given on the theme of socialism and the trade union movement. On Vitebsk see Dvinov, *Vitebsk*. Not all shop assistants' organizations, it should be pointed out, went over to the Bund; in Riga, for example, their society remained apolitical. See *Di arbayter shtime*, No. 40 (September 1905), 31.

was arrested shortly after the Dvinsk conference.[1] It would appear that the conditions under which the shop assistants worked did not require an inter-city organization; their problems could be handled just as well by local organizations like the artisans' 'kassy'.

Undoubtedly, the description offered in this chapter of the organization of the Jewish proletariat during the agitation period is somewhat idealized. 'Kassy', agitation assemblies, and even central committees were hardly stable organizations. A few untimely arrests might, and on occasion did, cripple the local organizations for years, while a number of unsuccessful strikes often resulted in mass desertion from the ranks of the 'kassy'. Both these factors combined, as we have seen, to weaken the bristle-workers' and the tanners' unions. In Kovno, to give another example, a police report from 1900 notes that 'There are no energetic leaders, no financial means, and the participants in the movement...have no desire to work for the success of the cause'.[2] Emigration, which reached mass proportions at the turn of the century, also sapped the resources of the local movements.[3]

Yet, as Litvak observed, 'Organization was always the strong point of the Jewish labor movement'.[4] What was remarkable was not that local organizations would occasionally collapse, but that the 'kassy' and the other institutions of the movement survived and even flourished under exceptionally difficult circumstances. Moreover, such organizational strength was quite unique within the Russian Empire. Just as they were correct in assuming that the Jewish artisan masses would welcome the slogans of agitation, so the socialists were vindicated in their view that the artisan character of the Jewish proletariat would promote organization.

---

[1] On the co-operative kitchen see the accounts in Botvinik, in *Hirsh Lekert*, 27, and A. Y. Goldschmidt, 'Khaver Aron', *Vayter-bukh* (Vilna, 1920), 70. The attempt to found a 'Union of Shop Assistants' is described in Litvak, *Vos geven*, 109 ff. According to Herts et al., *Di geshikhte*, I, 225, 'In 1900 there was...an attempt to establish a centralized union of shop assistants (in Vilna there was a conference of delegates from a number of cities), but it did not last long'. No proof is offered for this statement. See also *Posledniia izvestiia*, No 14 (24 May 1901), and *Der idisher arbeter*, No. 12 (1901), 103.

[2] 'Konstruktsiia partiinoi organizatsii "Bunda"', in Rafes, *Ocherki*, 326.

[3] See also Chapter 3, 46. In Dvinsk, Berman was made a member of the carpenters' 'kassa' at a very young age because the older workers had emigrated to America (Berman, *In loif fun yorn*, 128).　　　[4] Litvak, *Vos geven*, 116.

CHAPTER 5

The Strike Movement

No, brothers, no I say! Things must be different,
different! We must realize that we are not animals,
that we are men with souls, men who wish with all our
heart and being to be free.

From *Der kampf*, organ of the Bund in Gomel, 1901

By rejecting the premises of the circle movement, adherents of the
agitation program hoped to create and promote a mass movement
based on the new forms of organization described above. Yet the
story of the Jewish labor movement is by no means the story only
of the 'kassy'. In fact, the 'kassy' members themselves constituted
a definite elite, though a much larger one than that of the circles.
While at times 'kassy' membership swelled to include the
majority of workers in a particular craft, on the whole the
organized worker was very much in the minority. Only the most
courageous and dedicated were willing to risk membership in
an illegal organization. This situation was recognized by the
Bund itself, which as early as 1899 charged that the 'kassy' were
rapidly evolving into elite worker organizations cut off from the
masses. The same complaint was made by delegates to the ninth
conference of the Bristle-Workers' Union.[1]

If the formal institutions of the labor movement did not attract the
worker masses, the latter were nonetheless active participants in
the agitation campaign. With much of the same intensity that the
circle workers had pursued education, the new recruits waged
strikes. And if the circle leaders, the 'philosophers' and 'teachers',
had been revered for their knowledge, the new leaders were
esteemed for their skill as 'stachechnikes', or 'strikers'.

The strike movement was naturally dominated by artisans,

[1] 'Unzer dritter tsuzamenfahr', *Di arbayter shtime*, No. 16 (March 1900), 3–4; 'Unzer
9-ten tsuzamenfahr', *Der veker*, No. 8–9 (March 1902), 2.

82

who had also formed the first cadres of worker-agitators. Gradually, as the movement proliferated, the more backward workers of the large cigarette and match factories were drawn into the wave of protest. (The cultural level of the cigarette and match factory workers was very low. Thus the majority at Shereshevsky's enormous factory in Grodno were illiterate).[1] In Vilna the first strike by factory workers occurred in 1895, three years after the artisans had begun their organized attack. A strike by several hundred workers at Edelshtein's cigarette plant, the largest establishment in Vilna, thus marked a new stage in the development of that city's labor movement. It was, in fact, the first time a major industrialist, rather than the owner of a small shop, had been challenged. In 1899, 800 women went on strike in Shereshevsky's cigarette factory in Grodno, much to the alarm of local 'public opinion'; the same year witnessed the first strike at Zaks' match factory in Dvinsk; and in Bialystok girls employed at Janovsky's cigarette factory were organized by an agitator from Vilna, a veteran of the Minsk 'circle' movement.[2]

The strike wave spread from the shops to the factories, and from the large centers to the smaller towns. Generally the labor movement in the small communities was sparked by the arrival of workers from the nearby cities, who were experienced in the techniques of agitation and were anxious to spread the new doctrines among the 'ignorant, almost primitive people' they encountered in these provincial towns. In Disna, a town in Vilna Province, the idea of the class struggle was introduced by several bristle workers from Kreslavka, an important center of the Bristle-Workers' Union. The labor movement in Ihumen was

---

[1] See *Rabochee delo*, No. 4–5 (September–December 1899), 113.

[2] On the Vilna event see Martov, *Zapiski sotsialdemokrata*, 247; see also Mill, *Pionern un boyer*, I, 71–2. On the strike itself see the brochure written by Gozhanskii, 'Der shtot magid', published in *Historishe shriftn*, III, 721–30. A Russian version (probably by Martov), entitled 'Evreiskie rabochie protiv evreiskikh kapitalistov', was published in *Rabotnik*, No. 1–2 (1896), 82–8. See also 'Taytikayts-berikht fun vilne 1896', published in *Unzer tsayt*, No. 6 (June 1928), 26, which comments that 'This was a remarkable strike, our city has never seen such a strike'. On the strike in Grodno see *Rabochee delo*, No. 4–5 (September–December 1899), 112–15; *Rabochaia mysl'*, No. 8 (February 1900), 6. The strike in Dvinsk is treated in *Di arbayter shtime*, No. 16 (March 1900), 5–7; the organization of workers at Janovsky's factory, in Blum, *Zikhroynes*, 133 ff., and in Kopelovich, 'Der onhayb', 4–5.

sparked by an agitator from Minsk, who came equipped with a suitcase full of illegal literature; and in Drohiczyn the first strikes broke out after several members of the Bund in Pinsk, a major city in Minsk Province, had held a meeting in the local synagogue. In Slutsk, a town in Minsk Province, a speech by the prominent Bund leader Litvak led to the formation of small circles and to the eventual outbreak of strikes. Once launched, the labor movement in a small town could count on assistance from the nearest local Committee of the Bund, which sent aid, both in the form of literature and manpower, to the 'provinces', and collected funds for the striking workers.[1]

Despite this assistance from 'outside agitators', it was the local workers themselves who led the movement in the provincial towns throughout Belorussia–Lithuania. Even in Suvalki (the capital of Suvalki Province) 'the local organization carried on its activities entirely through its own resources...the guidance of the local movement, all of its propaganda work, was carried out by the workers themselves'.[2] The lack of local radical intellectuals reversed the evolution of the movement. Strikes were dominant from the very beginning, while only later were circles formed. In Veshenkovichi, a town in Vitebsk Province, the movement commenced with a series of strikes in 1899; later a circle was established for 'systematic reading and the discussion of questions concerning the theory and practice of the labor movement'.[3] Interestingly enough, the untutored activists of the small towns were eventually to repay their debt to the cities. Many partici-

[1] The quotation is from Grinberg, *Der veker*, VI, No. 309 (15 October 1927), 20. He describes workers he encountered in Vilkovishki after he had learned the techniques of agitation in Vilna. On the origins of the movement in Disna see *Posledniia izvestiia*, No. 180 (22 April 1904); on Ihumen and Drohiczyn, see Presman, *Der durkhgegangener veg*, 30 ff. and Gedaliah Kopelman, 'Der bund', in Dov B. Varshavsky (ed.), *Drohiczyn, finf hundert yor yidish-lebn* (Chicago, 1958), 272. On Slutsk see Moshe Tulman, 'Di antshtayung fun "bund" un zayn untergang', in *Pinkas slutsk u-vnotehah* (New York–Tel Aviv, 1962), 301–12. For other examples, G. Orinsky, 'Gezelshaftlikhe bavegungen in pruzhene', in M. Bernshtein (ed.), *Pinkes fun finf fortilikte kehiles* (Buenos Aires, 1958), 117 ff.; Kril Bunem-Idel, 'Derinerungen fun a rokisher sotsialist', in M. Bakaltshuk-Felin (ed.), *Yizker-bukh fun rokishok un umgegent* (Johannesburg, 1952), 115 ff.

[2] *Posledniia izvestiia*, No. 192 (28 August 1904). Levin, *Untererdishe kemfer*, 116, also makes this point.

[3] *Posledniia izvestiia*, No. 136 (3 July 1903).

pated in the steady stream of migration from the towns to the major centers, and thus provided a source of 'revolutionary energy for the cities'.[1]

A statistical study of the Jewish labor movement by Ber Borokhov, a leading Zionist–Socialist, estimates that between 1895 and 1904 at least 2,276 Jewish strikes were held by workers in the Pale of Settlement. The number of strikes during 1900–4 alone is estimated at 1,673, an average of more than one strike per day. In comparing these figures with the incidence of strikes throughout Russia and other countries, Borokhov concludes that the strike movement of the Jewish workers in the Pale was of far greater intensity than any in the Western world.[2]

This unparalleled strike activity was due not to the extraordinary aggressiveness of the Jewish proletariat, but to the fragmented nature of its structure. The typical strike by Jewish workers occurred in small shops, and on a statistical table a strike by three Jewish tailors in Minsk figures as large as one by three thousand steel workers in Pittsburgh. Moreover, as Gozhanskii and Kremer noted in their polemics with the 'opposition', the artisan not only was more apt to risk the consequences of a strike than was the worker in a large factory, but to strike time and again. Indeed, Borokhov's point in surveying these statistics is that, far from making any impressive gains, the Russian Jewish class struggle was essentially bankrupt from the start. Taking a position similar to that of Gordon and Liesin, he characterizes the Jewish labor movement as 'poverty-stricken', and insists that in light of the general decline of the Jewish craft industries and the failure of the artisans to become 'proletarianized', the strikes were meaningless.[3]

Whatever its accomplishments, or lack of them, a question which will be considered below, the Jewish strike movement was undeniably a mass movement. The chief aim of the struggle

---

[1] *Ibid.*, No. 176 (5 April 1904).

[2] Ber Borokhov, 'Tenuat ha-poalim ha-yehudit be-misparim', in L. Levita and D. Ben-Nahum (eds.), *Borokhov, Ketavim* (Tel Aviv, 1958), II, 274–5, 283.

[3] *Ibid.*, 286 ff. As a Zionist Borokhov sought to prove that the Bund's economic program was completely inadequate and the situation of the Jewish proletariat in Tsarist Russia hopeless.

was to secure a 'normal working day'; in Minsk workers were geared to action by the slogan, 'Brothers and sisters, let us not delay, but let us shorten the working day';[1] in 1897 the battle cry in Bialystok was, 'From seven to seven'. Such slogans were echoed by workers throughout the Pale. Both in the small towns and in the large cities the labor movement invariably began with a rash of strikes aimed at curtailing the working day. For example, in Parachi, a small town in Mogilev Province, in 1902 all the Jewish workers, servants included, went on strike for a twelve hour day.[2] In Vitebsk, to cite another example, the movement in 1898 'rapidly embraced almost all the crafts, strike followed strike. The struggle began primarily because of overtime work, and therefore the demand raised everywhere was to shorten the working day to twelve hours (including rest periods and two hours for breakfast and dinner).'[3]

The twelve hour day represented to the Jewish worker what the eight-hour day came to mean to American labor. As a Bialystok carpenter explained it:

Before that I hardly knew my own children; I would leave for work when they were still asleep, and when I returned from work they were asleep again; only on Saturday did I have time to hold my child. Now I come home at 7.00 in the evening and have time to play with the children and then go to the synagogue for the evening prayer.[4]

For some the twelve hour day meant sufficient leisure to read and become educated: 'We have no time and no means to study', a 'kassa' statute from Vilna declared. When asked by their employers what they would do with the free time they had won, the bristle workers of Mezrich (Miedzyrzec) replied: 'Do you see these little booklets? (socialist literature issued by the Bund). This is our Torah, which we shall study in our free time.'[5]

---

[1] Quoted in Presman, *Der durkhgegangener veg*, 38; see also *Posledniia izvestiia*, No. 157 (24 November 1903).　　　　[2] *Iskra*, No. 40 (15 May 1903), 6-7.

[3] 'Bor'ba vitebskikh rabochikh', in Agursky (ed.), *Di sotsialistishe literatur*, 338. Aynzaft, *Der ekonomisher*, 105-7, lists 60 carpenters' strikes between 1896 and 1905, 43 of which were aimed at shortening the workday. A list of 12 strikes in Bialystok in 1900 indicates that four contested the workday issue; see *Der idisher arbeter*, No. 10 (1900), 64.

[4] Quoted in *Der idisher arbeter*, No. 4-5 (November 1897), 29.

[5] Litman Geltman, 'Der ershter bershter-shtrayk', *Mezrich zamlbukh*, 242. The first quotation is from 'Der statut', *Unzer tsayt*, No. 2 (5 February 1928), 88.

As the movement progressed, workers added new demands. Wages, working conditions in shops and factories, the problem of middlemen, of piece work, and of the arbitrary firing and ill-treatment of workers by their employers—all of these became crucially important in the labor campaign. Despite the multiplicity of aims, however, one major theme is clearly discernible. In its broadest and most general sense, the Jewish strike movement was directed squarely against the anarchical, chaotic conditions that prevailed in the Jewish shops and factories. Above all, it demanded uniform, well-regulated conditions of work, a twelve hour day being the most fundamental requirement. Previously, as the expression had it, a worker labored 'without end', his workday depending upon the whim of his employer. In Minsk the artisans in one shop were not free to leave until the master had finished telling his favorite stories, for 'who can leave when the boss is talking?' In the smaller towns the situation was especially grim. In Bielsk, one activist wrote, 'The concept of a workday did not exist at all, everything depended on the desire of the employer. When there was less work one labored 12–14 hours a day; when there was more, 16–17 hours. Before holidays, when everything had to be finished, the workers could not go home to sleep.'[1] By instituting a regular twelve hour day, with allotted time for meals, the workers hoped to eliminate such abuses.

The same desire for well-regulated conditions applied to the wage issue. The workers naturally demanded higher wages, but they were equally anxious to eliminate inconsistencies in the wage system—for example, the failure of employers to pay wages promptly and at regular intervals, and the widespread practice of paying by the piece. To the demand 'From seven to seven' workers of Krynki added the slogan 'Money every week'. In Kreslavka 230 workers went on strike because their employer wished to pay them by the season rather than by the week. A major tanners' strike in Vilna in 1905 demanded, among other things, that wages be paid every week rather than in a haphazard,

---

[1] Shtern, *Zikhroynes*, 23; *Der minsker arbeyter*, No. 3 (June 1901), 9, contains the anecdoto about the garrulous master.

irregular fashion.[1] The workers often sought a more well-defined period of employment, the right 'to conclude a contract for a specific period of time', as one group put it.[2]

In addition to a strictly defined workday and a strictly defined wage system, a third object of the movement was the demand for strictly defined relations between worker and employer. At Zaks' match factory strikes were held because workers 'were called abusive names and were often dealt slaps and blows'; in Bialystok weavers were incensed because their bosses addressed them contemptuously as 'du'. In Pinsk 200 carpenters demanded 'more respectful treatment' from their employers; a strike by a number of artisans in Gomel in 1900 was directed in part 'against the employer's (practice) of insulting the workers'.[3]

The Jewish labor movement, therefore, aimed at instituting 'modern' relations between employer and employee, relations based on contract, not on habit and whim. We turn now to the movement itself, to an examination of the means workers used to secure their ends. How were the strikes organized, and what tactics were employed? To what extent was the strike movement dependent on the formal institutions of the local organizations? What opposition did workers encounter in their struggle for improved conditions? And, finally, how successful were workers in realizing their goals?

The majority of strikes by Jewish workers were small undertakings that required neither advanced planning nor the intervention or support of the organized labor movement. A participant in the Minsk labor movement, for example, wrote: 'Joseph and I called a strike in our workshop...we demanded that work be stopped at 10.00 p.m.... We went out on strike and the other boys (in the shop) came along with us.' This, one can safely assume, was typical of hundreds of strikes that erupted in small shops throughout Belorussia–Lithuania, many of which pitted a

---

[1] *Der idisher arbeter*, No. 4–5 (November 1897), 38; *Rabochee delo*, No. 8 (November 1900), 68; *Di letste pasirungen*, No. 23 (18 October 1905), 2–3.

[2] See *Rabochee delo*, No. 8 (November 1900), 68.

[3] *Di arbayter shtime*, No. 16 (March 1900), 5; *Der bialystoker arbeter*, No. 1 (April 1899), 47; Aynzaft, *Der ekonomisher*, 107.

single worker, or possibly a journeyman and his apprentice, against a master artisan.[1]

In the case of the larger strikes, the local organization rendered vital assistance. For example, the local Committee of the Bund in Bialystok decided to organize a bakers' strike in 1901. Bakers were generally recognized as among the most 'backward' of the Jewish workers; conditions in the bakeries were atrocious, relations between employer and employee were 'paternalistic' to the extreme. 'The Bialystok bakers', the local organ of the Bund reported: 'were...from the very beginning condemned to live in hell, and not only after their deaths but during their lives as well.'[2] Since bakers had never been exposed to propaganda and had no sense of 'class consciousness', a skillful program of indoctrination was required to draw them into the labor movement. The first step was to call a special meeting of the bakers on the outskirts of the city, where 200 workers were lectured on the importance of 'unity and struggle'. A month later 'kassy' (or 'skhodkes', as they were called in Bialystok) were organized in the various districts, circles were set up to educate the workers, and proclamations made their way into the bakeries. During the Passover holiday the 'kassy' made five basic demands the issue of a strike: a twelve-hour day; an end to eating and sleeping in the bakeries (some bakers were obliged to live on the premises); an increase in wages and in the amount of free bread distributed to workers; regular payment of wages; and respectful treatment of workers (this demand applied especially to the apprentices). When, after a general strike by the bakers, the employers were forced to concede their demands, the local Committee announced the bakers' victory in a special proclamation.[3]

Other examples can be found of expert planning by the local

---

[1] Presman, *Der durkhgegangener veg*, 28–9. Borokhov cites several examples of strikes limited to one or two workers who declared war on their 'capitalistic' employer; see 'Tenuat ha-poalim', in Levita and Ben-Nahum (eds.), *Borokhov*, 288–9. According to him, two-thirds of all the strikes by Jewish workers had fifty or less participants (288).

[2] *Der bialystoker arbeter*, No. 6 (September 1901), 11. In 1903 the bakers in Lodz still had not participated in the labor movement; see the proclamation *Tsu alle lodzer beker*, October, 1903, which appeals to them to strike for higher wages and a twelve-hour day.

[3] Bentsel Tsalevich, 'Erinerung fun 1-tn bialystoker beker shtrayk in yor 1901 khoydesh may', typescript located in the Bund Archives, New York City.

organizations, which were particularly helpful in collecting funds for the strikers. During a strike at Shereshevsky's factory in Grodno the organization obtained contributions from workers throughout the Pale as well as from Baku and from socialist groups abroad.[1] When workers at Zaks' match factory in Dvinsk went on strike, their appeal for aid was published in the socialist press: 'Help us, dear comrades,' it read, 'write to other cities, help us in our struggle which continues stoically, despite the sacrifices.'[2] The considerable aid given the strikers is revealed by the fact that within a twelve month period, the Foreign Committee of the Bund collected 1,567 rubles for strike purposes from socialist organizations in such cities as New York, London, Berlin and Lyon. The local 'kassy' were themselves able to raise considerable sums. Between July and December 1903, 20 rubles were collected in Vilna for a shoemakers' strike, 23 for a bristle-workers' strike, and as much as 137 rubles for a general bakers' strike. Without such assistance the larger strikes would scarcely have been possible.[3]

When it came to matters of tactics, the local organizations headed by the socialist intellectuals and the agitators had much to offer. Workers were taught to strike only during the 'busy season' when their employers were least able to withstand the challenge.[4] Further, new methods of strategy were engineered by the local committees. In Bialystok, for example, the committee decided to use the boycott as a weapon against Janovsky, the owner of the local cigarette factory, and as preparation for this published an article entitled 'A New Method in the Struggle of the Bialystok Workers' in the local socialist newspaper. The article explained how the new tactic was to be employed, and

---

[1] *Der bund*, No. 3 (April 1904), 8; contributions were received from the following cities in Russia: Riga, Kiev, Lodz, Gomel, Warsaw, Bobruisk, Bialystok, Mogilev, Dvinsk, Vilna, Minsk, Baku, Vitebsk, Kreslavka and Krynki.

[2] 'Pis'ma rabotnitsy', published in *Rabochee delo*, No. 4–5 (September–December 1899), 87.

[3] *Posledniia izvestiia*, No. 60 (13 March 1902); 'Rekhnung fun vilner komitet 15-yuli-15-dets. 1903', *Flug-blettel, heroisgegeben fun vilner sotsialdemokratishen komitet fun bund*, No. 4 (January 1904).

[4] See, for example, the proclamation *Tsu alle grodner stoliares* (1903?), in which the carpenters of Grodno are urged to strike in the summer, the busy season, when employers are most in need of labor.

even went so far as to provide a scholarly analysis of the derivation of the word 'boycott'. A special proclamation, entitled 'To the Public', explained the reason for the boycott (Janovsky had fired 45 Jewish girls without notice and had replaced them with peasants from the nearby rural areas) and appealed for cooperation. 'Feival Janovsky', the proclamation stated:

Is a pious Jew; he goes to the synagogue regularly, and with all his heart prays to God. He is a Jewish nationalist, a patriot and perhaps even a Zionist. He no doubt is upset by the persecution of the Jews, and sheds crocodile tears over the Jews' desperate situation. But all this, as we see, does not prevent him from cruelly exploiting his Jewish workers.

The Bialystok committee, the proclamation continued, had decided to 'wage war against Janovsky' by boycotting his cigarettes. 'If the public supports us, if all those whose feeling for justice has not been extinguished completely, whose conscience has not been lulled to sleep entirely, rally to our call...success will be complete.' The proclamation was distributed throughout the cities where Janovsky's cigarettes were sold, as were special cards with the slogan: 'A boycott on Janovsky's cigarettes. Do not buy Janovsky's cigarettes.' Announcements of the boycott were made in the synagogues by agents of the organization; in Krynki, not far from Bialystok, picket lines were set up, and when someone bought a box of the tobacco, sympathizers demonstrated by seizing the merchandise and burning it in the street. After a month, the boycott forced the factory owner to concede. Faced with financial ruin, he agreed to re-hire the workers and promised to keep them on until the Passover holiday. Thus ended what the committee termed the first boycott on goods in the Russian Empire.[1]

[1] According to An-man, 'Bialystoker period', 50, the Bialystok leaders were attracted to the idea of a boycott because lengthy strikes often cost the workers their jobs and were very expensive. This tactic had been used by the tailors of the city, who boycotted an unreasonable artisan master for 14 weeks until he made certain concessions. See 'A nayer mittel tsum kamf bay bialystoker arbayter', *Der bialystoker arbeter*, No. 6 (September 1901), 10–11. The two proclamations are published in Rafes, *Ocherki*, 335–7; and the cards announcing the boycott in *Posledniia izvestiia*, No. 41 (n.d.). On the pickets in Krynki, see Lev, 'Vospominaniia o tov. Sikorskom', *Katorga i ssylka*, No. 41 (1928), 144; also 'Der boykot gegen yanovsken', *Der bialystoker arbayter*, No. 7 (January

The boycott was a skilfully planned operation, the committee employing the considerable resources at its disposal to secure maximum co-operation from workers and 'public opinion' in other cities and towns. It was perhaps the single most outstanding achievement, in the struggle against the employers, of that alliance between the socialist intelligentsia and the masses which Gozhanskii and Kremer had advocated in the early 1890s to ameliorate the economic plight of the Jewish working class.

The Jewish strike movement as a whole, however, rarely demonstrated such expert planning, nor was the organization always able to control the activities of workers. In 1900 the local organization in Bialystok had to admit that the strike movement had become 'too big' for it to supervise. This may well have been because the strike movement there was fairly atypical; unlike the working class elsewhere in Belorussia–Lithuania, the proletariat in Bialystok had a history of spontaneous revolt. In 1895 a huge strike was staged by 8,500 weavers (both Jews and non-Jews) who refused to accept factory books, which they regarded as a threat to their mobility. The strike had not been authorized by either the Jewish or Christian socialist groups in the city but was an instance of spontaneous protest by the masses.[1] Subsequent attempts by the weavers to take matters into their own hands met with a rebuke from the socialists. The weavers, they maintained, were wrong to think that 'a strike is an isolated incident and that when

1902), 506. One reason for the boycott's success, according to An-man was that the 'petty-bourgeoisie' were willing to smoke Shereshevsky's cigarettes instead; the latter owner, who was himself a frequent target of the workers, profited by their actions on this occasion. See also Mikhalevich, *Zikhroynes*, I, 132 ff., who notes that 'The boycott greatly increased the prestige of our organization'. In subsequent years the boycott was used against other prominent factory owners, most notably against the well-known tea firm of Wissotsky; see 'Der boykot oif der te-firme fun visotsky', *Di letste pasirungen*, No. 22 (19 September 1905), 4. In 1903 two 'loynketniks' in Lodz were boycotted by the tailors because they had informed on two of their employees: see the proclamation *Tsu alle lodzer arbayter un arbayterinen. Der boykot gegen di loyn-veber*, August 1903.

[1] The quotation is from *Der idisher arbeter*, No. 10 (1900), 63. The strike is described in *Rabochee dvizhenie v Rossii v XIX veke*, IV, Part I, 1895–7 (Moscow–Leningrad, 1961), 183–5, and in Kalabiński, 'Początki', III, 118 ff. The strike began in the large factories of Christian workers and, according to a police report, 'even spread to the Jewish (factories)'. The workers believed that the factory books which recorded their wages would have the effect of enslaving them to the owners. On the law covering the use of these books see I. I. Shelymagin, *Fabrichno-trudovoe zakonodatel' stvo v Rossii vo vtoroi polovine XIX veke* (Moscow, 1947), 88 ff.

the strike ends so does the entire struggle...' If the weavers wished to succeed, the leaders added, they must unite and affiliate with the organized labor movement. However, the majority of the weavers went their own way, thereby incurring further criticism from the socialist press. An article in *The Bialystok Worker* attacked them for their failure to pay dues to the 'kassy', claiming that 'Most weavers are of the opinion that only during a general strike is it necessary to support (the workers) by paying dues, and that during the small strikes such dues can be dispensed with'. Much to the annoyance of the socialists, the weavers sometimes refused to support their fellows in strike activities. When a group of 'shpuliarkes' (women who assisted at the looms in the factories) went on strike and refused to clean up under the looms at the end of the workday, the weavers' reply was: 'What's going on, have you become countesses?' The factory promptly hired Christian girls to do the dirty work, and the strike was broken.[1]

The Bialystok weavers, however, were not the only workers to disregard the advice and guidance of the organized movement. In 1901 a strike by 1,300 Jewish and Christian tanners in Smorgon caught the organization completely by surprise. The socialists rebuked the tanners for their failure to organize and reminded them that 'in order to carry on a strike connexions must be established with the tanners in other cities, there must be a permanent organization...'[2] Similarly the leaders of the Bristle-Workers' Union complained that their members disregarded the Union's order and struck too frequently, thereby forcing owners to close their factories and fire hundreds of workers. For many workers, the Union publication observed, the strike had become a 'custom' which like all Jewish customs was hard to eradicate. 'The (unorganized) masses are ignorant.' an article in *The Awakener* complained, 'They handled themselves badly in the strike, and therefore lost.'[3] In Vilna, several years after the mass strike

[1] 'Umziste sinah', *Der bialystoker arbeter*, No. 7 (January 1902), 6–8; the quotations are from 'Di oifgaben fun di veber', in No. 3 (December 1900), 5, and 'Der fakh veber', No. 4 (April 1901), 4.

[2] *An oifruf tsu alle garber*, November 1901; a proclamation published in Dubnov-Erlich, *Garber-bund*, 64–5.

[3] 'Aynige verter vegen shtrayken', *Der veker*, No. 5 (May 1900), 5; and 'Di bershter zind' in No. 10 (August 1901), 6–8.

movement had begun, a number of strikes were defeated because workers failed to time them properly and struck in the off-season. The dilemma was summed up by the Bund's publication in that city, which in 1900 noted that 'strikes had become so commonplace, they often attracted people who had no experience at organized protest' and who therefore failed to appreciate the need for discipline and planning.[1] This confession clearly demonstrates that the formal institutions of the movement were unable to control the wave of strikes which erupted in the wake of the agitation program.

If unauthorized strikes broke out continuously, it is also of some interest to discover that the tactics employed by the strikers often contradicted the ideological premises of the socialists. The organized Jewish labor movement began on a legal basis, but the socialist leaders assumed that the workers ultimately would be forced to resort to illegal strikes. This was generally the case, but many workers continued to operate within a legal framework by announcing their strikes two weeks in advance. This was equivalent to giving two weeks notice to their employers, and was perfectly legal. The bristle workers often employed this tactic: in the words of one participant, 'Usually we struck at the beginning of a "zman" (period of employment), we sought legal methods in order to appear to be in the right to the police.'[2] In Kishinev 80 mill employees announced a strike two weeks in advance; in Bialystok, 3,000 weavers in shops and factories struck in 1898 'on the basis of the law', that is, by giving their employers two weeks notice before quitting the looms.[3]

The use of such tactics scarcely advanced the socialists' hopes that through economic struggles political consciousness would emerge; nor did the willingness of many workers to collaborate with government factory inspectors. The latter encouraged the workers to use legal methods. 'If you wish to strike', an inspector told a group of cigarette factory employees in Priluki, 'it is

[1] *Der klassen-kampf*, No. 2 (May 1900), 2; 'Materialy', Agursky (ed.), *Di sotsialistishe literatur*, 417.
[2] 'Aynige verter vegen shtrayken', *Der veker*, No. 5 (May 1900), 6; see also No. 3 (January 1900), 7.
[3] *Posledniia izvestiia*, No. 83 (28 August 1902); *Listok 'Rabotnika'*, No. 6 (February 1898), 18.

necessary to announce this two weeks in advance.'[1] In Minsk, during a strike of cigarette makers, the inspector persuaded the workers to return to their jobs for two weeks, promising that he would then make a judgment as to 'who is right'.[2] Naturally, the socialists had a profound distrust of these inspectors. An editorial in the Bund's Warsaw organ cautioned the workers: 'The truth is that factory inspection is not intended to protect the workers, but the employers.' The inspectors, it was assumed, were simply Tsarist spies, whose chief function was to root out conspiracies against the factory owners.[3] Many workers shared this opinion, and in 1895 a police report on a strike in Bialystok noted: 'They regard the factory inspectors as instruments of the factory owners, and...foresee nothing but an endless series of fines and punishments.'[4] On the other hand, Jewish workers often looked up to the inspector as a kind of 'father-protector', and turned to him when problems arose.[5]

In fact, many inspectors proved to be important allies of the workers during labor disputes, as the socialists themselves were forced to admit.[6] In Vileika, a little town in Vilna Province, the carpenter employers appealed to the local inspector for aid against the workers. The latter refused to comply, saying it was not his job to intervene. During a strike by the bristle workers in Vilkovishki, the inspector 'Officially...warned the workers against

---

[1] *Posledniia izvestiia*, No. 146 (18 September 1903). See also *Di arbayter shtime*, No. 30 (October 1902), 12.

[2] See *Der minsker arbayter*, No. 1 (December 1900), 6.

[3] 'Fabrika-inspektsie', *Der varshaver arbeter*, No. 5 (August 1900), 3. The Russian socialists' attitude toward factory inspection is discussed in 'Fabrichnaia inspektsiia v Rossii, Po povodu novago polozheniia 7 Iunia 1899 g.', *Rabochee delo*, No. 4–5 (September–December 1899), 28–43. For general information see Theodore von Laue, 'Factory Inspection under the Witte System', *American Slavic and East European Review*, XIX, No. 3 (October 1960), 347–62; Frederick C. Giffin, 'The Formative Years of the Russian Factory Inspectorate', *Slavic Review*, XXV, No. 4 (December 1966), 641–50.

[4] *Rabochee dvizhenie v Rossii v XIX veke*, 183.

[5] 'Fabrika-inspektsie', *Der varshaver arbeter*, No. 5 (August 1900), 3; *Di arbayter shtime*, No. 4–5 (23 September 1897), 11, 14. See also Gaston Rimlinger, 'The Management of Labor Protest in Tsarist Russia: 1870–1905', *International Review of Social History*, v, Part a (1960), 239.

[6] See the article 'Fir vemen zorgt unzer tsarishe zelbstherrshung?' in *Flug-blettel, heroisgegeben fun vilner sotsialdemokratishen komitet fun bund*, No. 3 (August 1903), 2–3. The article compares the inspectors favorably to the gendarmes, and notes that the former frequently intervened on the workers' behalf in labor disputes.

breaking their contracts, but in a private letter to the factory owner, persuaded him to satisfy the workers' just demands'. Similarly in Vilna, during a general tailors' strike in 1893, workers had the support of the inspector who assured them that they were entitled to leave their shops after twelve hours.[1]

There were, of course, instances of inspectors and employers uniting against the workers. 'How dare you rise up against the boss?' an inspector in Minsk shouted at several hundred match factory workers as he ordered them back to work.[2] The socialist press also charged employers with sabotaging the work of honest inspectors. In Vilkovishki, we are told, the owners of the bristle factories would instruct their workers how to reply to the questions of the inspector. This tactic was countered by an agitator who told the inspector the truth about conditions in the factory and coached the workers, who knew no Russian, to respond in unison 'tochno tak' ('exactly so') to each of his criticisms.[3]

Given their willingness to trust the benevolent impulses of the inspectors who, after all, represented the government, it is no wonder that some Jewish workers extended this trust to the Tsarist police. An article in the Bundist press quotes the workers as saying: 'When the regime finds out how oppressed we are it will not permit such inhuman robbery.'[4] Although the socialists had lectured workers on the inevitability of conflict with the police, who could be counted on to protect the interests of the capitalists, many Jewish workers hoped to enlist the aid of these officials in their struggle. When the bakers in Vilna announced a general strike, they first appealed for assistance to the chief of police.[5] In a few instances, at least, the police were helpful. During a strike of Jewish workers in Kovno the chief of police

---

[1] *Posledniia izvestiia*, No. 176 (5 April 1904); *Rabotnik*, No. 3–4 (1897), 91; 'Materialy', Agursky (ed.), *Di sotsialistishe literatur*, 416; *Di arbayter shtime*, No. 22 (March 1901), 8.

[2] *Posledniia izvestiia*, No. 55 (6 February 1902); see also *Der klassen-kampf*, No. 3 (October 1900), 4; *Rabochee dvizhenie v Rossii v XIX veke*, III, Part 1, 1885–9 (Moscow–Leningrad, 1952), 165. According to the latter source, the workers of Petrokovsky Province were dissatisfied with the factory inspectors because they 'do not investigate the situation sufficiently (and) are bribed by the factory owners'.

[3] Grinberg, *Der veker*, VI, No. 309 (15 October 1927), 20. The agitator was promptly fired by his irate employer.

[4] 'Di yudishe arbayter bevegung in varshe', *Der varshaver arbeter*, No. 2 (1899), 2.

[5] *Der klassen-kampf*, No. 3 (October 1900), 5.

tried to persuade the employers to concede their demands; in Bialystok fifty weavers won their strike largely because the chief of police intervened on their behalf.[1]

The attitude of the police toward the strike movement was unpredictable. At times mass arrests were made, especially during strikes at the larger factories. During a strike at Janovsky's factory in 1901 the police swooped down upon the workers 'like wolves' and many of them were sentenced to jail; similar instances occurred at cigarette factories in Vilna and Grodno.[2] However, the police were reluctant to intervene in the smaller strikes by Jewish artisans, and in the early years of the labor movement often preferred to treat these as minor struggles 'within the family'. In Gomel, up to 1897 the police and gendarmes remained indifferent to the quarrels between Jewish employees and their bosses. They intervened in Vilna only after requested to do so by the employers. In a little town like Bielsk no arrests whatever were made during the artisan strikes.[3] Known members of the organization, of course, were in constant danger, and as the movement increased even the unorganized were sometimes arrested. By 1903 such arrests were common in Vilna, for example.[4] Nonetheless, for the typical Jewish artisan, who confined his relations with the movement to an occasional strike, the risk was relatively slight. This may well explain why the average worker did not necessarily become an inveterate enemy of the police, as the socialists had expected, but was perfectly willing to trust and co-operate with them and with the inspectors. For such workers the slogan 'from economic to political struggle', the very basis of the agitation program, had little meaning.[5]

It was the employer, however, and not the police, who was

---

[1] *Der bialystoker arbeter*, No. 7 (January 1902), 14; *Rabochaia mysl'*, No. 14 (January 1902), 16.

[2] *Der bialystoker arbeter*, No. 5 (May 1901), 8; *Posledniia izvestiia*, No. 79 (24 July 1902), 1; 'Der shtot magid', *Historishe shriftn*, III, 721.

[3] On Gomel see 'Gomel'skoe rabochee', in Agursky (ed.), *Di sotsialistishe literatur*, 359; *Iskra*, No. 40 (15 May 1903), 6; on Vilna *Posledniia izvestiia*, No. 58 (27 February 1902). On Bielsk see Shtern, *Zikhroynes*, 24 ff. (in this case the employers requested police intervention, but failed to secure it). See also Martov, *Zapiski sotsialdemokrata*, 194–5.

[4] *Posledniia izvestiia*, No. 161 (11 December 1903). During a strike of 25 factory workers the report observes, 'The police, as usual, intervened.'

[5] See below, pp. 134 ff., for additional comments on this subject.

the real enemy of the Jewish strike movement, and his reaction was particularly interesting. We should not lose sight of the fact that the Jewish employer was often not much better off than his workers—this was certainly true in the little shops. Nor should we forget that our information on the behavior of these employers is derived from the hostile accounts of labor activists. The evidence suggests, however, that the struggle between Jewish worker and Jewish employer, though often the struggle of 'pauper against pauper', was extremely bitter. While traditional historians, writing of Russian Jewry, have emphasized the unity of the community as against its gentile oppressors, the community was in fact rent by internal dissension of great magnitude.

At first it appears that the Jewish employers were stunned at the spectacle of their employees, their 'wards', rising up against them, so much so that they seem to have offered little resistance. But in due time the employers demonstrated their own skill in organizing against the new threat. In the tanning and bristle-making trades, as we have seen, employers' unions preceded those of workers; in other crafts it took aggressive attacks by the workers to galvanize the employers into action. Once the masters of the carpenters' shops in Lodz were confronted by a union of workers, they set up a committee of employers whose signatures were required before a carpenter could be hired in any of the shops; they also came to an agreement on a policy of uniform wages and hours to be used throughout the city.[1] In Smorgon, employers formed a 'Union of Industrialists' which kept a close watch on workers' activities; in Minsk, members of a baker masters' 'union' had their own arrangement for weekly dues and guarantees of mutual support during strikes. Likewise in Bialystok a 'union of bosses' followed the weavers' strikes of 1898; in Dvinsk store owners formed a union in response to actions by rebellious shop assistants.[2]

[1] *Der frayhayts-glok*, No. 3–4 (November 1902), 6.

[2] *Posledniia izvestiia*, No. 34 (27 September 1901); Peskovoi, 'V smorgoni', 17 (Smorgon); *Listok 'Rabotnika'*, No. 6 (February 1898), 17 (Minsk); *Rabochee delo*, No. 2–3 (August 1899), 99 (Bialystok). In Gomel, after a number of strikes in various crafts, an 'employers' coalition' was formed; 'They all swore on a holy book in the synagogue never to give in to the workers.' ('Gomel'skoe rabochee', in Agursky (ed.), *Di sotsialistishe literatur*, 356.) In Vilna the establishment of a union of middlemen in the

Blacklisting was a favorite weapon, and workers like Avram 'The Bristle Worker', who were suspected of being agitators, were 'boycotted' by the factory owners.[1] More serious, however, was the employers' attempt to exploit the traditional hostility between Jew and Christian and therefore undermine the unity of the labor movement. We have already seen how the existence of Christian workers in the tanneries impeded the emergence of the 'Tanners' Union'. Wherever Jewish and Christian workers labored side by side—and this occurred only in Jewish-owned factories, never in the small Jewish shops—a weapon of great usefulness was placed in the hands of the employer. To cite one example of how this opportunity was exploited, we quote the following report from Berdichev: 'A Jewish factory owner made a speech to the Christian workers. He told them that the Jews are disloyal to the Christians and are only out to harm them; therefore, they should break the strike and go back to work.' In Bialystok, too, an employer urged his Christian hands not to co-operate with the rebellious Jews. He is quoted as having used 'all his eloquence in order to rouse a strong hatred on the part of the Christians toward the Jews, so that they would not be able to confer together and make a strike at his factory'.[2]

In other cases, gentile workers were imported by Jewish employers to break all-Jewish strikes, 'to teach the strikers a lesson'.[3] They could be so used because, in Belorussia–Lithuania, the Christian labor force was proverbially lacking in organization. 'Christian workers', we read, 'are now cheaper than Jews, because their class-consciousness is not as developed and they allow themselves to be more exploited.'[4] Neither the Polish nor the Russian socialist movements had much of an impact in that

tailoring industry touched off a general strike of 200 tailors; see *Der klassen-kampf*, No. 4 (April 1901), 11.

[1] Bernshtein, *Ershte shprotsungen*, 92; Grinberg, *Der veker*, VI, No. 309 (15 October 1927), 19, writes that at the age of fifteen no one in Vilna would hire him since he was known as a 'rebel'.

[2] The first quotation is from *Di arbayter shtime*, No. 28 (August 1902), 9; the second is from *Der bialystoker arbeter*, No. 4 (April 1901), 6. See also *Der frayhayts-glok*, No. 3–4 (November 1902), 7.

[3] 'Evrei-kapitalisty v bor'be s evreiami-rabochimi', published in *Iskra*, No. 10 (November 1901), 3. The preference for non-Jewish labor has already been discussed in regard to the situation in Bialystok.   [4] *Der klassen-kampf*, No. 4 (April 1901), 1–2.

region, at least in the period under discussion. The Bund itself determined, in 1902, to 'found and support Christian social democratic organizations among the Christian proletariat', but was unable to do so. That these efforts were largely unsuccessful is acknowledged in an editorial in *The bund*, published in 1905, entitled 'An Old Question'. 'What meaning can our Jewish movement have', the editorial reads, 'when in the regions of the Bund the movement of the non-Jewish workers is so weak[1]?' Just as the old circle leaders had been unable to communicate withChristian workers, so the Bund's organizational efforts could not reduce the threat of Christian strike breaking.

This is not to say that non-Jewish workers were always willing to intervene. There were instances of genuine co-operation between the two groups. In Bialystok, for example, in 1882, German weavers not only refused to replace Jewish workers who had been laid off at the factory but gave them financial assistance during the strike; at Shereshevsky's factory in Grodno, non-Jewish workers refused to act as strike breakers, saying: 'Here Jew and Pole do not exist, we are all workers.'[2] During a strike at the Zaks Match Factory in Dvinsk 'The Christian workers from a nearby leather factory held a demonstration and hailed the strikers, as they urged them to stand firm and wished them success'.[3]

Such instances of solidarity were doubtlessly encouraging to the socialists, but they could not counterbalance the far more frequent

[1] *Der idisher arbeter*, No. 14 (October 1902) 162; *Der bund*, No. 6, (May 1905). On the activities of the Polish Socialist Party in Belorussia–Lithuania see Menachim Wajner, 'Do historii P.P.S. na Litwie', *Niepodległość*, IX, No. 2 (22) (January–June 1934), 221–35; on the Russian Social Democrats, the documents published in *Dokumenty i materialy po istorii Belorussii (1900–13)* (Minsk, 1953), III, 337 ff., particularly documents numbered 391, 396, 398. The failure of the P.P.S. to organize the Polish workers of Belorussia–Lithuania is illustrated by Joseph Pilsudski's report to the Fourth Congress of the party which met in Warsaw in 1897. According to Pilsudski there was no important P.P.S. organization either in Bialystok or Vilna, two of the most important centers of the Jewish labor movement. See Jósef Pisludski, *Pisma zbiorowe* (Warsaw, 1937), I, 186. See also *Posledniia izvestiia*, No. 141 (14 August 1903); *Di arbayter shtime*, No. 29 (September 1902), 10; *Der klassen-kampf*, No. 4 (April 1901), 1–2.

[2] *Di arbayter shtime*, No. 40 (September 1905), 30; co-operation by German workers in Bialystok is described in *Nedel'naia khronika 'Voskhoda'*, II, No. 2 (16 January 1883), 36.

[3] See *Posledniia izvestiia*, No. 152 (25 October 1903). See also *Di arbayter shtime*, No. 16 (March 1900), 7.

occurrence of blacklegging by non-Jewish workers. Sometimes the use of Christian strike breakers backfired on the owners, as it did with Janovsky, the cigarette manufacturer in Bialystok, whose product was subsequently boycotted in the city. On the whole, however, this weapon was extremely effective, as it served not only to break the strikes, but to intensify the animosity between Jewish and Christian workers. To cite but two examples out of the hundreds available: in Bialystok a labor dispute was won by an employer because Christian workers agreed to blackleg; in Dvinsk, strikes in the factories often were broken by hiring Russians to replace the Jewish workers.[1]

Employers were also accused of hiring bands of hooligans to attack the strikers. A dispatch from Kaidan complained of 'bands of crooks' who beat up workers suspected of belonging to the local strike organization;[2] in Lodz the 'loynketniks' were charged with employing members of the 'lumpenproletariat' to persecute the striking weavers. Levin, too, writes of this in his memoirs: 'The bosses stopped at nothing in their struggle against the workers. They turned for help to the underworld, to the hooligans, who beat up the workers.'[3] According to Daytsh, in Dvinsk the factory owner Zaks '...had connexions with hooligans, thieves, pimps, and gangsters' whom he paid to attack the strikers.[4] The 'hooligans' scarcely needed any encouragement to assault the workers. Well organized themselves, they seem to have regarded the new movement as a threat to their authority and responded with predictable violence. 'Hooligans,' Medem wrote, 'wild kids, were set upon us, who were looking for an opportunity to beat us up. Several fights in fact did take place between the Jewish "black hundreds" and our comrades. Our organization seriously considered the question of how to arm

---

[1] *Der bialystoker arbeter*, No. 1 (April 1899), 30; *Posledniia izvestiia*, No. 76 (3 July 1902). The use of one group of workers to hamper the advancement of another, more organized group is familiar to labor historians. One thinks, for example, of the employment of Irish strike breakers in 19th-century England, or of Negro strike breakers in America. See E. P. Thompson, *The Making of the English Working Class* (New York, 1964), 432; Herbert G. Gutman, 'Reconstruction in Ohio: Negroes in the Hocking Valley Coal Mines in 1873 and 1874', *Labor History*, III, No. 3 (Fall 1962), 243–64.

[2] *Posledniia izvestiia*, No. 87 (25 September 1902).

[3] *Der frayhayts-glok*, No. 2 (April 1902), 2; Levin, *Untererdishe kemfer*, 98.

[4] Daytsh, 'Vegn', 3.

ourselves against the toughs.' In Vilna, we are told, a group of roughnecks, led by Motke 'The Tanner', 'waged war against the "philosophers"', and in Dvinsk similar instances of terrorism are said to have occurred.[1] Curiously enough, many of the attackers eventually joined the movement, where they were put to work against the strike breakers.[2]

The frequent use of strike breakers, the assaults by hooligans, contributed to an atmosphere of violence and terror which pervaded the Jewish strike movement, even in the smaller shops. One of the workers who participated in the small strike in Minsk described at the beginning of this chapter wrote:

The boss found other boys to employ...the only thing to do was to go into the shop and kick the blacklegs out by force. I was the strongest; I took a drink to screw up my courage and strength, and entered the shop. Four boys were working. I began to scream at them that they should get out or they'd have their heads broke.[3]

The workers themselves used violence to oppose those who were unwilling to strike. In Kovno workers who refused to participate in strikes had their windows broken. 'I learned', said one of the leaders there, 'that such means were unpleasant and unethical, but that they brought good results.'[4] During one of the earliest strikes in Minsk the organizers actually beat up workers who refused to participate; in Vilna, where violence was habitually directed toward the strike breakers, the fights often ended with 'split heads and bloodied faces'.[5] Anticipating the possibility that workers from Dvinsk would blackleg, strikers in Kaidan wrote to them: 'We, the workers in the Kaidan factories, tell

[1] Medem, *Fun mayn leben*, I, 210; Bernshtein, *Ershte shprotsungen*, 27; Berman, *In loif fun yorn*, 121. The term 'black hundreds' refers to the Russian organizations which, among other things, participated in pogroms during the 1905 revolution. See also Shkliar, 'Onhayb', 194 ff. The best treatment of this is to be found in Litvak, *Vos geven*, 160 ff.

[2] Motke 'the Tanner' joined the Vilna organization where he became 'another man'. He began to read Yiddish books for the first time and formed a group of young workers to fight the strike breakers. See Bernshtein, *Ershte shprotsungen*, 27–8.

[3] Presman, *Der durkhgegangener veg*, 29. Although a bloody fight ensued, the workers won their strike.

[4] Shkliar, 'Onhayb', 198.

[5] 'Der ershter shtrayk in minsk', *Royte bleter* (Minsk, 1929), I, 26; Elie Raytshuk, *Royte bleter*, 3.

you not to dare come here to work, but if you are tired of life come, and you shall soon take leave of it...'[1]

Special squadrons were organized to fight the blacklegs. In Bielsk 'shrek-otriaden' (literally 'fright-detachments') were used against both the masters and the strike breakers; in Vilna the cause was fought by groups known as 'boeviks' (fighters). It was from this background that Hirsh Lekert, a young shoemaker, emerged to make his famous assassination attempt on the Governor of Vilna in 1902.[2]

These outbreaks of violence during strikes alarmed the socialists, who tried to convince the workers that terrorist tactics were 'shameful', and that the strike breakers acted out of ignorance.[3] An article in the Bund's publication in Vilna stressed the idea that violent attacks on Christian strike breakers were not only an offense to 'moral feelings', but intensified the hatred of gentile for Jew. 'We hope', the article added, 'that in time Christian workers will also come to understand who the real enemy is, and that together with their growth of awareness and their increasing needs...they will no longer replace Jewish workers and will demand the same working conditions we have won now.'[4]

Violence, directed against various targets, nevertheless continued to plague the Jewish labor movement throughout the period under discussion. By and large it was perpetrated by new recruits to the movement, uneducated workers who had little respect for party discipline and whose means of expression in disputes was often physical rage. Lekert, for example, the first great folk hero of the Bund, was an illiterate shoemaker who represented a world and a mentality completely alien to the elite of the circle period. The agitators disapproved of violence because

---

[1] *Listok 'Rabochego delo'*, No. 1 (June 1900), 9. The letter was written by employees of a match factory and addressed to workers in the same industry in Dvinsk.

[2] See Y. A. Khatovitsh, 'Dos vos ikh vays vegn Hirsh Lekert', in *Hirsh Lekert, tsum 20-ten*, 13. On Bielsk, see Shtern, *Zikhroynes*, 24; on the role of the Vilna 'boeviks', see Lev, 'Aynike bamerkungen tsu kh. Raytshuks zikhroynes vegn der arbayter-bavegung', *Royte bleter*, 2.

[3] 'Vos darfen mir ton gegen shtraykbrekher?' *Der frayhayts-glok*, No. 2 (April 1902), 5; *Minsker flug-blettel*, No. 5 (March 1902).

[4] 'Vegen bruns shtrayk', *Der klassen-kampf*, No. 4 (April 1901), 2.

it could not be controlled; yet violence was inevitable once the masses joined the movement.[1] And it is clear that the mass Jewish strike movement in general was not under the control of the official organization. The leadership during the agitation period must have occasionally felt that it had created a Frankenstein monster, a force quite alien to the ideals of the Marxist intelligentsia.

The gap between the leadership and the masses is also revealed in the fact that religious orthodoxy, long forgotten by the former, maintained its hold over the latter. The socialists recognized this problem and instituted a campaign to wean the workers away from the old values. In essence, this was an attempt to discredit the ancient notion of Jewish solidarity, the idea that 'all Jews are brothers', and to replace this with the Marxian notion of class struggle. In a brochure concerning the cigarette workers' strike in Vilna in 1895, Gozhanskii has one character pose the following question:

Are the Jews no longer one people, a people strongly united by its frightful troubles, which all have shared, which it has experienced over thousands of years in the darkness of exile? Are not all Jews the children of a single father with a single belief, with a single Jewish heart? Children, who gather on the Sabbath in the synagogue...to forget all their pains and sorrows, which give them not a moment's rest, and to pour out their heart in prayer and in pleas to God?[2]

To this Gozhanskii and other socialist leaders answered that the wealthy Jews, the factory owners, 'have their own God', while 'our God is unity'. 'We workers lament on the ninth of Ab (the fast day commemorating the destruction of the Temple in Jerusalem) not because we are Jews, but because we are workers.'[3] Over and again the socialists explained to the workers that 'the factory owner is our blood-sucker, our exploiter, not our benefactor as was previously believed'. They tried to convince workers of the inevitable clash of interests between the capitalists and the

[1] See also below, pp. 130 ff.
[2] 'Der shtot magid', *Historishe shriftn*, III, 723–4.
[3] 'Tsu di idishe arbeter in varshe', 1896, published in *Historishe shriftn*, III, 752; 'K grodnenskoi rabochei messe', in Lev, 'Pervye shagi', in Dimanshtein (ed.), *Revoliutsionnoe dvizhenie*, 280.

workers, despite the Jewish tradition both classes shared.[1] Employers, they warned, wished to appear to the workers as 'brider fun ayn folk' (brothers of a single people), but this was merely the lie they used to hold on to the 'good old days', to justify wealth in the midst of poverty.[2]

Anti-religious propaganda of the type indulged in by the Jewish anarchists of New York was eschewed by the Bund.[3] Rather, the socialists attempted to discredit the Jewish clergy by exposing the rabbis as friends of the bosses and the police. The 'Magid' (preacher) of Vilna, for example, was reported to have appeared in the synagogue during the cigarette workers' strike in 1895. There he 'severely castigated the strikers, beseeching them with great solemnity to preserve the national-religious unity of the Jewish people'. He was interrupted by members of the audience, which included some of the local activists, who shouted: 'Rabbi, how much were you paid for your sermon?' Cries of 'shame, shame' by other members of the congregation rang through the hall.[4]

Once again we must remember the nature of our sources. But it is clear that the rabbis were in general unfriendly to the labor movement, and that this attitude in part stemmed from a fear that the radicals would play into the hands of the anti-semites. Thus after an anti-Tsarist demonstration a rabbi in Minsk exclaimed: 'How can we Jews, who are equal to crawling worms, be involved in such deeds? Consider, sons of Israel, reflect well on what you are doing.'[5] They were also disturbed that many of the workers who had been drawn into the movement were abandon-

---

[1] *Der bialystoker arbayter*, No. 1 (April 1899), 3–4. The quotation is from the proclamation *Ko vsem grodnenskim rabochim i rabotnitsam*, published in Dimanshtein (ed.), *Revoliutsionnoe dvizhenie*, 278.

[2] *Der kampf*, No. 1 (September 1900), 12; *Rabochee delo*, No. 6 (April 1900), 60.

[3] Bernshtein, *Ershte shprotsungen*, 29. Among other things, the anarchists held banquets on Yom Kippur (the Day of Atonement).

[4] *Ibid.*, 30; the first quotation is from Martov, *Zapiski sotsialdemokrata*, 246. The incident inspired Gozhanskii to write the brochure 'Der shtot magid', referred to above. For a similar occurrence see A. Baylin, 'Zikhroynes', *Royte bleter*, 7; according to him the rabbi in Mstislav delivered a sermon accusing the local activist of having 'forsaken almighty God' and profaned the Sabbath, forgotten that poverty and wealth rest with God alone.

[5] Quoted in *Posledniia izvestiia*, No. 73 (12 June 1902).

ing orthodoxy. A special rabbinical proclamation, issued in Mezrich in 1903, warned the community as follows:

Let it be known to the inhabitants of our city, that according to rumor there are many places here where young people hold meetings and assemblies, especially on the holy Sabbath at the time of the morning prayer. In each of these a young man has in his charge many students, whom he teaches to abandon the paths of justice and law and to go against the regime.[1]

Ideological opposition sometimes drove the rabbis to collude with the police. In Mezrich a special society was established known as the 'Guardians of the Law', whose function was to spy on workers who attended socialist meetings and to inform on them to the police. During a major strike of tanners in Krynki, the local rabbi declared that such acts of protest would 'turn the world upside down', and he rebuked the workers saying: 'Your unity is also a dangerous thing and your leaders must be arrested.' In Smorgon, local clerics of all faiths joined the 'Union of Industrialists'; and in Lodz, the rabbi threatened the striking workers with imprisonment if they persisted in protesting.[2] Sometimes these clashes of view erupted in violence, as in Vilkovishki where the police, the employers and the local rabbi were attacked by workers during a strike. In another town, the rabbis made a funeral the occasion to remind workers that 'all problems derive from the sins of the "atheists", from "unity"', thus inciting the mob against certain members of the local organization.[3]

The rabbinical attitude toward the labor movement was not entirely hostile; even the socialist press reported occasional incidents of clerics who were sympathetic to workers' demands, if not to the ideas of socialism. Rabbi Mohilever, for instance, the

---

[1] *Posledniia izvestiia*, No. 161 (23 December 1903), 7.

[2] On Krynki see *Di arbayter shtime*, No. 4–5 (23 September 1897), 13; on Smorgon, Peskovoi, 'V smorgoni', 83; on Lodz, *Der frayhayts-glok*, No. 1 (September 1901), 7–8. According to the latter source the workers were pleased when their rabbi intervened in the strike and hoped to win him over to their side. 'Naive men', comments the article. For other instances of the rabbis' stand against the workers see *Di arbayter shtime*, No. 15 (December 1899), 13–15, and *Der minsker arbayter*, No. 3 (June 1901), 5.

[3] Grinberg, *Der veker*, VI, No. 310 (22 October 1927), 14; *Di letste pasirungen*, No. 25 (3 December 1905), 7.

well-known Zionist leader from Bialystok, was prepared to accept the Bund as the 'representative of the Jewish proletariat'.[1] But this was clearly a minority view. In 1903 a special conference of rabbis, held in Cracow, denounced the movement and passed a resolution against Jews who violated the precepts of Judaism by breaking the laws of the state. A similar conference planned for Grodno that same year inspired a savage attack on clericalism by the socialists. In an article entitled 'Religious Slavery, or the Rabbis in the Service of the Gendarmes', the latter referred to the Jewish religious leaders as 'cursed slave-charlatans' and 'servants of the knout and of theft'.[2]

The rabbis had some justification for fearing that workers who entered the movement would reject the traditional Jewish practices. To be sure, those who did break away from orthodoxy found it extremely difficult. In describing the serious conflicts which rent the families of the circle members, Gordon, the leader of the Vilna opposition group, complained that the intellectuals showed little sympathy or understanding of this problem.[3] Most contemporary observers agreed, however, that workers who were committed to the movement quickly shed the external trappings of orthodoxy. 'Our workers', Bernshtein wrote:

Stopped praying, stopped using the prayer book and phylacteries (small leather cases worn on the person in which certain biblical texts

[1] *Posledniia izvestiia*, No. 186 (9 July 1904). According to Daytsh, 'Vegn', 20, who was sentenced to prison for his participation in the movement, a rabbi said to him: 'Despite the fact that (you) are on the wrong road (you) are a good Jew.' In Dvinsk a local preacher set up special worker societies, mainly of an educational nature, which were of great benefit to the artisans of that city. Ironically, many of the activists were veterans of these societies. See Berman, *In loif fun yorn*, 68 ff., who adds that a pioneer of the labor movement, the tailor Mendel Skutelskii, was 'the right-hand man of (the preacher) Eliakum Getsl'.

[2] 'Di religieze shklaferay oder di rabonim in der dienst fun zhandarmn', *Flug-blettel, heroisgegeben fun grodner sotsialdemokratishen komitet fun bund*, No. 3 (November 1903). On the resolution of the Cracow conference see *Der fraynd*, No. 176 (8 August 1903), 4. The Grodno conference seems not to have taken place, although an anti-socialist proclamation signed by a group of Vilna clerics was circulating in the city late in the summer of that year. See *Posledniia izvestiia*, No. 162 (31 December 1904); and No. 143 (29 August 1903). On the proposed Grodno conference see also the proclamation *Po povodu s'ezda ravvinov v Grodne*, November 1903.

[3] Avram Gordon, *In friling*, 15 ff. A feuilleton in *Der klassen-kampf*, No. 6 (December 1901), discusses the difficulties encountered by a revolutionary whose father happened to be a pious Jew, and who was torn by the idea that he must not only obey God but also the law of the land.

are written) and even stopped eating kosher food...A young man at a meeting smokes a cigarette on Saturday, something he has never done before. Next, he begins to ask questions about religious customs. Then he begins to question the essence of religion, etc. Our world naturally freed itself from clericalism and religious customs.[1]

According to a circle leader, 'Our workers were never religious, even those with whom we quarreled had already abandoned religion, they could go off to study on Saturday...to gather in the circles'. Members of the Bristle-Workers' Union, an article in *The Awakener* claimed, had given up 'the stupid belief in miracles' that characterized their parents and those of the workers who had not yet become enlightened.[2] The article goes on to contrast the younger generation of bristle workers with their parents: 'Israel's father is certainly an ignorant man, who does not know the wisdom of the Talmud, but he wants to know it, he envies the learned man, he desires to learn—at least, passages of the Mishnayot (parts of the Talmud)...Israel, however, is no longer concerned with legends...Israel is seeking another type of education.' In 1903, workers in Mezrich openly ate and drank on the Day of Atonement.[3]

It seems clear that actual membership in the organization was incompatible with orthodox practices. Yet many workers, who remained on the periphery of the movement, retained their religious beliefs. In Vitebsk such workers attacked organizers whose activities seemed to them heretical.[4] These attitudes were particularly evident among the older workers; the factory owners and masters often discouraged their employees from participating in strikes by telling them that the young, atheistic workers, who were merely out to secure their own interests, would cause

---

[1] Bernshtein, *Ershte shprotsungen*, 29; see also Litvak, *Vos geven*, 132, who claims workers quickly broke with tradition, ate on the fast day of Yom Kippur (the Day of Atonement), and rejected God.

[2] *Der veker*, No. 3 (January 1900), 2.

[3] *Posledniia izvestiia*, No. 161 (23 December 1903): according to this report, the rabbi 'called together all the factory owners of the city (a center of the bristle-making industry) and prepared a "black list" of all the rebels and apostates. The employers agreed not to hire them, and many workers now go hungry.'

[4] See Ginzburg, 'Nachalnye shagi', 108, who claims he was once 'beaten up severely' by a group of carpenters whom he had attempted to draw into the movement. See also Shkliar 'Onhayb', 194, 197.

irreparable damage to the older workers. 'Enough of this submission to the young', one employer is quoted as saying, and he
added: '...the young leaders are (the older workers') true
enemies.'[1] In Gomel young shop assistants declared their allegiance
to the 'Bund', while the older workers formed a politically
neutral 'Union for the Protection of Shop Assistants' Interests'.[2]
Those pious workers who chose to listen to the agitators were
sometimes confused by the new message. Thus, after hearing an
activist hold forth on the glories of the socialist order to come, a
bristle worker asked: 'Tell me "reb" (Mr) Preacher, what will
happen if the Messiah comes before we achieve freedom and
introduce socialism?'[3]

Many of the workers who were caught up in the labor movement tried to combine the new ideology with the old traditions.
Thus a group of bristle workers, who had not been fully
indoctrinated by the leaders of their union, 'swore on a Torah
scroll during a strike that they would not serve as strike breakers'.[4]
The boycott in Bialystok, described earlier, was interpreted
by some as a religious act; thus, in one of the synagogues of
Bialystok a member of the congregation announced: 'Jews, it is
forbidden to buy Janovsky's cigarettes, there is a ban on them!'[5]
During a strike in Minsk when a workers' meeting was being
held in a synagogue, an elderly Jew 'swore by God and the
Torah that his name had been mistakenly confused with that of a
strike breaker, and requested that this shame be removed (from
him)'.[6]

Perhaps the most interesting example of the attempt to combine
the new ideology with the practices of orthodoxy was the

---

[1] *Posledniia izvestiia*, No. 151 (3 October 1903).

[2] *Ibid.*, No. 53 (24 January 1902). During a strike at Shereshevsky's factory in Grodno the
older workers refused to participate; in Horodok, a town near Bialystok, a factory owner
promised the older workers a raise if they would agree not to join the young 'rebels'.
See *Der bund*, No. 3 (April 1904), 8–9; *Der bialystoker arbeter*, No. 4 (April 1901), 10.
Being heads of families, the older workers naturally were less anxious to take risks.

[3] Lazar Kling, 'Epizodn fun der amoliker bundisher tetikayt', *Buletin fun bund arkhiv*,
No. 3 (19) (October 1964), 10.

[4] *Ibid.*, 11.

[5] Avram der Tate, *Bleter*, 56. The term he used ('herem') was employed by the socialists
to mean a 'boycott'. In a religious context it means 'excommunication'.

[6] *Der bund*, No. 6 (May 1905), 16.

reaction of 300 Jewish tanners to a general strike in Krynki in 1897. The workers, we are told, held an outdoor meeting to discuss strategy: 'The weather was bad, it began to rain; everyone stood in the rain for more than two hours. All swore by a pair of phylacteries that they would stand firm and support those workers who had been fired, and everyone sang the "Oath", the official hymn of the Bund.'[1] Thus a solemn religious ceremony was followed by the singing of a revolutionary song.

As the labor movement progressed, of course, the established ideas about Jewish unity showed signs of giving way. One Bialystok employer remarked: 'Formerly, the factory owner and the workers would gather together every day for the morning and evening prayers, they would meet each other in the synagogue on Saturdays and on the holidays...and come together on a more personal level.' But things have changed, and today, 'there is no neutral meeting ground, they have become completely estranged.'[2] In one sense, then, the socialist campaign of agitation had achieved its end: the strike movement had definitely driven a wedge between the two classes. But when we examine the changes it made in the economic condition of the Jewish proletariat we find that while considerable gains were achieved, they were for the most part short-lived. In the small shops, particularly, employers did not put up much resistance at first and workers usually won their demands for a twelve hour day and higher wages. An official report from Vilna in 1896 lists in detail substantial improvements workers achieved with respect both to wages and the length of the working day.

A noticeable improvement of material conditions...occurred among the following workers: (1) spatmakers, (2) glovemakers, (3) lacemakers, (4) shoemakers, (5) turners, (6) bristle workers and several others. In these crafts wages increased from 25 to 50 kopeks a week or from 13 to 26 rubles a year. Among the following workers the workday was shortened by one hour after the founding of the 'struggle

---

[1] *Der idisher arbeter*, No. 4–5 (November 1897), 35. The influence of traditional Jewish customs on the labor movement is discussed by Menes, *Historishe shriftn*, III, 56 ff.; he deals with this too in his article 'Der onhayb fun der idisher arbeter-bevegung un ihr shoyresh in idishen folks-leben', *Di tsukunft*, XL, No. 9 (September 1935), 534–44.

[2] Landau, *Unter jüdischen Proletariern*, 55.

kassy': (1) engravers, (2) glovemakers, (3) turners, and others. By
1½ hours: (1) shoemakers, (2) 'tandetniki' (tailors producing for
stores), (3) tailors working by order, (4) female glovemakers, and
others. By 2–3 hours: (1) lacemakers (a small craft, consisting of nine
men in all), (2) bristle workers, and others.[1]

These held true for most cities in which the labor movement
flourished. By 1899 the following changes had been instituted in
Vitebsk:

Almost everywhere...there is a clearly established workday; on
Thursdays one leaves work at the usual time, on Saturdays there is no
work at all, and overtime has been completely abolished. With a few
exceptions the workday does not exceed 13–14 hours (including
breaks) and in a great many shops one works only twelve hours (ten
hours without breaks). Moreover, everywhere there is a regularly
established time for eating and for rests of 1½–2 hours, whereas previously one ate while working. Together with this wages have been
raised 30–100%; payments everywhere are given at specific times,
while previously they were paid by the month, particularly in the
women's crafts.[2]

In Gomel extraordinary gains were made:

Wages have been raised: 30% for tailors, 35–40% for piece workers;
for the carpenters piece work has been abolished completely, weekly
wages have risen 50%; there are practically no workers now who are
paid yearly...prices for piece work among shoemakers have risen
15%, yearly wages 30–40%. Locksmiths' wages have increased almost
50%. The workday has undergone the following changes: for the
tailors formerly it was 16–17 hours, now it is 14–15 hours; for the
carpenters it now lasts from 6.00 a.m. to 9.00 p.m. in the summer,
and from 7.00 a.m. to 8.00 p.m. in the winter, instead of 17 hours
(5.00 a.m. to 10.00 p.m.). For the shoemakers it lasts from 6.00 a.m.
to 9.00 p.m., instead of 18 hours as before. The locksmiths have a
14-hour day. Rests for mealtime are provided in almost all shops.
Improvements have occurred also in the relations between the employer and the workers: payments are made accurately, treatment is
more decent.[3]

[1] 'Materialy', Agursky (ed.), *Di sotsialistishe lituratur*, 417.
[2] 'Bor'ba vitebskikh rabochikh', in Agursky (ed.), *Di sotsialistishe literatur*, 336.
[3] See 'Gomel'skoe rabochee', in Agursky (ed.), *Di sotsialistishe literatur*, 350.

As we have seen, such uniformity of working conditions was precisely what the workers had hoped to achieve.

Nonetheless these gains proved none too permanent, and in some cases they were completely reversed within a few years. Carpenters in Vilna, for example, won their strike for a twelve-hour day in 1897, but by 1901 they were working fourteen to fifteen hours a day and all night on Thursdays; in 1897 all the Bialystok artisans had won a twelve-hour day, yet by the early 1900s they were clearly losing the struggle to hold on to these gains.[1] Six years of struggle found the carpenters, plasterers, locksmiths, and other artisans in Minsk no better off than they had been before the strike movement began. According to the socialist journal in that city, in 1902 the great majority of workers were still working fourteen to sixteen hours a day and being urged to continue the fight for a twelve-hour day.[2]

The Bialystok weavers who, as we have seen, were among the most aggressive workers in the strike movement, had two major aims: to increase wages and to rid themselves of the 'loynketniks'. Although they persisted in their fight throughout the 1890s and the early years of the twentieth century, they managed only for brief periods to reduce the number of middlemen.[3] In fact, by 1901 the labor organization had to admit that the number of 'loynketniks' was actually on the rise; in that year, too, the Bund's publication in Bialystok was obliged to defend the very policy of the strike from attacks by the weavers, who blamed their declining economic situation on the movement. The real problem, the socialists insisted, was that the Jews were not hired in the modern factories, and they could only suggest to the workers that

[1] *Der klassen-kampf*, No. 4 (April 1901), 4–5, 9–10, 10–12; for other examples from Vilna, see *Der bialystoker arbeter*, No. 1 (April 1899), 20, and *passim*. The tailors who had won a twelve-hour day in 1896 were fighting to preserve it in 1900: *Der bialystoker arbeter*, No. 3 (December 1900), 9; in the same year the workday for carpenters was increased from 12 to 14 hours (10).

[2] *Der minsker arbayter*, No. 1 (December 1900), 1; and No. 2 (January 1901), 1, 5. As in 1894, a number of strikes were waged in 1901 to attain a twelve-hour day; see No. 4 (November 1901), 10–13.

[3] See 'Bor'ba tkachei v Belostoke s masterami-posrednikami, po povodu proshlogodnei stachki', *Rabochee delo*, No. 4–5 (September–December 1899), 83–9; 'Di oifgabes fun di veber', *Der bialystoker arbeter*, No. 3 (December 1900), 3–5. In 1899 a major victory was won when 200 'loynketnik' looms were transferred back to the factories.

they agree to work on Saturdays. This, of course, was a most inadequate solution.[1]

The weavers' dilemma was merely one example of the dilemma confronted by the Jewish labor movement as a whole. As the movement continued, it was all too apparent that improvements were possible only within severely circumscribed limits. The bristle workers had an excellent union, and had won by 1900 a twelve-hour day in at least twelve different towns and cities.[2] Yet it was increasingly difficult to maintain these gains. In 1902 the workers' situation was said to be 'desperate'. Four years of struggle had not eliminated rampant exploitation; working conditions were still bad, and further strikes had achieved nothing. Factory owners apparently were unable to make additional concessions without going under themselves. 'We can't live any more,' they complained to the workers, 'we are paying a good deal; others outside Vilna pay less, why don't you go to them?'[3] Many of the factory owners were threatened with bankruptcy after the numerous strikes and were forced to leave the city.

Throughout the cities of Belorussia–Lithuania the strike movement could scarcely hope to effect permanent gains for the workers. Depressions often robbed them of what they had won through long, costly strikes. In 1904 massive unemployment in Bialystok completely wrecked the labor movement.[4] In Kovno gains won by a strike of raft workers in 1902 were promptly reversed when a depression set in.[5] The situation in Pinsk was typical of many cities. Tailors there had won a twelve-hour day during the summer of 1904, but quickly lost this and were once again forced to work 'without limit'.[6]

---

[1] See 'Der fakh veber', *Der bialystoker arbeter*, No. 4 (April 1901), 3–5; 'Der dampf-shtul', *Der bialystoker arbeter*, No. 5 (May 1901).

[2] 'Di tsushtand fun der bershter produktsion nokh'h statistik in 1900-ten yahr', *Der veker*, No. 5 (May 1900), 13.

[3] Grinberg, 'Erinerungen', 19; 'Vos zollen mir tun', *Der veker*, No. 11 (March 1902), 1; see also 'Di bershter zind', *Der veker*, No. 10 (August 1901), 6–8; workers were told that indiscriminate strike activity was self-defeating since it would bankrupt the employers.

[4] *Di arbayter shtime*, No. 38 (September 1904), 18; *Der bund*, No. 4 (July 1904), 14–15. In Lodz, workers were still laboring sixteen to eighteen hours a day in 1903; see *Flug-blettel, heroisgegeben fun lodzer sotsialdemokratishen komitet fun bund*, No. 3 (July 1903), 1.

[5] *Rabochaia mysl'*, No. 14 (January 1902), 16.

[6] *Posledniia izvestiia*, No. 170 (25 February 1904).

With respect to the carpenters in Grodno, an official report stated in 1898: 'The shortened workday, which the workers won through their strike in the summer, was lengthened by the employers in the winter, as soon as the season was over.'[1] The same held true in Dvinsk, where workers literally were starving during the winter. The socialist leaders were powerless to help them. 'Everyone turned to us, to the leaders of the crafts. What will happen?...We too did not know.'[2]

By the turn of the century the problems of the strike movement were all too apparent to the socialist leaders. The report from Grodno quoted above noted: 'It is impossible to conduct an economic struggle in Grodno.'[3] Leaders of the Bristle-Workers' Union advised their members to strike only when absolutely necessary; and in 1904 the Polish section of the Union announced that no further gains were possible at the time.[4] Moreover, the fourth congress of the Bund resolved in 1901 to support strikes only in places where the economic struggle had not yet begun, or where the 'employers attempt to worsen existing conditions or to cancel gains already won by the workers'. In short, only defensive strikes were approved. The resolution went on to state: 'In those crafts where, given the local conditions, strikes have achieved the maximum possible results...new strikes should not be organized.'[5]

Thus while the strike movement brought some important improvements in workers' conditions, it was incapable of effecting radical and permanent changes. It was more a palliative than a cure. And while depressions and crises could be surmounted, the general decline of Jewish crafts and the failure of the artisans to enter the factories proved insurmountable. If the weavers of Bialystok won a shorter workday, such temporary gains were offset by their failure to eliminate the 'loynketnik' system. The artisans achieved a certain degree of regularity in their workshops, but they were constantly threatened with a return to the 'old

---

1 'Der leben un kampf', *Der idisher arbeter*, No. 10 (1900), 66.
2 Berman, *In loif fun yorn*, 189.
3 'Der leben un kampf', *Der idisher arbeter*, No. 10 (1900), 66.
4 'Unzer 9-ten tsuzamenfahr', *Der veker*, No. 6 (July 1900), 2; *Flug-blettel, heroisgegeben fun der komitet fun poylishen bershter-rayon*, No. 1 (January 1904), 1.
5 The resolutions are published in *Di arbayter shtime*, No. 24 (August 1901), 1.

regime' by conditions outside their control. The cigarette and match factory employees, whose strikes were among the most dramatic of the agitation period, continued to work long hours for meagre wages. The long months of unemployment in the off-season constituted a problem for which the labor leaders had no solutions. Emigration, the only escape from the impossible economic conditions of the Pale, continued unabated.

The above evidence suggests that the members of the circle opposition, as well as the Zionists were right to criticize the tactics of agitation. The strike movement did not solve the economic problem of the Jewish proletariat in Belorussia–Lithuania.

CHAPTER 6

On the Cultural Front

Within (the last) two years there has been a marked
increase in the cultural needs of the workers. The request
for books has grown to such a degree that the two
workers' libraries (Russian and Yiddish) are unable to
satisfy the demand.

From an official report on the Minsk labor
movement, 1897

In 1897 the Minsk activist and 'opposition' leader Abraham
Liesin, newly arrived in America, was interviewed by the editor
of the Yiddish daily *Forverts*. Discussing the 'kassy', Liesin is
quoted as saying: 'The practical revolutionary work these groups
are capable of is fairly insignificant. Even their strikes are often
very childish. First of all, the employers are not capitalists, but are
themselves extremely poor, so that a struggle goes on between
the poverty-stricken and the indigent; secondly, the hired artisans
are future employers...' What is really important, Liesin argues,
is the cultural work the organization carries on: 'Some workers
have become pretty fair intellectuals and well-read men, and their
lives have taken quite a different course than they would have
under normal circumstances.'[1]

We have already stressed the importance attached to education
during the circle period. While the transition to agitation shifted
the emphasis from learning to direct action, it did not mean the
end of cultural work, as Gordon and his supporters had feared.
Liesin's description, as noted, dates from the year 1897, five years
after the socialists had launched the agitation program. In Minsk,
to cite another source, a compromise was eventually reached
in the controversy over agitation. 'True,' a participant writes,

[1] Ab. Cahan, 'Bildung un sotsialistishe propagande bay yidishe bale melokhes in di
litvishe shtet', *Historishe shriftn*, III, 396–7.

116

'teaching the workers Russian, arithmetic, and the natural sciences was not emphasized as much as before. But propaganda circles to develop activists for the movement were continued.'[1] In 1901 circles in that city were still occupied with questions of socialism, private property, primitive communism, slavery, capitalism, and nationalism.[2] A complex system, operating on three different levels, was in effect. On the most elementary level workers were taught to understand the inherent contradictions of interests between employers and employees; they were also lectured on the concept of the workday, wages, surplus value, and the need for organization. After this introduction to 'economic' affairs they would advance to the level of 'political' theory, where they studied constitutional government, revolutionary ideology, and the like. The final, or 'socialist' stage of the program took up such problems as the class struggle, various types of social structures, the division of labor, social democracy, and Zionism.[3] In Vitebsk numerous circles continued to function, 'teaching their members Russian grammar and giving them their first inkling of political economy'.[4]

At first glance it would appear that the educational work of the circle period had continued unchanged. This, however, was not the case. As a result of the new agitation program and the influx of new recruits, cultural work reached a much larger audience. Furthermore, it was now conducted in the native language of the workers. In Riga, for example, by the late 1890s the educational campaign was conducted entirely in Yiddish.[5] In 1893 a Yiddish library was established in Vilna for organized workers who knew no Russian; the library contained the works of the well-known Yiddish novelists and short story writers Mendele Moicher Sforim (Mendele the Book-Seller) and Sholem Aleichem, as well as a few popular novels and books in translation.[6] Gradually, new literary

---

[1] Levin, *Untererdishe kemfer*, 104. He adds that while several workers accepted the agitation program, they continued to study, only that they did so on the sly so as not to irritate the champions of the new program.

[2] See Bukhbinder, *Krasnaia letopis'*, No. 5 (1923), 139.

[3] 'Programma zaniatii s rabochimi kruzhkami', in Rafes, *Ocherki*, 329–31. Theoretically, at least, this was the program for 1900.

[4] Dimanshtein (ed.), *Revoliutsionnoe dvizhenie*, 126.

[5] See Abramovich, *In tsvay revolutsies*, I, 55.   [6] See Litvak, *Vos geven*, 71 ff.

works were made available: stories by Y. L. Peretz and David Pinsky, who were among the first Yiddish writers to describe proletarian life, were extremely popular. This was particularly true of the works of Peretz, the great Hebrew and Yiddish man of letters, who for a certain time was closely connected with the socialist movement. His 'Yon-Tev Bletlekh' ('Holiday Pages'), which appeared in the 1890s, 'passed from hand to hand'.[1]

We have had occasion to mention that the emphasis on Russian in the early circles was partly the consequence of a dearth of appropriate material in Yiddish. By the turn of the century, however, a Yiddish 'renaissance' was under way, and had already produced a considerable original literature. At the same time the European classics were translated into the Jewish vernacular. By turning to the masses, the new movement had committed itself to Yiddish, and this commitment was naturally extended to the cause of Yiddish literature. The Bundists became the champions of 'Yiddishism', the noble 'language of the people', which they supported over the 'bourgeois' Hebrew of the Zionists.

It was natural, then, for a close bond to be established between the labor movement and the new Yiddish literature. In Vilna this alliance was marked by the formation in 1895 of a 'Jargon Committee', whose aim was 'to distribute good literature among the Jewish workers, to found Jewish worker-libraries...and to publish popular scientific books and fiction in Yiddish'. The 'Committee' functioned for three years, and its leaders combined literary and socialist activities.[2]

The need for propaganda materials in the vernacular encouraged those of the leaders who knew Yiddish to undertake translations and to write their own material. Thus Gozhanskii asked Litvak, a leader of the 'Jargon Committee', to translate some works of Karl Kautsky, the German socialist, which he wished to use in his circles.[3] Gozhanskii himself was a prolific

---

[1] Levin, *Untererdishe kemfer*, 115. See also Mill, *Pionern un boyer*, I, 25; especially Mikhalevich, *Zikhroynes*, I, 72 ff. For a sensitive account of Peretz' relation to the revolutionary movement see Maurice Samuel, *Prince of the Ghetto* (New York and Philadelphia, 1959), 171–6.

[2] The quotation is from Litvak, *Vos geven*, 96, who was also the principal historian of the 'Committee' ('Jargon' means simply 'Yiddish').

[3] Litvak, *Vos geven*, 86 ff.

writer of popular brochures which dealt in a homely, simple way with various themes of proletarian life. His pamphlet 'The Jewish Question in Russia under Alexander the Third' concerned the disabilities Jews faced in Tsarist Russia, while his 'A Speech on Purim' compared Haman of biblical times with the modern oppressors of the Jews and the working class in general.[1] Similar to these were the feuilletons which were extremely popular with readers of the socialist press. The story 'No, A Thousand Times No (The Tale and Declaration of an Artisan)', which appeared in *The Struggle*, the Bund's publication in Gomel, portrayed a typical Jewish journeyman rebelling against the intolerable conditions of the workshop; 'Haim the Weaver', a story in *The Bialystok Worker*, concerned a pious, orthodox Jew who, in the twilight of his life, converts to socialism and devotes himself to the labor movement. 'All Jews Are Friends', a feuilleton in *The Minsk Worker*, attacked the idea of Jewish unity.[2] Educational articles on a somewhat higher level were also published in the local press and above all in the Bund's journal abroad, *The Jewish Worker* (*Der idisher arbeter*). A regular reader of that journal would find articles such as 'The Importance of the Petersburg Strikes for the Labor Movement in Russia and in Western Europe', 'Anti-

[1] A list of Gozhanskii's brochures is published in Herts *et al.*, *Di geshikhte*, I, 98. The above-mentioned works are published in *Historishe shriftn*, III, 685-94, 705-21. See also his 'A Discussion Concerning Fate' (694-705), which consists of a dialogue between Shimon and Zerakh; the former insists that poverty is inevitable and permanent, the latter describes the march of history which will abolish poverty; 'Good Holiday, A Short Story' (679-85), discusses the importance of May Day; 'The Worker Revolution' (665-78) is a simple exposition of Marxism. Among the other socialists to write brochures for the workers was Arkady Kremer, the initiator of the agitation program, who wrote 'The Workday' and 'Wages'.

[2] 'Nayn, un toyzend mol nayn (ertzehlung un erklerung fun a bal melokhe)', *Der kampf*, No. 3 (March 1901), 1-17. 'Haim der veber', *Der bialystoker arbeter*, No. 1 (April 1899), 3-4. 'Kol yisroel khavarim', *Der minsker arbayter*, Nos. 1, 3-4. The following, too, are examples of this genre of literature: the story 'Tsvay ferbrekher' ('Two Criminals'), *Der minsker arbayter*, No. 3 (June 1901), 3-8, concerns a socialist who is arrested for participating in a strike and a pickpocket. The former convinces the thief that criminals are made by their environment and that socialism will create a world in which robbery will be unnecessary. In the feuilleton 'A kholem erev yon-tev-dem ershten may' ('A dream on May Day eve') which appeared in *Der veker*, No. 4 (May 1900), 3-4, a bristle worker abandons religion and becomes a socialist; for him God has come to mean the proletariat and Satan the police. In 'Der shtrayk (Vy der fabrikant fershraybt zayne tsores)' ('The strike (How a factory owner writes about his troubles)'), *Der veker*, No. 5 (May 1900), 8-11, despite the help he receives from the local rabbi and from the police, the employer is unable to break down the workers' solidarity.

Semitic Disorders in Galicia', 'Friedrich Engels on Anti-Semitism', 'Social Democracy in Denmark', etc. That material of this sort was made available in Yiddish proved to be of great help in propagating socialist ideas among the masses who knew no other language.[1]

The feuilletons in the socialist press, the popular brochures, Yiddish translations, and original works of Yiddish literature, all were made available to the organized workers through the medium of special libraries. Ideally, there were both 'kassa' libraries, which catered to a particular craft, and general libraries used by all the workers in a given city. In Dvinsk:

Aside from the craft libraries, there was also a central library which would buy new books, distribute them, and exchange them for others in the craft libraries. The central library had its own special librarian whose identity was a closely guarded secret. Only the other librarians and those high up in the organization knew him. Despite their illegal status, the librarians functioned extremely well and performed their task in the best possible way.[2]

In Minsk much the same arrangement was in force. 'I was the representative of the illegal library', writes Levin. 'We already had a large number of brochures in Russian and Yiddish, especially in Yiddish...we would distribute them to the representatives of the crafts and they would pass them on to the members. Every brochure had to be returned.'[3] In Vilna, intricate regulations were established to govern the use of the illegal libraries:

(1) The aim of the libraries is to develop knowledge and understanding among the masses. (2) The library commission consists of representatives chosen in each of the craft commissions...(3) A representative is one who has had experience with literature and knows which books are needed in his craft; he must also be an honorable person who knows how to operate in secret.... (5) The elected representatives constitute a joint library commission. The Library Commission selects from its members a Librarian, a Treasurer and a Controller. (6) The Librarian

[1] A list of 25 Yiddish brochures available to the Jewish workers in 1901 is published in *Der idisher arbeter*, No. 11 (1901).
[2] Berman, *In loif fun yorn*, 146. The libraries were illegal because of their connexion with the illegal organization.
[3] Levin, *Untererdishe kemfer*, 144.

is to distribute and receive books from each library and to be certain that the books are in order... The literature must be kept in his home. (7) The Librarian is forbidden to distribute torn books, and he must be certain that torn books are not brought in. When a representative brings in a torn book, he must pay (a fine). (8) The Treasurer is to receive money from each Library Commission. (9) The Controller is to record the books and money which the Library Commission receives or distributes, and to give receipts to each representative for the money and books he has received from him...[1]

The libraries were well-stocked and were always much frequented by workers. In 1897 workers in Minsk had two libraries available to them; and in Vilna, in addition to two general libraries containing 500 books, there were also individual 'kassa' libraries. In 1904 the city of Libau, hardly a center of socialist activity, had an illegal library that stocked 100 books; even the little town of Verzshbolov in the bristle-making region had, it was said, a 'very rich' library.[2] Aside from the popular literature described above, the libraries usually carried basic texts on socialism by Marx, Guesde, Lafargue and Lassalle. In the Dvinsk libraries Yiddish translations of Jules Verne and Tolstoy were available (in American editions), as were translations of popular scientific books. Workers in Minsk also had available to them the writings of the well-known American-Yiddish poets Rosenfeld and Edelshtadt.[3] For those who knew Russian, of course, the selection was somewhat wider, and although a special effort to teach the workers Russian was abandoned for the most part

[1] 'Ustav rabochei organizatsii', in Rafes, *Ocherki*, 321–2. Many other details are recorded; it is stipulated, for example, that books could be kept only for the length of time it took to read them, after which they were to be returned immediately.

[2] See *Der veker*, No. 12 (March 1903), 16. Prior to 1902 the Bristle-Workers' Union had a number of 'legal libraries', which were condemned at the Union's 10th conference as part of the general crackdown on non-socialist activities; see 'Unzer 10-ter tsuzamen-fahr', *Der veker*, No. 8–9 (March 1902), 2. On Minsk, see 'Nachalo rabochego dvizheniia v Minske 1894–97 g.', in Agursky, *Di sotsialistishe literatur*, 28; on Vilna, 'Der leben un kampf', *Der idisher arbeter*, No. 11 (1901), 43. In 1900 only one library seems to have been in existence in Kovno; this was also true of Vitebsk; see 'Konstruktsiia partiinoi organizatsii "Bunda"', in Rafes, *Ocherki*, 327, and Ginzburg, 'Nachalnye shagi', 111. In Kiev each 'kassa' founded its own library, and in Zdunska-Wola (Kalish Province) both legal and illegal libraries were in existence in 1904. See *Di arbayter shtime*, No. 8 (5 February 1898), 7, and *Der bund*, No. 5 (October 1904), 20.

[3] See Levin, *Untererdishe kemfer*, 107, and Berman, *In loif fun yorn*, 147.

during the agitation period, Russian literature continued to be read. In Vilna, for example, workers read Dostoevsky, Turgenev, Shchedrin, Pisarev, Dobroliubov, and Chernyshevsky.[1]

Like the 'kassy' organizations, the libraries held special evening gatherings to commemorate their anniversaries; these were made the occasion for speeches and fund raising. What follows is a description of one such celebration in a small town in Vilna Province:

On Saturday, the 20th of October, the Shirvinty organization celebrated a library holiday. Twenty people gathered together. Speeches on the importance of the library, on Zionism, and on local affairs were given. 8.45 rubles were collected for illegal literature...Revolutionary songs were sung and many toasts offered...The celebration began at 12.00 noon and lasted until late in the evening. It ended with the singing of the 'Oath'.[2]

Somewhat larger was a celebration in Smorgon to honor the seventh anniversary of the 'Yiddish Workers' Library'; 170 workers gathered to hear speeches on the interrelation of literature and socialism, the career of Hirsh Lekert, anti-semitism, the Kishinev pogrom, and problems of organization in the labor movement.[3]

Circles, as we have noted, continued to operate during the agitation period, and were known popularly as 'Saturday readings'. In Dvinsk, according to one account, 'a group of young carpenters would gather early on Saturday mornings in a "kruzhok". At the circle a young intellectual would read and explain...Bogdanov's "Political Economy" or other works which a worker could not understand alone.'[4] 'Saturday readings' were supplemented by lectures and 'evenings', at which various

---

[1] See the list in 'Materialy', Agursky (ed.), *Di sotsialistishe literatur* 401. For other lists of reading material see Fogorelsky, 'Zikhroynes'; Lev, 'Vospominaniia', *Katorga i ssylka*, No. 41 (1928), 143; Kopeovich, 'Der onhayb', 3; Bronisław Szuszkiewicz, 'Organizacja grodzieńska P.P.S. w latach 1898–1910', 517.

[2] *Posledniia izvestiia*, No. 154 (10 November 1903).

[3] *Posledniia izvestiia*, No. 136 (3 July 1903); see also Nos. 80 (9 August 1902), and 90 (16 October 1902). In one major city in the Pale (not specified in the source) a library celebration netted as much as 45 rubles; see *Der idisher arbeter*, No. 2–3 (February 1897), 40.

[4] Berman, *In loif fun yorn*, 148. 'Saturday readings' in Smorgon are described in Peskovoi, 'V smorgoni', 81.

topics were discussed before the members of the organization. In Bialystok the best of the lectures prepared for the workers by a special 'Intellectuals' Commission' were selected for use by the 'Propaganda Commission'.[1] Workers were encouraged to discuss their readings with the librarians whom they would often meet with on the 'birzhe', the favorite arena for propaganda. 'When books were exchanged', wrote Berman, 'the librarian...would ask the readers what they had understood of their reading... "What does the author mean by this?" was the question most commonly asked of the readers.'[2]

Libraries, lectures, 'Saturday readings' and 'evenings' were of benefit mostly to the organized workers—the 'kassy' members who were firmly committed to the movement. Other methods were required to reach the unorganized mass of workers. By far the most widespread and successful of these was the presentation of illegal 'spectacles', or plays. The drama had great appeal to the circle members of the pre-agitation period, who were among the first Jewish workers to attend the theater. But the theater also appealed to the masses, and during the agitation period a variety of plays were used by the local organizations as platforms for propaganda. In Vilna, for example, organized workers produced a play based on Litvak's translation of a text by An-sky (the author of the well-known play the 'Dybbuk').[3] In Kovno one of the local agitators adapted a story by Peretz for the stage; equipped with scenery constructed by some of the carpenters affiliated with the organization, the play is said to have made a profound impression on the mass of workers there.[4]

[1] Boris Tsifir, 'Zikhroynes fun a bialystoker bundist (1901–5)', in Herman Frank *et al.* (eds.), *Natsionale un politishe bavegungen bay yidn in bialystok (material tsu der geshikhte)* (New York, 1951), I, 38 ff. In Minsk, according to 'Nachalo rabochego dvizheniia', in Agursky (ed.), *Di sotsialistishe literatur*, 29, 120 workers took part in the 'readings' held by the organization. For a description of one of these 'evenings' see *Posledniia izvestiia*, No. 115 (20 March 1903).

[2] Berman, *In loif fun yorn*, 146.

[3] Litvak, *Vos geven*, 93. The participants were promptly arrested but they were released after three days in prison. The play was produced in 1897, the year the Bund was founded.

[4] Shkliar, 'Onhayb', 213 ff. Interestingly enough, the play was presented at Purim, when Jewish plays based on the Scroll of Esther are traditionally given. According to Gold-schmidt, 'Khaver Aron', 75, Hauptmann's famous play *The Weavers* was also given in Vilna in 1897 (in Yiddish translation).

Such illegal presentations were staged throughout Belorussia–Lithuania. In Ponevyezh a play entitled 'In Struggle', by a local author, was presented before an audience of 200 people, 50 of whom were not members of the organization. A 'spectacle' offered in Shklov was based directly on a socialist feuilleton. Particularly popular was a play entitled 'The American Worker', which was staged by local organizations in Kovno, Vilkomir, Borisov, and Rezhitsa (in the latter city it was performed twice before an audience of 300 spectators).[1]

In addition to the plays presented by the local organizations, many workers attended the city theaters, which frequently became the scene of demonstrations against the regime. In 1903 a play by Gorky was presented several times in Bialystok; at the first performance workers shouted, 'Hurrah for Gorky', at the second they added, 'Down with autocracy'.[2] In Kovno a spontaneous demonstration broke out in 1904 in the city theater during a performance of a play by Gorky; several days later a 'patriotic play' was given, but since people feared there might be further demonstrations few attended.[3] Berman's memoirs of Dvinsk describe how important theater was to the workers. Every Friday evening after work, he tells us, members of the local organization would rush off to the Russian theater in town. 'In the dim light that reached the gallery, people recognized friends whom they had not caught sight of before. They called to one another, greeted each other...in a word, one felt free, as though one were at home...' Being a gathering place also for the librarians and the workers they instructed, the theater served not only as a cultural center, but as a substitute 'birzhe', a place for discussion and political intrigue.[4]

The cultural work conducted by the Jewish labor movement was strictly intended to further the cause of socialism, and there

---

[1] *Posledniia izvestiia*, No. 104 (4 January 1903); No. 108 (6 February 1903); No. 116 (25 March 1903); No. 151 (3 October 1903); No. 161 (23 December 1903); No. 180 (1 May 1904). A play entitled *Stachka* (*Strike*) was performed in the little town of Krozhki (Vilna Province) in 1904: *Posledniia izvestiia*, No. 194 (22 September 1904).

[2] *Posledniia izvestiia*, No. 113 (7 March 1903). Twenty arrests were made after the performance.

[3] See *Flug-bletter, heroisgegeben fun kovner sotsialdemokratishen komitet fun bund*, No. 2 (February 1904), 3–4.   [4] Berman, *In loif fun yorn*, 156, 159.

were no champions of 'art for art's sake' within the organization. In Dvinsk the leaders rejected works that had no 'message' to convey, insisting that 'Reading must enlighten, educate'—in short, stimulate social protest.[1] But the impact of the cultural activities sponsored by the labor movement was not limited to the creation of class-conscious socialists. Of course, many did become radicals as a result of what they read; for others, the impact was more difficult to define. As one worker commented after reading a pamphlet by Tolstoy in Yiddish translation: 'From then on I was not sure of anything any more.'[2]

The cultural campaign of the agitation era, considerably broader than that of the circle period, made it possible for thousands of Jewish workers to enter a new world, hitherto closed before them. And if cultural work was less emphasized than strikes, its impact was perhaps more permanent. A tailor might lose his twelve-hour day; he could not be so easily robbed, however, of what he learned at the 'kassa' library or at the 'Saturday reading'.[3]

[1] *Ibid.*, 146; see also comments by Litvak, *Vos geven*, 24. Berman notes (158) that workers who went to the theater viewed plays as protests against 'the world of falseness and hypocrisy'.

[2] Raskin, *Tsen yor lebn*, 15.

[3] A few attempts at writing were made by the workers themselves. One of 'Khaver Aron's' (Devenishsky's) dreams was to create a 'proletarian theater' in Vilna, but it was never realized. At the fourth anniversary of the tailors' 'kassa' in Kovno, one of the members read a story based on a worker's life; in another instance a Jewish worker wrote a story attacking the 'good old days' when paternalistic relations prevailed between employer and workers. See *Posledniia izvestiia*, No. 99 (28 November 1902); 'Rabochii pishet-stikhotvorenie v proze (perevod s evreiskago)', *Rabochee delo*, No. 6 (April 1900), 60–2.

CHAPTER 7

The Opposition Movements

Kick the intellectuals out of the Committee.

A slogan of the Dvinsk 'opposition', 1901

The labor movement is one thing, and social democracy
—another.   From a letter by Zubatov, 1898

The Russian Jewish labor movement, as we already know, was
composed of various elements, distinguished from one another
both by class (intelligentsia or proletariat) and by function. There
were intellectuals and 'one-half intellectuals', circle members,
'kassa' activists, and the unorganized masses who participated in
strikes. There were members of local committees and 'kassy'
officials. When the various elements co-operated, the result was
an efficient if complex organization. But oftentimes the interests
of one group clashed with those of another, and disputes broke
out. The most serious dispute of the circle period was that
between the intellectual proponents of agitation and the circle
workers. Many of the ideas engendered by that clash continued
to exercise influence during the agitation period, while the new
campaign gave birth to opposition movements of its own.

One such movement involved the problem of democracy,
which rank-and-file 'kassy' members believed was being eroded
by the largely intellectual leadership. In the early years of the
agitation period the organizational structure of the movement had
allowed for fairly widespread application of democratic practices.
Elections were the rule and ambitious workers managed to enter
the higher echelons of the movement, often becoming members
of the local committees. To some observers the Bund seemed to
achieve a remarkable degree of democracy. 'From the experience
of the Bund', a Russian socialist wrote, 'we see that a democratic
organization *is able* to function properly...in Russia despite all

the obstacles from the police and gendarmes.'[1] Democracy, however, could scarcely flourish under conditions of extreme secrecy and illegality, and in time complaints were raised that workers' rights had been abused. In comparing the local organizations in Minsk and Bialystok, Levin observed that while the two were similar in structure, 'in Bialystok the organization knew nothing about democracy'. Composed of three men, the committee appointed the members of the agitation assembly who, in turn, 'sought out the more developed workers in the crafts and organized them in craft "skhodkes"'.[2] Boris Frumkin, an activist from Minsk, has described the changes that occurred in the workers' relationship to the institutions of the organized labor movement during this period:

In the beginning...the institutions were close to the masses: work was carried on in the open, general meetings were held often, and at them almost all of the less complicated issues of the movement were discussed. With the passage of time the functions of the institutions became more complex; many of these (such as relations with other cities, illegal literature, etc.) became concentrated in the hands of a few people who made up the local committee. Together with the agitation assemblies, these committees...gradually began to impose on the masses prepared directives which the agitators issued under their guidance.[3]

Under such conditions voices of protest were heard. Workers insisted that the head of each institution be elected by the masses to whom he would be responsible, that power be not vested in the hands of the intellectuals and the professional agitators.[4] A variety of opposition movements soon arose throughout Belorussia–Lithuania, demanding more democracy and attacking the intellectual leadership. Thus, during the early years of agitation, a 'second opposition' emerged in Vilna. 'It had', wrote Peskin, 'a more organized basis: workers who had joined the "kassy" in the struggle against their employers already felt sure of

---

[1] This comment was made as late as 1902. See B. Krichevskii, 'Po povodu IV-go s'ezda Bunda', *Rabochee delo*, Nos. 11–12 (February 1902), 114.
[2] Levin, *Untererdishe kemfer*, 154.
[3] Frumkin, 'Ocherki', *Evreiskaia starina*, VI, No. 1 (January–March 1913), 260.
[4] *Ibid.*

themselves; they wanted to have influence on the movement, and they attacked the "despotism" of the intellectuals.'[1] Bernshstein also notes the workers' desire to free themselves of the intellectuals. 'Our workers want to run the library alone, without the intellectuals.' The author was allowed to join the library committee, 'because I was friendly with a number of workers'.[2] In Minsk, Frumkin remarks, 'There was not a shop in which heated debates were not held on the state of the organization. Arguments were conducted on the "birzhes", and in workers' apartments; at every meeting of the organization, at every "evening", this question...was discussed.'[3]

In Dvinsk the opposition was composed of young workers, activists who accused the intellectuals of taking over the organization and of dictating terms to the workers whose rights they had usurped. One intellectual who was particularly disliked by the workers was warned that if he did not leave the city, he would be beaten up. Another (non-intellectual) leader of the movement, Zalman Itshke 'the Bristle-Worker', was likewise charged with having refused 'kassa' workers their rightful place in the organization and was assaulted one Saturday by members of the opposition. 'We followed him for several blocks and, near his home on Kreslaver Street, threw ourselves at him as if he were our archenemy, and beat him up.'[4]

One reason for the opposition in Dvinsk, Berman informs us, was that workers disliked the extreme measures of conspiracy which they interpreted as a sign of the leaders' refusal to trust them. In Gomel, too, this was a source of tension, and leaders there found they were forced to defend their policy of secrecy to the workers. 'Our Gomel comrades', they claimed, 'do not wish to understand forms of conspiracy, and this is their undoing and

[1] Peskin, 'Di "grupe"', 554.
[2] Bernshtein, *Ershte shprotsungen*, 138.
[3] Frumkin, 'Ocherki', *Evreiskaia starina*, VI, No. 1 (January–March 1913), 261; the intellectuals and agitators were popularly known as 'men with epaulettes'. On the 'second opposition' in Minsk see also Bukhbinder, *Krasnaia letopis'*, No. 5 (1923), 126–7. Much of his information derives from Frumkin's account.
[4] Berman, *In loif fun yorn*, 165–6. Ginzburg, 'Nachalnye shagi', 112, notes that two years earlier, in 1899, among the masses in Dvinsk there was a 'feeling of enmity toward the intelligentsia'.

the undoing of our sacred cause. Many of us desire to know who, what, how, and when everything is done. *This cannot be!'* The statement then goes on to exhort workers not to 'take our sacred cause so lightly' or 'to play with the word "democrat"'.[1]

The so-called 'second opposition' was symptomatic of the growing restlessness of workers who had been recruited during the period of mass participation and who now felt themselves excluded from positions of power. It represented the newcomers' challenge to the established leaders. But it was also symptomatic of a growing frustration with the strike movement itself. Workers who had entered the movement to improve their economic condition often discovered that the class struggle was an exercise in futility: today's gains might well be lost tomorrow, and there was little the leaders could do to forestall this pattern. Naturally the more ambitious and energetic workers sought new outlets and demanded to have a greater say in shaping the policies of the movement.[2]

Sometimes these accusations of 'despotism' could be resolved simply by giving the workers a greater share of control—as in Vilna, where more of the workers were elected to the local Committee.[3] But hostility toward the leaders, particularly the intellectuals, continued, and was reinforced by the Bund's emphasis on centralization and political control of the labor movement. At the party's fifth conference in 1902, it was decided that economic issues should be firmly controlled by the local social democratic organization, that the revolutionary and political struggle was to have priority over the fight for better wages and a shorter workday.[4] The new organizational program of the party was attacked mainly because it seemed to workers to repudiate the democratic principle on which the movement had

---

[1] 'O konspiratsii', January or February, 1902, published in Bukhbinder, *Krasnaia letopis'*, Nos. 2–3 (1922), 80–1. In Vilna leaders of the movement went to extreme lengths to keep everything secret; see Litvak, *Vos geven*, 86.

[2] See Frumkin, 'Ocherki', *Evreiskaia starina*, VI, No. 1 (January–March 1913), 259 ff.; Peskin, 'Di "grupe"', 554.

[3] *Ibid.*, 554; according to Blum, *Zikhroynes*, 45–6, a report by Kremer in 1896 noted that there were 'too few workers' in the local Committee. In accordance with his wishes, new elections were held and three workers were placed on the Committee.

[4] The resolutions are published in Rafes, *Ocherki*, 80–1.

been founded. In Lodz the emissary of the Bund's Central Committee met with opposition when he attempted to carry out party orders.[1] Akimov describes the changes which took place in the Grodno organization: 'There are now at the head of the entire movement an agitation assembly and a Committee which are not elected.' Previously democratic elections had been held for these offices.[2] In 1903 an opposition group in Minsk demanded not only that workers head the labor organization, but that intellectuals be relegated to the job merely of propagandists and teachers—precisely the demand of Gordon and his adherents in Vilna.[3] If police reports of the time can be trusted, the new opposition seceded from the party and formed a group known as 'The Workers' Organization of the Bund'. Largely a reaction to the resolutions of 1902, the group opposed the 'introduction here of a new type of organization which represents a departure from the previous (system) of electing leaders'.[4]

An opposition group of quite another order was made up of the proponents of terrorism. As a Marxist social democratic party, the Bund was on principle opposed to terrorism, whether of a political or economic nature, and it denounced the violence that so frequently accompanied the class struggle.[5] Pro-terrorist sentiment, however, continued to be widespread, not only among the masses engaged in the daily struggle for a livelihood, but among certain of the leaders as well. The terrorist heroes of the 'People's Will' (the Russian terrorist organization which assassinated Alexander II in 1881) were venerated by many Jewish activists within the organization as they were, also, by the Russian Marxists. In a feuilleton published in the Bundist press the main character is depicted as treasuring the memory of the martyrs. 'Each was engraved in his heart, each did he invest with the highest qualities.' This attitude, of course, did not lead automatically to terrorism, but it may well have contributed to a

---

[1] See Herts, *Di geshikhte fun bund in lodz*, 78.

[2] Akimov, in his article 'Stroiteli budushchago', *Obrazovanie*, XVI, No. 4 (April 1907), 115. On the reorganization in Vilna see Rafes, 'In Lekerts tsayten (zikhroynes)', in *Hirsh Lekert, tsum 20-ten*, 34 ff.

[3] Bukhbinder, *Krasnaia letopis'*, No. 5 (1923), 145.

[4] *Posledniia izvestiia*, No. 162 (31 December 1904).

[5] See above, Chapter 5, pp. 102 ff.

willingness, on the part of individuals, to resort to such tactics.[1] In 1901 the Bund's fourth Congress issued a stern warning against the use of terrorism which, it said, 'blunts workers' social-democratic consciousness, worsens their material situation, and discredits the labor movement'.[2] Nonetheless, only a year later Hirsh Lekert made his unsuccessful assassination attempt on the Governor of Vilna Province; the reaction revealed the extent to which pro-terrorist sympathies prevailed in the movement. The Governor's mistreatment of political prisoners had provoked workers to seek revenge through certain terrorist groups whom they asked the Vilna Committee to assist. Although the Committee seriously considered backing their request, it decided finally to remain neutral—at least officially. 'The Committee', declared its most influential member, 'cannot lend assistance to terror, but certain members who sympathize with the proposed act may aid it—that is their personal affair.'[3] According to another source, the Committee helped Lekert's group 'unofficially'. One of the participants reports the following discussion with a representative of the Committee: 'Listen,' he told me, 'do what you like...that means, in private...the organization as such knows nothing...meanwhile here is 60 rubles.'[4]

The tense atmosphere created by the attempted assassination, and the subsequent execution of Lekert, only increased pressure on the party to endorse terrorist tactics. Lekert was immediately raised to the rank of a folk hero, and the Committee in Vilna was bitterly attacked by some of the workers for having remained neutral.[5] At the Bund's fifth conference in Berdichev revolutionary passions triumphed over the traditional restraint, the party officially adopting a resolution calling for 'organized revenge' to fight abuses. 'It is perfectly clear', the delegates

[1] 'A brif tsu Berel'n', *Der bund*, No. 1 (January 1904).
[2] 'Der fierter kongress fun algemaynen idishen arbayter bund in russland un poylen', *Der idisher arbeter*, No. 12 (1901), 98.
[3] Isak Mitskin, 'Di vilner organizatsie fun bund un Lekerts attentat', in *Hirsh Lekert, tsum 20-ten*, 45.
[4] Herts, *Hirsh Lekert*, 50. Pages 17 ff. describe the Governor's attitude toward the labor movement.
[5] Mitskin, 'Di vilner organizatsie', 45; Herts, *Hirsh Lekert*, 54. According to Herts, many workers believed the assassination attempt would have succeeded had the Committee itself organized it.

declared, 'that we must protest with all our strength against such wild acts (those used by the Governor of Vilna)...The honor of a revolutionary party demands revenge for the oppression of its members.' However, only those acts of reprisal were permitted which the party itself organized.[1]

This resolution was as far as leaders of the Bund had ever gone to support pro-terrorist sentiments.[2] Understandably they were attacked by the party's Foreign Committee which, being far removed from the scene, had not been caught up in the surge of revolutionary sentiment. Fearing that the resolution would encourage unbridled terrorism, the Bundists abroad reproached their colleagues in Russia for having adopted so dangerous and unwise a policy.[3] A special brochure issued by the Foreign Committee noted that there was little difference between 'organized revenge', and 'organized terror', and that official sanction of such tactics would lead inevitably to the degeneration of the movement.[4] After a cooling-off period the Bundists in Russia admitted they had been wrong; at their fifth Congress in 1903, they proclaimed 'organized revenge' a form of terrorism, and rescinded the resolutions of the fifth conference.[5] As far as the leaders were concerned, the issue had been resolved.

The rank-and-file workers, however, were not so ready to abandon terrorism; if anything, the assassination attempt in Vilna had only exacerbated their conflict with the leaders over this issue.

[1] The resolutions of the fifth conference are published in Herts *et al.*, *Di geshikhte*, I, 245–6. The decision to approve 'organized revenge' was passed by a 'great majority of votes'. See Bentse Levin, 'Di 5-te konferents fun bund, zikhroynes', in *Hirsh Lekert, tsum 2-ten*, 60. The conference drew a line between systematic terror of the Populist variety, which it continued to oppose, and organized acts of revenge against officials, like the Governor of Vilna, who were judged personally responsible for the ill-treatment of workers.

[2] Mikhalevich, *Zikhroynes*, I, 148. Commenting on the general mood of the conference, B. Levin, 'Di 5-te konferents', 58, notes that Gozhanskii arrived with revolver in hand. The conference was attended by several delegates who had recently returned from exile in Siberia and were among the most outspoken supporters of 'organized revenge'.

[3] Medem, *Fun mayn leben*, I, 318; for the reaction to Lekert's act abroad, see 315 ff.

[4] *K voprosu o terrorizme* (London, 1903). The brochure attacks the position of the Social Revolutionaries and re-publishes the resolutions on 'organized revenge'. See especially 'K voprosu ob "organizovannoi mesti"', 43–53.

[5] See *V-yi s'ezd vseobshchago evreiskago rabochago soiuza v Litve i Pol'she i Rossii* (London, 1903), 29–30. Apparently there was scarcely any debate on the subject; see the account in Herts *et al.*, *Di geshikhte*, II, 110–11.

Considerable bitterness had been aroused by the Vilna Committee's reluctance to aid Lekert, but outside of Vilna, too,
terrorists groups occasionally became sufficiently powerful to
challenge the party's leadership. In Riga a terrorist group comprised of former Bundists was organized in 1903.[1] And during a
labor dispute at the Shereshevsky factory in Grodno, workers
quit the party when it refused to sanction their plan to 'beat up the
masters'.[2] Similarly in Lodz, police reprisals, culminating in the
execution of Lekert, induced 60 Bund members to adopt the
terrorist program of the Social Revolutionary (Populist) Party,
which condoned terrorism. They formed a group known as the
'S.R. (Social Revolutionary) Bundists', and only rejoined the
Bund when it approved (albeit temporarily) of 'organized
revenge'. The strength of this group was revealed during its
negotiations with the Bund: 'The negotiations at first were
fruitless. On the contrary, the group became stronger...Money
was collected for a printing press.'[3]

Being a great proletarian center with a history of violent labor
protest, Lodz had witnessed enough police oppression to become a
breeding ground for terrorism. Sympathy for such actions ran
sufficiently high in some instances for even the Social Democratic
leaders to back the terrorists, though by and large they tried to
discourage outbreaks of violence.[4] Next to Lodz, Bialystok was
the major center of terrorist opposition. In 1899 an alleged
informer in that city was murdered by a group of workers. The
Bund denounced the act, insisting that workers struggle 'not

[1] Its program ('Programa rizhskoi sotsial-demokraticheskoi boevoi organizatsii') is
published in Bukhbinder, *Istoriia*, 262–4. According to the program the Riga group had
its own legal and illegal libraries. It was organized because 'At the present time the
government has resorted to measures which, even under our autocratic regime, are
extremely shocking'.

[2] *Der bund*, No. 3 (April 1904), 9.

[3] From the memoirs of Yudel Rozen, pseud. (Bukhbinder), as quoted in Volf A. Yasni,
Di geshikhte fun bund in lodz (Lodz, 1937), 214–15. The group ceased all its activities with
the appearance in Lodz of the November 1902 edition of *Di arbayter shtime* which
covered the Bund's fifth conference.

[4] Shortly after Lekert's execution a well-known informer (a 'loynketnik') in the town of
Pabianice, near Lodz, was stabbed by a Bundist who sought revenge for the textile
workers. When he returned to Lodz the terrorist was given money by the local
committee to escape from Russia. See Yasni, *Di geshikhte*, 215–16; also *Posledniia
izvestiia*, No. 31 (4 September 1902).

against gendarmes, not against Governors, not even against Nicholas II as individual persons...they struggle against absolutism'.[1] But the terrorism let loose in Bialystok could hardly be checked by such admonitions. Eventually a rift was created between the leaders of the Bund and the more uncontrollable segments of the local Jewish proletariat, who wanted to take direct action against police brutality. The latter were attracted to the anarchist movement in the city, which was organized in 1903 with the establishment of the 'Bor'ba' ('Struggle') group. The anarchists began to win recruits among workers who had formerly been affiliated with the Bund. By 1904 the anarchist movement was decidedly a force to reckon with; its popularity undoubtedly reflected the widespread dissatisfaction workers felt with the Bund's 'conservative' stand on the issue of terror.[2]

We have, then, two radically different opposition tendencies. One expressed the frustrations of the 'kassy' workers who desired a greater share in decision making. The other expressed the frustrations of those who became impatient with Marxist scruples. The former objected neither to party discipline (so long as it was based on 'democracy') nor to party ideology, while the latter represented a rough and ready section of the proletariat which desired to take direct action to redress grievances.[3] A third opposition tendency was to have more serious consequences. This opposition centered around the all-important issue of political versus economic action.

According to the program of agitation laid down by Kremer and Gozhanskii, a growth of political 'consciousness' would

---

[1] 'Der mord fun a loynketnik in bialystok', *Der idisher arbeter*, No. 7 (August 1899), 20. See also *Der bialystoker arbeter*, No. 1 (April 1899), 45.

[2] On the anarchist movement in Bialystok see Benjamin Shtufler, 'Tsvay pionern fun der revolutsionerer arbeter bavegung in bialystok', in Frank *et al.*, *Natsionale un politishe bavegungen*, 47–55, and Belostochanin, 'Iz istorii anarkhicheskago dvizheniia v Belostoke', in *Almanakh, Sbornik po istorii anarkhicheskago dvizheniia v Rossii* (Paris, 1909), I, 5 ff. In 1902, a year before the founding of the 'Bor'ba', a group of Jewish workers joined the Social Revolutionary Party in Bialystok; see I. F. Zil'berblat, 'Moi vospominaniia o tov. Simone Vul'foviche Sikorskom', *Katorga i ssylka*, No. 41 (1928), 149. One of the members of this group greatly admired the 'heroic acts of the immortal heroes' who had been active in the 'People's Will' Party; he was also inspired by Lekert's act (148–9).

[3] See comments by Rafes, 'Hirsh Lekert i ego pokushenie', *Krasnyi arkhiv*, II (xv) (1926), 89.

inevitably follow from the economic struggle. Hence, they reasoned, agitation need concern itself primarily with the economic injustices of the age; leaders might enlighten workers about political goals, but they would not stress political action. The aims of the agitation program, according to Gozhanskii's 'Letter to the Agitators', were to: '(1) improve the living conditions of the Jewish artisan masses, (2) develop their need for education, (3) further in the masses an understanding of their economic interests, (4) develop their political consciousness'.[1] The socialists at first were extremely cautious in their approach, stressing the economic struggle and playing down the need for anti-Tsarist activities; frequently, during the initial stages of agitation, no mention whatever was made of political goals. In Pinsk, at a time when the labor movement was still at an elementary stage, workers were urged to fight for a twelve-hour day simply because 'We must have time to develop, to understand where we are in the world and who our enemies are'.[2] Political goals seemingly did not figure in this exhortation. In a proclamation to the workers of Vitebsk in 1901 five demands are listed: a ten-hour day, higher wages, better conditions in the shops, an eight-hour day for apprentices, and political freedom. The last is written in tiny letters, in contrast to the bold print used for the first four.[3] Yet as the movement advanced, the socialist leaders began to make explicit the connexion between economic and political goals. In 1904 the workers in Lodz were told: 'Thus we have concluded that both the struggle for socialism and for daily improvements in the workers' situation can bring results only in a free political order.'[4] An example of the techniques used to link the two problems can be seen from the proclamation 'To All Male and Female Workers in Grodno', issued in 1900. After discussing a strike in the Shereshevsky factory, the proclamation continued:

Let us remember the role played by the factory inspector and the gendarmes. At first the inspector agreed to satisfy several demands, but

[1] Gozhanskii, 'A briv', 632.
[2] *Tsu alle pinsker idishe arbayter un arbayterinen*, September 1903.
[3] *Tsu alle vitebsker arbayter un arbayterinen*, 1901.
[4] *Tsu alle lodzer arbayter un arbayterinen*, January 1904.

later...he went back on his word. The gendarme also promised to help them (the workers), but when he saw that they wanted to return to work, he changed his mind... [1] We already know about Russian laws. When we workers wish to improve our life, to feel like men, to study and gather together to discuss our interests, this is forbidden... Russian laws are identified with the factory owner. He can do everything, we can do nothing. The law, the police, the gendarmes, and the entire regime are for him, and no one is for us. And so, workers must protect themselves...let us unite, workers not only of Shereshevsky's factory, but of all Grodno, of all Russia and Poland, and all other lands which suffer under the Russian regime...and then we will achieve victory over our powerful enemy—the autocratic regime and its police and gendarmes. Then we will enjoy human rights, we will be able to publish and to assemble freely...truth and justice alone will rule over the world. Down with the autocratic regime, long live the labor movement! [2]

Faced with increasing difficulties in the strike movement the Bund's leaders had, by the early 1900s, come to stress the primacy of political over economic goals. The Bristle-Workers' Union noted that its organization had deteriorated because 'we have taken too little account of the necessity and value of political struggle'. 'Our movement', we read in a statement from Minsk, 'up to now has been primarily an economic struggle, but the time has come to place more weight on political slogans.' [3] In 1902, at the Bund's fifth conference, it was resolved that the local organizations 'must consider in their activity the general interests of the entire revolutionary proletarian movement and must therefore regard themselves not as representatives of a trade union organization, but of a revolutionary organization that is representing the principles of international revolutionary social democracy'. [4]

Obviously, there was far less opportunity for mass participation

---

[1] During the strike some of the workers decided to return to work; the implication here is that the police officer went back on his word as soon as he realized that the strike would be broken.

[2] 'Ko vsem grodnenskim rabochim i rabotnitsam', in Dimanshtein (ed.), *Revoliutsionnoe dvizhenie*, 278–9.

[3] *Minsker flug-bletel*, No. 5 (March 1902), 2; *Flug-bletel, heroisgegeben fun komitet fun poilishen bershter rayon*, No. 1 (January 1904), 2.

[4] As quoted in Rafes, *Ocherki*, 81.

in political activities—which consisted mostly of clandestine operations—than in the strike movement. Obviously, too, political action required a much stronger commitment to the ideals of the movement than participation in a strike; the risks were greater, particularly the possibility of severe prison sentences. Upon occasion the Party was compelled to cancel demonstrations for fear of reprisals. On May Day, 1901, the local organization decided not to sponsor a demonstration in Bialystok because the city was 'swarming' with police spies and gendarmes.[1] In part this explains why the political activities of the Party were less impressive than its conduct on the economic front—at least in its ability to stimulate mass response. In 1901 the Vilna Committee was forced to admit that 'only a small segment of the Vilna proletariat has considered the idea of political freedom and engaged in the decisive struggle against Tsardom'. Even on May Day, the organization complained, only small contingents of workers joined the demonstrations.[2] And in Bialystok only in 1901, after years of labor disputes and police repression, was the Party able to organize a political demonstration.[3]

Political activities, therefore, were usually confined to the elite of the 'kassa', who commemorated events such as the abolition of serfdom, the Decembrist revolt, and the assassination of Alexander II, and who occasionally would hold secret meetings

[1] See 'Vy hot der regirung unz geholfen fayern dem i-ten may'! *Der bialystoker arbeter*, No. 5 (May 1901), 1–2.

[2] 'Unzere letste demonstratsionen un der politisher kampf', *Der klassen-kampf*, No. 5 (July 1901), 6.

[3] *Der bialystoker arbeter*, No. 4 (April 1901), 1–3. The demonstration occurred at a funeral of a bristle worker; according to the journal, some 3,000 people participated, both Jews and Christians; they sang revolutionary songs and shouted 'Down with autocracy'. The demonstration made a great impression on the city. 'What a great funeral,' people said, 'there has never been its like in Bialystok.' When it was ascertained that the dead man was not a great religious leader, nor a wealthy man, but only a poor worker, there was much indignation. The employers, we are told, were furious that Jews should attend a funeral with their heads uncovered, and called the demonstration 'shameful'. See Serere Saymon, 'Di ershte demonstratsie (erinerungen vegen der onhayb fun der revolutsionerer bavegung in bialystok)', *Bialystoker shtime*, VI, No. 13 (March 1926), 37–9. Funeral demonstrations were rather common during the course of the labor movement, and were often marked by shows of solidarity between Jewish and Christian workers. See, for example, A. Chemerinskii, 'In lodz in 1905', *Royte bleter*, I, who comments that 'The revolutionary funerals were the major expression of international solidarity and collective struggle'.

in the forests where, undetected by the police, they listened to speeches on political themes.[1] Great pains were taken to insure secrecy. Berman writes:

In order to organize a forest meeting a special group was formed in the organization, which was very familiar with the area around the city, knew all the paths and trails in the woods. Two weeks before the meeting, this group would go to the forest and find a suitable place... it was usually in a deep valley, surrounded by small and large hills. They would make signs on the paths so that it would be easier to find them later. Sometimes they would visit the place several times—until everything was ready. Then the work in the organization itself would begin. The masses were divided into little groups—each group with a leader.[2]

Each group would then be guided by special 'patrols' to the appointed site by different routes. With such intricate planning the police were usually thwarted, and the meetings proceeded without interference. Action by the non-affiliated workers, however, was usually minimal. Not only were they unwilling to shoulder the risks of involvement in anti-governmental demonstrations, but, in marked contrast to their behavior in the strike movement, they were often apathetic or even hostile to the idea of political protest. For this reason certain members of the Bialystok organization bitterly opposed the inclusion of political goals in a proclamation appealing to the shop assistants to unite: 'the masses are frightened off; one can win them over by appealing to their daily, elementary needs—for higher wages, a shorter workday, and so forth'.[3] A socialist in Lodz claimed the Jewish masses there had an 'indescribable fear of "politics"' which augured poorly for the acceptance of the organization's political platform.[4]

---

[1] Such a meeting is described by Levin, *Untererdishe kemfer*, 125.

[2] Berman, *In loif fun yorn*, 168.

[3] An-man, 'Bialystoker period', 65. He claims, however, that the attitude of the masses changed and became more politically-oriented.

[4] Y. M. Pasakhson (An alter bekanter, pseud.), 'Der onhayb fun der yidisher arbeter-bevegung in lodz', *Royter pinkes*, II, 161. One explanation for this state of affairs in Lodz was that a demonstration by workers in 1892 deteriorated into a pogrom. Mikhale-vich, *Zikhroynes*, I, 14, notes that a general fear lingered that each May Day would bring another anti-Jewish riot (the Lodz excesses grew out of a May Day strike).

The frequent preference by Jewish workers for legal strikes and their faith in the goodwill of the authorities, which we have already observed, were another indication of their negative attitude toward political activism, an attitude that manifested itself in hostility toward those who advocated political protest. In Warsaw, for example, some of the workers actually accused the Bund of fomenting police repressions and insisted that 'workers should not be involved in politics'.[1] Others, in Vilna, refused to join May Day demonstrations, demanding 'strictly workers' holidays'.[2] In Grodno, workers at the Shereshevsky factory who had grown impatient with the political disputes there between the Bund and the Polish Socialist Party decided to establish a politically neutral union.[3] According to a Bundist proclamation from Bialystok in 1905, 'Many workers now say that there should be no party, no political organization: the workers alone can lead strikes'.[4]

Such attitudes were encouraged by the Zubatov campaign of legalism that was launched in the Pale of Settlement during the early years of the twentieth century. By then S. V. Zubatov, head of the Moscow section of the 'Okhrana' (secret police) and the originator of police socialism in Russia, had succeeded in making certain inroads into the Moscow labor movement, setting up unions that had no affiliation with political parties but were controlled by the authorities. The purpose of these organizations, presumably, was to improve the cultural and material conditions of workers' lives without recourse to illegal activity.[5] Zubatov hoped to duplicate these unions among the Jewish workers of the Pale, and in part succeeded during 1901–3.

In 1898, a year after the founding of the Bund, some of its leading activists were arrested and interrogated by Zubatov, who sought to convince them that under autocracy legal trade unionism

[1] 'Vi kumt an arbeter tsu politik'? *Der varshaver arbayter*, No. 7–8 (May 1901), 1.
[2] *Posledniia izvestiia*, No. 135 (9 July 1903).
[3] *Di arbayter shtime*, No. 40 (September 1905), 30.
[4] *Der letste veber shtrayk*, June 1905.
[5] On the Zubatov movement in general see S. Ainzaft, *Zubatovshchina i gaponovshchina* (Moscow, 1925); K. Tidmarsh, 'The Zubatov Idea', *The American Slavic and East European Review*, xix, No. 3 (October 1960), 335–46; A. Morskii, pseud. (von Stein), *Zubatovshchina, stranitsa iz istorii rabochago voprosa v Rossii* (Moscow, 1913).

would be of greater benefit to the working class than a socialist-oriented party. He had, as he put it, 'brilliant success' with some of the prisoners, and was encouraged to try and divert the Jewish movement into legal channels. In 1900 new arrests were made, primarily in Minsk, the prisoners being again subjected to long harangues by Zubatov on the efficacy of legalism. Finally in 1901 Zubatov's ideas found embodiment in the founding of a 'Jewish Independent Labor Party' in Minsk.[1]

Zubatovism, at least in the form presented to Jewish workers, was based on the notion that workers are, like everyone, motivated entirely by enlightened self-interest. Since their only aim is to better their material and cultural conditions, they will, if allowed to pursue these aims in peace, remain indifferent to politics. It followed from this reasoning that the proletariat could not hope to profit from an alliance with the intelligentsia who, while they might be of service as teachers, all too often tried to engage workers in a senseless political struggle which could only defeat their demands for economic and cultural improvements. These demands, Zubatovism insisted, could only be won were workers to abandon illegal schemes and ally themselves with the government. In short workers should establish unions, based on democratic principles, and should not permit the interference of the intelligentsia; the government itself would willingly support their struggle for decent wages, shorter hours, and better cultural opportunities.[2]

These same points were stressed in a manifesto issued by the 'Independents' in 1901. The Jewish working class, it stated, demanded nothing more than 'bread and knowledge' and there-

[1] For a list of those arrested in 1898, and on their talks with Zubatov in Moscow, see Bukhbinder, 'Nezavisimaia evreiskaia rabochaia partiia', *Krasnaia letopis'*, No. 2–3 (1922), 208–9; Frumkin, 'Zubatovshchina i evreiskoe rabochee dvizhenie', *Perezhitoe* (1911), III, 199 ff.; see pages 205–6 on the arrests of 1900; the experiences of A. I. Chemerinskii, who was arrested in Minsk in 1900 and later became a leader of the 'Independents', are recounted in his memoirs in 'Novoe o zubatovshchine', *Krasnyi arkhiv* (1922), I, 315 ff.

[2] This account is based on a typescript of a lecture delivered at the Zubatov 'ferayns' (unions) in Minsk. The typescript is signed 'Gruppa soznatel'nykh rabochikh' ('A Group of Aware Workers') and is available in the Bund Archives, New York City. See also Zubatov's remarks quoted by David Zaslavsky, 'Zubatov i Mania Vilbushevich', *Byloe*, No. 3 (31) (March 1918), 110 ff.

fore rejected political ideas which were 'foreign' to these aims. The program formulated by the new party read as follows:

(1) The Jewish Independent Labor Party has as its aim the elevation of the material and cultural level of the Jewish proletariat through cultural-economic organizations, legal or illegal...In practice this entails: (*a*) the development of broad economic organizations (trade-unions, funds, clubs, associations), (*b*) the diffusion of scientific and technical knowledge among the working class...(2) The party deliberately sets for itself no political goals, and deals with political problems only to the degree that they affect the daily interests of workers. (3) In its economic and political activities the party unites workers of all political views, as well as those who hold no views whatever. (4) The organization of the party is democratic, that is, it is ruled from below and not from above.[1]

That this platform would elicit a positive response from the Jewish proletariat is hardly surprising. The Zubatov doctrine was sufficiently broad to attract both the proponents of the original opposition program (such as Gordon's followers) and the members of the various opposition groups that had emerged during the agitation period (except, of course, those who advocated terrorism). On the one hand, Zubatov's scheme held out the possibility of peaceful, cultural activity; on the other, it denounced political action, championed legalism, and appealed directly to the economic interests of the masses. Furthermore, it advocated greater democracy within the organization and rejected the intellectuals' control over the labor movement.[2] While the intellectuals were to play a role in the labor movement, that role would be restricted to the enlightenment of the workers. The notion of legalism, as we know, was no stranger to the Jewish labor movement. And to many workers Zubatov's message was quite acceptable. As one Minsk craftsman is reported to have said: 'If one may appeal to a factory inspector, why should this be forbidden with regard to police officers?'[3]

[1] The manifesto is published in Bukhbinder, 'Nezavisimaia', *Krasnaia letopis'*, No. 2-3 (1922), 242-3.
[2] Frumkin, 'Zubatovshchina', 208, notes that 'Zubatov's energy was directed toward convincing everyone of the harmful role of the intellectuals'.
[3] Quoted in Mikhalevich, *Zikhroynes*, II, 14.

Zubatovism's appeal was enhanced by the crisis within the strike movement and the Bund's new emphasis on political action. The economic struggle, which attracted so many workers to the movement, was growing less and less effective, and many were prepared to look elsewhere. There was some reason to believe that Zubatov's legalist doctrine held out greater chances for success than the Bund-affiliated 'kassy'.[1]

The actual inroads made by Zubatovism are difficult to assess. We know that 'Zubatovite tactics' were employed by officials in Belorussia–Lithuania even before Zubatov appeared on the scene, and such tactics continued to be used after his departure. In 1904, for example, the Governor of Mogilev called the printers and their employers together for a friendly talk to settle their differences; in Bialystok in the same year the Chief of Police appealed to the weavers in an address that smacked of the 'Zubatov style'.[2] Early in 1904, when the Governor of Grodno addressed a group of factory owners in Bialystok, he stated: 'Strikes of a purely economic nature must be settled by the factory heads themselves, as their own private affairs, with no appeal for police aid. This (police aid) will only make the strike take on a political character.'[3]

According to the local organ of the Bund in Gomel, Zubatov's ideas had merely won over some 'stupid workers'.[4] No doubt the Bund's evaluation lacked objectivity; certainly the doctrine of legalism seems to have had adherents in many cities. The leaders of the locksmiths' organization in Vitebsk may well have been influenced by Zubatovism when, in 1904, they refused to join a May Day demonstration. 'And when, together with the class-conscious workers of Vitebsk, hundreds of non-organized workers celebrated the sacred workers' holiday, when they thus

[1] See remarks in Frumkin, 'Zubatovshchina', 212–13; 'Novoe o zubatovshchine', *Krasnyi arkhiv* (1922), I, 327–8; Zaslavsky, *Byloe*, No. 3 (31) (March 1918), 100–1. A report in *Posledniia izvestiia*, No. 113 (7 March 1903), attributed much of the success of the 'Independents' to the great unemployment in Minsk.

[2] *Der bund*, No. 2 (March 1904), 8; and No. 1 (January 1904), 12. Both incidents occurred after the official demise of Zubatovism in Minsk, but the officials involved were clearly influenced by the experiment.

[3] *Posledniia izvestiia*, No. 164 (13 January 1904). See also the proclamation *Tsu alle bialy-stoker arbayter un arbayterinen: Di letste pasirungen*, November 1903.

[4] *Der kampf*, No. 1 (September 1900), 16.

demonstrated their solidarity, their unity with the workers of the entire world—to the joy of their employers and gendarmes the organized "class-conscious" locksmiths worked.'[1] In Grodno, Mania Vilbushevich, perhaps the most important Jewish Zubatovite, propagated the views of legalism among the local proletariat. 'The printers at Lapin's print shop considered holding a strike,' she wrote, 'I persuaded them to do it legally, so that no one would be arrested.'[2] In Bobruisk, a survey claims, the Zubatov program had about 200 adherents in 1903.[3]

It was in Minsk, however, that Zubatov's ideas really took root. During his discussions with the Bundists who had been arrested there, Zubatov came to the conclusion that Minsk was the key center of revolution, and he concentrated the arrests made in 1900 in that city. In Minsk's chief of police, Vasil'ev, he found a ready ally to promote the idea of legalism; Vasil'ev's energetic support of the Zubatov doctrine was certainly one explanation for its success in the second most important city of the Jewish labor movement. 'At the end of April of the past year, 1900,' wrote Zubatov, 'I met the head of the Minsk Province gendarmerie Captain Vasil'ev, who was travelling through Moscow, and in his subsequent trips our identical understanding of the current so-called labor movement drew us together.'[4]

Attracted by the goals of legalism, and the appeals of former socialist intellectuals who had been converted to the doctrine, organized worker 'kassy' in Minsk went over en masse to the 'Independents'. 'Four major crafts—' wrote one of Zubatov's correspondents, 'the carpenters, locksmiths, binders, and bristle workers—rebelled against the (revolutionary) organization and wished to leave it...the masons are almost all ours, so are the

---

[1] *Der bund*, No. 2 (March 1904), 8–9.

[2] From a letter to Zubatov quoted in Zaslavsky, *Byloe*, No. 3 (31) (March 1918), 115; for Vilbushevich's activities in Grodno see pp. 124 ff.

[3] Bukhbinder, 'O zubatovshchine', *Krasnaia letopis'*, No. 4 (1922), 319. For evidence of the influence of Zubatovism elsewhere see An-man, 'Bialystoker period', 51–2, who notes that despite the failure of the legalists in Bialystok 'our committee member Khatsi Munves...was powerfully stung by the poison of Zubatovism'.

[4] From a letter by Zubatov quoted in Bukhbinder, 'Nezavisimaia', *Krasnaia letopis'*, No. 2–3 (1922), 213. See also Frumkin, 'Zubatovshchina', 213 ff.

binders; the locksmiths—to a man, the carpenters—half, the shop assistants—half, the tinsmiths—almost all.'[1]

The 'Independents' made special efforts to attract bristle workers and shop assistants to their organization. Zubatov offered the Union 20,000 rubles to publish a legal journal. Writing to Zubatov from Kreslavka during a bristle-workers' strike in that town, one of the leaders of the 'Independents' stated, 'I am convinced that the Bristle-Workers' Union would (given encouragement by Zubatov) change its tactics fundamentally and become entirely legal.'[2] Zubatov himself was much impressed with the Bristle-Workers' Union and hoped to transform it into a legal union. Though he failed to do this, he did manage to convert a considerable number of the bristle workers to his cause.[3] For his part, Vasil'ev made the shop assistants the subject of an intensive propaganda campaign. In 1901 he organized a mass meeting of shop assistants, during which he spoke of 'the harm of political struggle', and encouraged the workers to dissociate themselves from the intellectuals and not to become involved in clandestine activities. He also promised them help were they to operate through legal channels.[4] *Iskra* noted in 1901 that Vasil'ev's

[1] Quoted in Bukhbinder, 'Nezavisimaia', *Krasnaia letopis*', No. 2–3 (1922), 219–20. In August, 1901, there were six 'Independent' workers' unions operating in Minsk (those of the carpenters, tinsmiths, bristle workers, binders, masons and locksmiths).

[2] Quoted in *ibid.*, 211. The Moscow 'Okhrana' leader, who was urged to intervene in this strike (apparently it occurred in 1901 though this is not certain), wrote to his superiors, 'At present this incident may have deep political significance in terms of a victory of faith, among the workers, in the impartiality of the central government'. The gendarmes in Kreslavka, however, refused to go along with Zubatov, and the strike ended without his intervention.

[3] See Frumkin, 'Zubatovshchina', 210. Chemerinskii, 'Vospominaniia', 316–17, attributes his conversion to Zubatovism to conversations he had with activists in Minsk, two of them bristle workers. See also Mikhalevich, *Zikhroynes*, II, 9, who describes how Zubatov donated a number of books to a bristle worker in the hope that they would form the basis of the Union's legal library. For the Union's reactions, see *Der veker*, No. 6 (July 1900), 7–8; and No. 12 (March 1903), 6.

[4] Quoted in Bukhbinder, 'Nezavisimaia', *Krasnaia letopis*', No. 2–3 (1922), 215. The shop assistants were warned also that workers who participated in illegal strikes would be punished severely. According to *Der minsker arbayter*, No. 4 (November 1901), 10, Vasil'ev's speech was unsuccessful. Many shop assistants, however, did adhere to the new party; according to a report by Vasil'ev, published in Bukhbinder, 'O zubatovshchine', *Krasnaia letopis*', No. 4 (1922), 327, there existed in 1902 a 'Society of Jewish Shop Assistants in Minsk' which was affiliated with the 'Independents'. In 1903 several shop assistants were 'boycotted' by the legal Party because they refused to affiliate—a sign of the 'Independents' general success in recruiting these workers. See the proclamation *A boykot oif di prikazshtsikes fun fraynkel's manifakturgesheft* (3 January 1903).

tactics 'have met with complete sympathy...among the petty-bourgeois masses of shop assistants'.[1]

The organizational structure of the 'Independents'' unions differed little from those sponsored by the Bund. Each craft comprised a 'ferayn' (union) which elected a 'soviet' (council) consisting of eight to ten people; dues of five kopeks a week went toward a strike fund, and each 'ferayn'—like its 'kassa' counterpart in the Bund organizations—had a library of its own. Representatives of the various councils constituted a 'Workers' Committee', which conducted the 'general affairs of the trade-union organizations' and included a special 'Cultural Commission', consisting of several workers and intellectuals.[2]

The new party differed radically from the Bund, of course, in its methods. And at the time when the social democrats were emphasizing political slogans, the 'Independents' were making a concerted effort to improve the economic conditions of the Jewish workers; a new wave of strikes—this time supported by the police—broke out in Minsk. As Bukhbinder put it, 'strikism' became a popular sport among the workers.[3] The 'ferayns' did their utmost to institute uniform working conditions and better relations between workers and employers; they also sought to eliminate the arbitrary, chaotic practices in the shops which had proved so troublesome to the artisans. When there were grievances, the 'councils' would send their demands in writing to the employers who would then meet with the 'ferayn' representatives. If no settlement were forthcoming, workers would usually strike.[4] As the following description indicates, these strikes had the full support of Vasil'ev; Zubatov wrote:

[1] No. 6 (July 1901), 4.

[2] The highest institutions of the party were the 'Party Committee (which consisted of representatives from Minsk, Vilna, and Odessa), and the 'Executive Bureau'. See Vasil'ev's report published in Bukhbinder, 'O zubatovshchine', *Krasnaia letopis'*, No. 4 (1922), 326–7; also the document entitled 'Professional'noe rabochee dvizhenie v gor. Minske', apparently by Zubatov, which discusses the organization of the party (Bukhbinder, 'Nezavisimaia', *Krasnaia letopis'*, No. 2–3 (1922), 255–9, especially 258). Zubatov stresses the democratic character of the 'Independent' Party, contrasting it to the 'conspiratorial-dictatorial power of the [Bundist] Committee' (256).

[3] Bukhbinder, 'Nezavisimaia', *Krasnaia letopis'*, No. 2–3 (1922), 212.

[4] See the publication of the 'Independent' Party, *Arbayts-mark*, three issues of which are located in the Bund Archives, New York City. One purpose of this paper was to provide

In May of the current year...several hundred locksmiths went on strike, demanding the working day be limited to the legal 12 hours (in accordance with statute 431 of the Artisans' Code) instead of 14 hours, as was then the case. Hearing about this, Captain Vasil'ev expressed a desire to meet with the representatives of the locksmiths, and at the same time also invited representatives of the employers...At the negotiations...the workers were informed that their work stoppage was completely illegal and arbitrary, and the employers were told that their demands were illegal...and it was suggested: first, a return to work, and second, the introduction of a legal working day, concerning which there would be an official announcement...by the Governor of Minsk Prince Trubetskoi, which would be posted in all the shops being struck. Toward evening such an announcement was posted, and in the morning work was resumed.[1]

The extent to which the 'ferayns' sought to govern worker-employer relations may be gauged from a document entitled, 'Rules concerning the relations between employers, their workers and apprentices', drafted by a mixed commission of 'ferayn' representatives and the Jewish photographers of Minsk.[2] A typical article reads: 'The employer is obliged to instruct the apprentice and is not allowed to give him any kind of work except photography.' In other articles, wages and hours are defined and the employers' rights with respect to hiring and firing are discussed. The document reads like a modern contract between union and employer. In some instances Vasil'ev went so far as to threaten the shop owners: 'You exploit the workers! You force them to labor to the point of exhaustion. You employ foreign labor.[3] You tell the workers that they are rebelling against

workers with detailed information on job possibilities and the economic conditions in various crafts. See the memoirs of Chemerinskii, 'Vospominaniia', 317; 'The Committee of the Jewish Independent Labor Party', it was announced in 1902: 'suggests frequent publication of a paper known as *The Workers' Market*, so that unions of organized workers will not only be able to organize strikes and to struggle against employers, but to lead the masses in times of peace and to show them what is possible in every situation, and so that workers will know what is happening in different trades, that nothing affecting the worker's life can escape a reaction on our part.' See 'Evreiskaia Nezavisimaia Rabochaia Partiia, "Rabochii rynok v Minske"', in Bukhbinder, 'O zubatovshchine', *Krasnaia letopis'*, No. 4 (1922), 324–5.

[1] Quoted in Bukhbinder, 'Nezavisimaia', *Krasnaia letopis'*, Nos. 2–3 (1922), 214.
[2] Published *ibid.*, 253–4.
[3] The reference is most probably to the practice of hiring strike breakers—Christian workers perhaps.

the government! I am the guardian of governmental order and I demand that you satisfy the workers immediately.'[1] No Bundist agitator could have put the matter more succinctly, and it is hardly surprising that employers in Minsk were cowed into submission. They resented the situation and complained. In May 1903, a group of tailor-employers sent a petition to the Ministry of the Interior objecting to the role of the police in the Minsk movement. According to the employers, the tailors' 'ferayn' was in the practice of levying fines against them if they were guilty of certain misdemeanors. 'The tailor Ruderman discharged a worker because he insulted...his wife, but by threatening him with a strike, the "ferayn" forced him to take this worker back.' Other examples of the journeymen tailors' 'reign of terror' are also presented, but as long as Zubatov and Vasil'ev remained in control, there was little choice but to submit.[2]

In addition to these police-supported strikes, the 'Independents' were actively engaged in cultural work. Workers needed 'know-ledge' as well as 'bread', and the new party was determined to supply this commodity. Zubatov himself recognized the need for cultural work among the Jewish workers, and believed that the education of the masses should be carried on 'through schools, lectures, special brochures, and newspapers'. He also favored the rise of Yiddish literature, which he felt would wean the workers away from the revolutionary movement while satisfying their cultural needs.[3] Thus the painters' 'ferayn' concentrated on rais-ing the 'cultural level' of its craft. 'We have now enlarged our library', the 'ferayn' announced in 1903. 'We have subscribed to the daily Yiddish paper, *Der fraynd*, which is always to be found in our own painters' quarters; our "ferayn" is also con-sidering the acquisition of new books, because the number of readers increases every day.'[4] Special legally authorized lectures

[1] 'Rabochee dvizhenie i zhandarmskaia politika', *Revoliutsionaia Rossiia*, No. 4 (February 1902), 12–13.

[2] The petition is published in Bukhbinder, 'O zubatovshchine', *Krasnaia letopis'*, No. 4 (1922), 330–4.

[3] See Zaslavsky, *Byloe*, No. 3 (31) (March 1918), 111–12.

[4] *Arbayts-mark*, No. 8 (15 February 1903). The *Protokol-bukh fun ferayn fun di stoliers, Minsk, Dets. 1902–2 Yuli 1903*, available in the Bund Archives, New York City, also indicates the concern for cultural work, especially 'gramota' (study of Russian).

were arranged for the members of the Party in the great assembly hall known as the 'Paris'. 'On Saturday, the 20th of October,' a correspondent of Zubatov's wrote, 'a literary evening was held for the workers in the "Paris" hall...There was an interesting program with speeches and a workers' chorus.'[1] 'Hundreds of workers affiliated with the Bund', reported one of the leaders of the 'Independents', 'eagerly attended lectures on Jewish history given by Berger on Saturdays at the "Paris" hall.'[2]

The success of Zubatovism hardly went unnoticed in the Bund. As early as 1900 the Party issued a special proclamation on the evils of an alliance between workers and the police. Polemics with the self-styled 'Independents' grew more heated as the years passed, reaching a feverish pitch in 1902, when the latter decided to expand their activities to Vilna, the stronghold of the Bund's organization.[3] Upon their arrival in the capital of Jewish Social Democracy, the delegates from Minsk met with an extremely cold welcome. The city had only recently experienced the traumatic events associated with Hirsh Lekert's assassination attempt and the Bund used public sentiment to marshal the workers and the population against what it called these 'Zubatov spies'. The socialists declared a boycott on the 'Independents',

---

[1] Bukhbinder, 'Nezavisimaia', *Krasnaia letopis'*, No. 2–3 (1922), 219; 1,000 workers attended. Cultural work was led by the intellectuals, who thus performed the very tasks that had been assigned to them by members of the first 'opposition'.

[2] From a document by Shaevich, leader of the 'Independents' in Odessa, published by Bukhbinder, 'O zubatovshchine', *Krasnaia letopis'*, No. 4 (1922), 318. See also Frumkin, 'Zubatovshchina', 223, who mentions lectures on the worker question, the labor movement, and history.

[3] On the first attack by the Bund and its effect on the workers of Belorussia–Lithuania see Zaslavsky, *Byloe*, No. 3 (31) (March 1918), 113 ff. A typical Bundist polemic against the 'Independents' is published in Bukhbinder, 'Nezavisimaia', *Krasnaia letopis'*, No. 2–3 (1922), 243–5. See also remarks by Frumkin, 'Zubatovshchina', 225: 'In the beginning Bundists would visit meetings of the "Independents" and the latter would go to those of the Bundists. But with the strengthening of ties between the "Independents" and Vasil'ev, this became impossible.' The question of the Bund's relationship to the Zubatov party in Minsk is debated in a mimeographed work by Solomon Schwarz and Y. Sh. Herts, *Zubatovshchina v Minske* (New York, 1962); Schwarz considers the Bund to have been rather 'soft' on Zubatovism, while Herts denies this. Schwarz's views may be read in English in his *The Russian Revolution of 1905* (Chicago, 1967), Appendix 5. Whatever the case, it is clear that the doctrine of legalism, by reserving a place for disaffected intellectuals, succeeded in transcending the limitations of a purely worker protest and thus represented a more viable alternative than the old worker 'opposition' led by Gordon.

warning the workers of Vilna neither to enter into debates with them, nor to accommodate them in their homes, nor even to greet them. 'You, Vilna workers,' a proclamation stated, 'must have no dealings with the "legalizatoren" (legalists); do not avail yourselves of the help which they offer, do not carry on any debates with them, (any) arguments with them, do not frequent their meetings, and...advise the great masses of the... total falseness of their shameful activity.'[1]

The delegates held several meetings in the city and won some support among the workers. Goldberg, an emissary of the Independents, describes how certain segments in the spatmakers' 'kassa' who were disillusioned with political activities were ready to join the new party, and how the older workers who had been alienated by the aggressive approach of the young Bundists welcomed Zubatovite tactics. 'I understood', he commented, 'that he (one of the old-timers) needed a different type of economic movement—not Bundist, not a movement which proposes as its principles war, war without end...but a movement which promises social peace, honorable conditions for the worker, humane relations on both sides.'[2] But they were unable to create anything like the organization they had established in Minsk. What with the hostility toward them (the threat, even, of violent reprisals), the 'Independents' might have predicted, as one of them was forced to admit later on, that 'their efforts would be fruitless'.[3] Under the influence of the Bund the masses had come to identify the 'Independents' with agents of the government, with those who had been responsible for Lekert's execution.[4]

[1] *Tsu alle vilner arbayter un arbayterinen,* July 1902.

[2] Published in Bukhbinder, 'O zubatovshchine', *Krasnaia letopis'*, No. 4 (1922), 298–9. In his memoirs, Chemerinskii ('Vospominaniia', 319) comments on the success he too had among the spatmakers.

[3] *Ibid.* For added material on the reception and activities of the 'Independents' in Vilna, see Bukhbinder, 'O zubatovshchine', *Krasnaia letopis'*, No. 4 (1922), 289 ff. The 'Vilna Group of the Jewish Independent Labor Party' published at least one issue of a newspaper in Vilna (*Flug-blettel, heroisgegeben fun der vilner gruppe fun a.a.a.p.*), but no organized 'ferayns' seem to have been established.

[4] See Vilbushevich's description of an 'Independents' meeting in Vilna in Bukhbinder, 'O zubatovshchine', *Krasnaia letopis'*, No. 4 (1922), 300. After an impressive speech by an advocate of legalism, a young man spoke of Lekert's heroic deed and death with great emotion and swayed the crowd against the 'cold logic' of the delegate from the 'Independents'.

Realizing that public sentiment there was overwhelmingly against them, the legalists abandoned their efforts in Vilna within a year.[1]

They had far greater success in Odessa, which became the scene of Zubatovite activity in 1902. An 'Independent Workers' Group' (later a 'Party') was established, and a program worked out for legal strikes and cultural activities in the unions.[2] Socialist opposition in this port city was in no way formidable; rather the chief enemy proved to be the police, particularly after a strike movement encouraged by the 'Independents' in 1903 got out of hand and its leaders were arrested. Without the support of the police the 'Independents' found it impossible to operate; ultimately they had no more luck in Odessa than their colleagues in Vilna.[3]

Apart from the failures it had suffered in Vilna and Odessa the 'Independents' party had too many obstacles against it to survive. Its identification with the regime was becoming more and more distasteful to the Jewish masses, a feeling that was to be greatly reinforced after the 1903 pogrom in Kishinev, when the Bund exploited public opinion to carry on a very effective campaign

[1] *Evreiskaia nezavisimaia rabochaia partiia, k nashim tovarishcham*, published *ibid.*, 302. The proclamation credits the Bund with the downfall of the Zubatovites in Vilna.

[2] *Ibid.*, 304–5, for the enthusiastic letter by the 'Independent' activist Volin; also the documents on 306–11. According to a police report published in Bukhbinder, 'Nezavisimaia', *Krasnaia letopis*', Nos. 2–3 (1922), 281–4, 2,000 workers belonged to the organization in Odessa. Many were non-Jews, it should be added, and the official name of the party therefore omitted the adjective 'Jewish'. However, the leaders were mostly Jewish, and the dominant figure, Shaevich, was a Zionist. Shaevich was converted to legalism while attending a Zionist conference in Minsk in 1902. At Zubatov's intervention this conference was held legally, and it is one of the more interesting facets of the Zubatov movement that it sought to ally itself with Russian Zionism. Encouraged by Mania Vilbushevich, Zubatov believed that Zionism might be used as a tool against the revolutionary movement (see the letter in Zaslavsky, *Byloe*, No. 3 (31) (March 1918), 119 ff.—Vilbushevich herself later became a pioneer settler in Palestine). A Zionist-Zubatovite alliance did, in fact, come into being, and the 'Independent' movement encountered Zionist support in Minsk, Vilna, and Odessa. See Chemerinskii, 'Vospominaniia', 319, and Bukhbinder, 'O zubatovshchine', *Krasnaia letopis*', No. 4 (1922), 305. The Tsarist regime turned against both Zionism and the 'Independent' movement simultaneously, in the summer of 1903. See Mishkinsky, 'Ha-"sotsializm ha-mishtari" u-megamot ba-mediniut ha-shilton ha-tsari legabay ha-yehudim (1900–3)', *Zion*, No. 3–4 (1960), 242–4. Frumkin, 'Zubatovshchina', 213, notes that some workers were attracted to the Zionist labor group 'Poale Zion' in Minsk because it concentrated on economic rather than on political affairs; see Mikhalevich, *Zikhroynes*, II, 15.

[3] See Bukhbinder, 'Nezavisimaia', *Krasnaia letopis*', No. 2–3 (1922), 229 ff.; Chemerinskii, 'Vospominaniia', 319 ff.

of propaganda against the party. Furthermore, the alliance
between the 'Independents' and the authorities had grown
weaker: the Zubatovites had not been able to turn up another
Vasil'ev either in Vilna or in Odessa (in the latter city the authorities were hostile to the movement from the very outset). By 1903
the Tsarist government represented by von Plehve had clearly
disassociated itself from the Zubatovite experiment. Without
governmental support, Zubatov's somewhat naive hopes for a
labor movement flourishing under police protection obviously
could not succeed.

In June 1903, the 'Jewish Independent Labor Party' of Minsk
declared its activities at an end, alleging hostility from the government as the reason for its disbanding.[1] While this may well have
been one explanation for the decline of the Minsk party, no less
important was the fact that even the Zubatov 'ferayns' supported
by Vasil'ev, which put considerable pressure upon the employers,
could not effect permanent changes for the Jewish artisan class.
The 'council' of the carpenters' 'ferayn', for instance, complained
that conditions in the shops were worse than ever. The apprentices 'heat the oven, carry water, and do everything, but they do
not learn the work'; the 'yoke' of the shop proved more difficult
to bear as wages dropped and competition from the factories
increased.[2] Thus the 'ferayn' was no more effective than the
'kassa' had been in reversing the inexorable decline of the Jewish
craft industries. The efforts of Zubatov, Vasil'ev, and the leading
'Independents' could not alter the fact that winter was still a
terrible season of unemployment for artisans, even those in the
'ferayns'. Nor were the 'Independents' particularly successful
with their strikes. The bakers' 'ferayn' went on strike for a
twelve-hour day in 1902; yet even though a number of employers
agreed to their demands, the eighteen-hour day was soon in
force again.[3] As one historian of the movement noted, 'at the

---

[1] *Tsu alle yidishe arbayter un arbayterinen,* July 1903; published in Russian in Bukhbinder,
'Nezavisimaia', *Krasnaia letopis',* No. 2–3 (1922), 265–6.

[2] *Tsirkular; tsu all minsker b"b stoliares,* 22 April 1903.

[3] *Arbayts-mark,* No. 8 (15 February 1903). On the failure of the 'ferayns' to mitigate the
horrors of the off-season see *Tsu alle minsker arbayter,* 21 May 1902. 'All hoped for
summer,' the proclamation states concerning the Minsk proletariat, 'for the dear
summer.'

first opportunity the employers reinstituted the former state of affairs'.[1] The Bundist press, commenting on the decline of legalism, claimed that the workers deserted the 'ferayns' because 'the economic struggle became more complicated and it was impossible to win the smallest successes under the existing political regime'. The failure of an important tailors' strike 'weakened the workers' belief in the all-saving strength of economic struggle'.[2] The implication that, after their unhappy experience, the workers became convinced political activists, may be open to doubt. It is clear, however, that the failure of even legalism to improve the condition of the Jewish artisans was a major reason for the decline of Jewish Zubatovism.

The various opposition tendencies we have discussed reflected certain deep-seated contradictions in the aspirations of those who had been attracted to the Jewish labor movement. The most important cleavage was that between workers and intellectuals, and the anti-intellectual theme connects the circle workers' opposition of the early 1890s with the rise of Zubatovism in the early years of the new century. In only two cases were the opposition movements sufficiently strong to pose a serious challenge, and both occurred when the leadership was promoting new programs. Thus Gordon's opposition emerged during the transition from propaganda to agitation, and legalism during the Bund's shift from an emphasis on economic struggle to a concentration on politics. The other opposition trends were merely reminders of dissent, albeit persistent ones, to the socialist leaders.

[1] Frumkin, 'Zubatovshchina', 228.
[2] *Posledniia izvestiia*, No. 143 (29 August 1903).

CHAPTER 8

Conclusion

I

We felt joy and pride in our newness: we eat and rejoice, while all Jews fast and cry.

> From a description by A. Litvak of a workers'
> gathering in Vilna on the Day of Atonement

What, precisely, did the Jewish labor movement offer its followers? This question has already been partly answered. The movement provided an opportunity for workers to express their grievances through an organized struggle against their employers, and to broaden their cultural (and, as a consequence, their political) outlook. This study has suggested that gains on the cultural front were more lasting.

The question, however, cannot be so easily dismissed. For the labor movement offered its members a completely new way of life, a new framework of conventions within which to live and work, a world unlike anything they had previously experienced. This world had its own unique institutions—the 'kassa' meeting, the 'birzhe', the secret gatherings in the woods outside the city, the illegal library, the Saturday 'reading', the educational circle. The movement had its own special holidays—celebrations commemorating the founding of a 'kassa', of an illegal library, or the memory of an important historical event. And it had its own ceremonies, the most stirring being the singing of the 'Oath', the Bund's anthem.[1]

Those who joined this new world were expected to become, in Bernshtein's words, 'different from what they had been', to give

---

[1] Compare the evaluation by Guenther Roth, *The Social Democrats in Imperial Germany* (Totowa, N.J., 1963), of the German movement: 'The labor movement came to offer to the masses of workers a way of life which was significantly different from that of other groups, especially those explicitly supporting the prevailing political and social system.' (159.)

153

up their old habits, whatever these might be—sexual license, participation in gang warfare, or love of religious ritual.[1] A new morality was practiced, one that stressed 'honorable' behavior. 'One's word within the socialist movement was considered holy,' commented a leader of the Bund. 'The Party was a Temple, and those who served socialism had to have clean hands, clean thoughts, pure qualities, and to be pure in their relations with one another.'[2] This new morality was especially evident in relations between the sexes. While participation in the movement enabled young men and women to meet and work together as equals, something that had rarely been encountered in the 'other' world, it imposed upon them a strict moral code which bordered on puritanism. 'Relations between men and women among the "bekante" (members of the organization) were more honorable than among the other workers. In our circles, friendship and comradeliness prevailed, rather than sex talk and vulgar jokes.'[3] To make declarations of love was considered by some to be a breach of revolutionary conduct, a 'betrayal of the revolution'.[4]

The inhabitants of this world regarded themselves as members of a new brotherhood, the bearers of a new mission. They called themselves 'bekante', literally 'known ones', who comprised one great family living by rule of 'one for all and all for one'.[5] The 'bekante' regarded themselves as 'new men', who had broken with the hypocrisy of the other world and were dedicating themselves to the future happiness of humanity. The best examples of these 'new people' were the agitators in the 'kassy'. Liza, 'the Tailor', we are told, '...carried on agitation among the workers. At the same time she was a member of the circle...She was occupied with the workers' library, which consisted almost exclusively of Yiddish books. She led strikes in various crafts,

---

[1] Bernshtein, *Ershte shprotsungen*, 24. Levin, *Untererdishe kemfer*, 119, notes that in Minsk workers ceased to visit prostitutes after they joined the movement. However, a few agitators recommended that workers visit prostitutes because it was a 'physical necessity' for them.

[2] Kossovsky, 'Zubatov "likvidirt dem bund"', 189.

[3] Bernshtein, *Ershte shprotsungen*, 25.

[4] Levin, *Untererdishe kemfer*, 149.

[5] See Bernsthein, *Ershte shprotsungen*, 23–5, for a discussion of the term 'bekante' and its significance.

organized circles for talented and active workers, and provided them with teachers from among the intellectuals.' But what showed Liza to be typical of the new mentality was that her concerns were not limited to economic and cultural work; she insisted that the agitation program establish a 'new moral and ethical level'.[1] In so doing, she emphasized one of the major aims of the Jewish labor movement.

We have spoken of 'new men', but it would be more exact to speak of 'new Jewish men'. Like Zionism, its great rival, the Jewish labor movement under the leadership of the Bund attempted to instill in its followers a new pride in their Jewishness. It insisted that Jews were a nation like any other, and elevated Yiddish to a new level of dignity. The socialists repudiated what they considered to be the traditional Jewish characteristics of indifference, apathy, and resignation. These, it was hoped, would be replaced by activism and struggle. The 'new Jewish man' was to regard himself as the subject, rather than the object, of history.

Indeed, the struggle itself, irrespective of the results, was vitally important. When in Vilna 230 people went on strike at a cigarette factory in 1902 for a raise of two kopeks a week, they persisted in a bitter dispute which lasted two weeks. Finally the owner himself commented: 'I know that the two kopeks are not important to you, but rather that you will be able to tell the whole world that you have won.'[2] The word 'fought' would have been equally appropriate; a raise of two kopeks a week, or a reduction in the workday from fourteen to twelve hours, might be won today and lost tomorrow, but the feeling of pride and exhilaration derived from the struggle was a permanent gain. This, perhaps, was the real meaning of the labor movement for thousands of Jewish workers who swelled its ranks.

[1] *Ibid.*, 80, 82.
[2] *Di arbayter shtime*, No. 32 (March 1903), 12.

II

From a certain point of view the Jewish workers may be considered the vanguard of the labor army in Russia.

From Georgii Plekhanov's report to the 1896
Congress of the Socialist International in London

The student of labor history in the Tsarist Empire cannot fail to be impressed by the contrast between the Jewish movement in Belorussia–Lithuania and the Russian movement of the interior. While in the former region the organized 'kassy' flourished, Russian workers found organization far more difficult. According to one observer, 'Until the spring of 1896, the term "labor movement" applied everywhere in Russia to a small elite of workers, mostly from the metallurgical industries, whose main concern was for education'.[1] In a city as important as Tsaritsyn (now Volgograd, formerly Stalingrad), whose population of 60,000 in 1900 included large numbers of workers, the 'broad worker masses' on the eve of the 1905 Revolution had not yet been organized or even affected by the movement.[2]

By pioneering in labor organization within the Russian Empire, the Jewish workers were doing precisely what their fellow artisans had done all over Europe. Throughout the continent it was the craftsmen who were the first to organize trade unions, leaving the factory workers behind. As Émile Vandervelde observed of Belgium in the 1840s, 'The workers in the great industries are still an amorphous mass, submitting passively to all the demands of the owners. But workers in manufacture—such as hat makers, printers, jewellers, etc.—...are beginning to understand the necessity to unite in order to maintain and improve their situation.'[3] A historian of the French labor movement remarks that 'The process of labor organization is clearly more rapid in those

---

[1] Pipes, *Social Democracy*, 99. On the early Russian workers' organizations, led by the Populists, see Venturi, *Roots of Revolution*, Chapter 19.

[2] K. S. Bogdanova *et al.*, *Ocherki istorii Volgogradskoi partiinoi organizatsii*, Book I (Volgograd, 1966), 24.

[3] Émile Vandervelde, *Enquête sur les associations professionnelles d'artisans et ouvriers en Belgique* (Brussels, 1891), 22.

crafts with a long artisan tradition than in the professions issuing directly from the industrial revolution'.[1]

We have already alluded to the reasons for the artisans' success—the guild heritage, the comparatively high level of culture, perhaps too the fragmented character of artisan production, which obliged more careful organization in order to wage strikes.[2] Even within the Russian Jewish labor movement it was the craftsmen who pioneered, and the cigarette and match factory workers who lagged behind. But the Jewish proletariat was overwhelmingly a proletariat of artisans, while the Russian working force, small as it might have been in relation to the West, was a proletariat of the great factories. We should not be surprised that the Jewish tailor was more likely to establish or join a 'kassa' than a Russian factory worker, who during the period under discussion was likely to be as much peasant as he was proletarian.

It is in this light that Plekhanov's statement, quoted above, should be understood. But if the Jewish artisans of Russia were the 'vanguard of the labor army' in the Empire, and if this phenomenon can be illuminated by reference to European labor history, the fate of the Jewish artisan class differed from that of the Western craftsmen. While the latter were eventually absorbed into the factories, the Jewish workers were not. And the Jewish labor movement must be understood by reference to two salient facts: the artisan composition of the Jewish proletariat, and the deteriorating economic condition of that class. These facts explain the labor movement's weaknesses as well as its strengths.

[1] Jean Montreuil, *Histoire du mouvement ouvrier en France, des origines à nos jours* (Paris, 1946), 111–16.

[2] This final point was made by Litvak, *Vos geven*, 117–18. If we employ literacy rates as a yardstick of cultural development, it is clear that the Jewish artisan was far ahead of the Russian worker. According to one estimate, in 1901 13% of all male Jewish masters in Minsk were illiterate (*Nedel'naia khronika 'Voskhoda'*, xx, No. 39 (21 June 1901), 19); a survey taken in Vilna in 1911 found that only 8·3% of the Jewish tailors were illiterate (Cherniovsky, *Der yidisher arbeter*, 140). A study of four cities in the Pale, published in 1913, reports that 1·7% of the male, and 27·3% of the female Jewish tailors were illiterate; see Rabinowitsch, 'Zur Bildungsstatistik der jüdischen Arbeiter in Russland', *Zeitschrift für Demographie und Statistik der Juden*, ix, 11 (November 1913), 153–60. By contrast, according to the census of 1897, only 40·2% of all Russian workers were literate; see A. G. Rashin, *Formirovanie rabochego klassa Rossii* (Moscow, 1958), 584. It may also be added that the Russian police was more interested, at least in the beginning, in the Russian than in the Jewish movement. See above, p. 97.

Bibliography

UNPUBLISHED SOURCES

Primary

Collection of proclamations, published, hectographed, and hand-written. New York, The Bund Archives.

Dvinov, B. *Vitebsk—1903-4 gg*. New York, The Bund Archives.

Protokol-bukh fun ferayn fun di stoliares, Minsk, dets. 1902-2 yuli 1903. New York, The Bund Archives.

Rukopis' T. Kopel'zona, 1907, ob oppozitsii 1893 g. New York, The Bund Archives.

Tsalevich, Bentsel. *Erinerung fun 1-tn bialystoker beker shtrayk in yor 1901 khoydesh may*. New York, The Bund Archives.

Typescript of a lecture read in the Zubatov unions in Minsk, signed 'Gruppa soznatel'nykh rabochikh'. (1902 or 1903?) New York, The Bund Archives.

Secondary

Frankel, Jonathan. *Socialism and Jewish nationalism in Russia, 1892-1907.* Ph.D. Dissertation, Cambridge University, 1961.

Herts, Y. Sh., and Schwarz, Solomon. *Zubatovshchina v Minske.* New York, 1962. Mimeographed.

Mishkinsky, Moshe. 'Regionale faktorn bay der oisforemung fun der yidisher arbeter-bavegung in tsarishn rusland.' New York, YIVO Institute for Jewish Research, 1965. Mimeographed.

Yesodot leumiim be-hithavutah shel tenuat ha-poalim ha-yehudit be-rusiah (mi-rashitah ve-ad 1901). Ph.D. Dissertation, The Hebrew University of Jerusalem, 1965.

Shukman, Henry. *The relations between the Jewish Bund and the RSDRP.* Ph.D. Dissertation, Oxford University, 1960.

Stone, Bernard B. *National and international currents in Polish socialism: The PPS and SDKPiL, 1893-1921.* Ph.D. Dissertation, The University of Chicago, 1965.

Tobias, Henry. *The origins and evolution of the Jewish Bund until 1901.* Ph.D. Dissertation, Stanford University, 1957.

Bibliography

PUBLISHED SOURCES

Brochures, reports and other sources

'Der ershter shtrayk in minsk.' *Royte bleter.* Vol. I, Minsk, 1929, pp. 25–8.

'Der leben un kampf fun di idishe arbayter in russland un poylen.' *Der idisher arbeter.* No. 10, 1900, pp. 51–74; No. 11, 1901, pp. 4–47.

'Der statut fun der kasse un baylage vegn der noytikayt ayntsuordnen biblioteken (algemayne yesoydes, vilne, 1894).' *Unzer tsayt* (Warsaw). No. 2 (5 February 1928), pp. 87–96.

Di geshikhte fun der idisher arbayter-bevegung in rusland un poylen. Geneva, 1900.

Gozhanskii, S. 'A briv tsu di agitatorn.' *Historishe shriftn.* Vol. III, Paris–Vilna, 1939, pp. 626–48.

   'A vikuakh vegen mazl.' *Historishe shriftn.* Vol. III, Paris–Vilna, 1939, pp. 694–705.

   'Der shtot magid.' *Historishe shriftn.* Vol. III, Paris–Vilna, 1939, pp. 721–39.

   'Erinerungen fun a papirosn makherke.' *Unzer tsayt* (Warsaw). No. 7 (July 1928), pp. 89–95; No. 8–9 (September–October 1928), pp. 110–28; No. 10 (December 1928), pp. 85–92.

K voprosu o terrorizme. London, 1903.

Kremer, Arkadii. *Ob agitatsii.* Geneva, 1896.

Mendlin, Wolf. *Ba-me nevashaya, 4 ma'amarim be-she'elat ha-matsav ha-homri shel yehuday rossia.* St Petersburg, 1883.

Pervoe maia 1892 goda. Chetyre rechi evreiskikh rabochikh. Geneva, 1893.

Plekhanov, Georgii. 'Nashi raznoglasiia.' *Sochineniia,* David Riazanov (ed.). Vol. II, Moscow–Petrograd, 1923, pp. 91–356.

   'O zadachakh sotsialistov v bor'be s golodam v Rossii.' *Sochineniia,* David Riazanov (ed.). Moscow–Petrograd, 1923, Vol. III, pp. 355–420.

'Taytikayts-berikht fun vilne 1896.' *Unzer tsayt* (Warsaw). No. 6 (June 1928), pp. 84–92.

V—yi s'ezd vseobshchago evreiskago rabochago soiuza v Litve i Pol'she i Rossii. London, 1903.

Bibliography

Newspapers, journals

Arbayts-mark (Minsk). 1902. Nos. 5–6, 8.

Der bialystoker arbayter (Bialystok). 1899–1902, Nos. 1, 3–7.

Der bund. 1904–5, Nos. 1–11.

Der frayhayts-glok (Lodz). 1901–2, Nos. 1–4.

Der fraynd (St Petersburg). 1903, Nos. 1–296.

Der idisher arbeter (Geneva, London, etc.). 1896–1904, Nos. 1–17.

Der jüdischer Arbeiter (Vienna). 1898, No. 1.

Der kampf (Gomel). 1900–1, Nos. 1, 3.

Der klassen kampf (Vilna). 1901–2, Nos. 2–6.

Der minsker arbeter (Minsk). 1900–1, 1905, Nos. 1–6.

Der varshaver arbayter (Warsaw). 1899–1903, 1905, Nos. 2–5, 7–10, 12–21.

Der veker. 1900–3, Nos. 3–6, 8–12.

Der yud (Cracow). 1899–1902, Nos. 1–52.

Di arbayter shtime (Vilna, Bobruisk, Warsaw, etc.). 1897–1905, Nos. 1–8, 11–12, 14–40.

Di letste pasirungen in rayon fun bund (Geneva). 1904–5, Nos. 1–26.

Dvinsker flug-bletel (Dvinsk). 1902, Nos. 1–2.

Flug-bletel fun bialystok (Bialystok). 1903, 1905, No. 2, un-numbered copy.

Flug-blettel, heroisgegeben fun der komitet fun poylishen bershter-rayon. 1904, No. 1.

Flug-blettel, heroisgegeben fun der vilner gruppe fun der a.a.a.p. (Vilna). 1902?, un-numbered copy.

Flug-blettel, heroisgegeben fun grodner sotsial-demokratishen komitet fun bund (Grodno). 1903, No. 3.

Flug-blettel, heroisgegeben fun vilner sotsial-demokratishen komitet fun bund (Vilna). 1903–4, Nos. 3–4, 6.

Flug-bletter, heroisgegeben fun kovner sotsial-demokratishen komitet fun bund (Kovno). 1903–4, Nos. 1–2.

Ha-magid (Lyck, Cracow, Berlin). 1856–1903, irregular volume numbers.

Iskra (Munich, Geneva, etc.). 1900–5, Nos. 1–112.

Letste nokhrikhtn (London). 1901, Nos. 1–47.

Listok 'rabochego dela' (Geneva). 1900–1, Nos. 1–8.

Listok 'rabotnika' (Geneva). 1896–8, Nos. 1–10.

Minsker arbeter bletl (Minsk). 1897, Nos. 1–9, *Historishe shriftn.* Vol. III, pp. 731–50.

Minsker flug-blettel (Minsk). 1903, Nos. 4–5.

Bibliography

Nakanune (London). 1899, Vol. I, No. 4–5.
Nedel'naia khronika 'Voskhoda' (St Petersburg). 1881–1903, Vols. I–XXII; known as *Voskhod* from 4 November 1899.
Posledniia izvestiia (London, Geneva). 1901–5, Nos. 1–256.
Proletariat 1902–5 r. Zbior artikułów (Lvov). 1905.
Przedświt (London). 1893–9.
Rabochaia mysl' (London). 1898–1902, Nos. 4–16.
Rabochee delo (Geneva). 1899–1902, Nos. 1–12.
Rabotnik (Geneva). 1896–9, Nos. 1–6.
Razsvet (St Petersburg). 1879–83, Vols. I–V.
Revoliutsionnaia Rossiia (London). 1902–5, Nos. 1–77.
Russkii evrei (St Petersburg). 1879–84, Vols. I–VI.
Vpered (London). 1875–6, Nos. 1–48.
Yudishes folks-blat (St Petersburg). 1881–90, Vols. I–X.

Memoirs (including articles)

Abramovich, Hirsh. 'Fun Hirsh Lekerts tsaytn, zikhroynes.' *Royter pinkes.* Vol. II, Warsaw, 1924, pp. 144–51.
Abramovich, Raphael. *In tsvay revolutsies.* 2 vols., New York, 1944.
Aksel'rod-Ortodoks, L. 'Iz moikh vospominanii.' *Katorga i ssylka* (Moscow). No. 2 (63), 1930, pp. 22–42.
An-man, P., pseud. (Pavel Rozental). 'Bialystoker period in lebn fun ts. k. fun bund (1900–2).' *Royter pinkes.* Vol. I, Warsaw, 1921, pp. 45–69.
Avram der Tate, pseud. (Leib Blekhman). *Bleter fun mayn yugent, zikhroynes fun a bundist.* New York, 1959.
'Zikhroynes fun der sotsialistisher un arbeter bavegung.' *Vitebsk amol*, Gregory Aronson *et al.* (eds.). New York, 1956, pp. 275–93.
Baskin, Y. 'Epizodn fun mayn leben.' *Y. Baskin, tsu zayn 70-yorikn yubilay.* New York, 1951, pp. 9–82.
Baylin, A. 'Zikhroynes', *Royte bleter.* Vol. I, Minsk, 1929, pp. 1–44.
Belenskii, E. 'Vospominaniia o bol'shevistskoi organizatsii v g. Minske v 1903 g.' *Proletarskaia revoliutsiia* (Moscow). No. 11 (34), November 1924, pp. 196–202; No. 8 (43), August 1925, pp. 65–96; No. 12 (47), December 1925, pp. 138–64.
Ben-Uziel. 'In baginen fun der bershter-arbet ba yidn in rusland.' *Virtshaft un lebn* (Berlin). Vol. I, No. 1, July 1928, pp. 54–9.
Berman, L. (Leibetshke, pseud.) *In loif fun yorn, zikhroynes fun a yidishen arbeter.* New York, 1945.

Bibliography

Bernshtein, Leon. *Ershte shprotsungen*. Buenos Aires, 1956.

Blum, Hillel Kats. *Zikhroynes fun a bundist*. New York, 1946.

Botvinik, H. 'Di vilner may-demonstratsie in 1902 yor.' *Hirsh Lekert, tsum 20-ten yortog fun zayn kepung*. Moscow, 1922, pp. 22–34.

Bunen-Idel, Kril, 'Derinerungen fun a rokisher sotsialist.' *Yizker-bukh fun rokishok un umgegent*, M. Bakaltshuk-Felin (ed.). Johannesburg, 1952, pp. 115–30.

Chemerinskii, A. 'In lodz in 1905.' *Royte bleter*. Vol. I, Minsk, 1929, pp. 1–3.

Memoirs in 'Vospominaniia o "evreiskoi nezavisimoi rabochei partii". Novoe o zubatovshchine.' *Krasnyi arkhiv*. Vol. I, 1922, pp. 315–22.

Daytsh, Mendel. 'Vegn mayn revolutsionere arbet.' *Royte bleter*. Minsk, 1929, Vol. I, pp. 1–24.

Dimanshtein, S. (ed.). *Revoliutsionnoe dvizhenie sredi evreev*. Moscow, 1930.

Fogorelsky, Mordechai. 'Zikhroynes fun a bialystoker "esesovits".' *Bialystoker shtime* (New York). Vol. XXI, No. 205, April 1941; No. 206, May 1941; No. 207, June 1941; No. 208, September–October 1941; No. 209, November–December 1941.

Frank, H. *et al. Natsionale un politishe bavegungen bay yidn in bialystok*. New York, 1951.

Frumkin, M. Memoirs in 'Vospominaniia o "evreiskoi nezavisimoi rabochei partii". Novoe o zubatovshchine.' *Krasnyi arkhiv*. Vol. I, 1922, pp. 327–28.

Gel'man, S. 'Pervaia podpol'naia tipografiia gruppy "Rabochee znamia".' *Katorga i ssylka* (Moscow). No. 6 (27), 1926, pp. 44–56.

Geltman, Litman. 'Der ershter bershter-shtrayk.' *Mezrich zamlbukh*. Buenos Aires, 1952, pp. 239–54.

Gershanovich, David. 'O Moise Vladimiroviche Lur'e.' *K dvadtsat-piatiletiiu pervogo s'ezda partii*. Moscow–Leningrad, 1923, pp. 165–74.

Ginzburg, A. M. (Naumov, pseud.) 'Nachalnye shagi vitebskogo rabochego dvizheniia.' *Revoliutsionnoe dvizhenie sredi evreev*, S. Dimanshtein (ed.), Moscow, 1930, pp. 100–26.

Goldschmidt, A. Y. 'Khaver Aron.' *Vayter bukh, tsum andenk fun A. Vayter*. Vilna, 1920, pp. 66–92.

Gordon, Avram. *In friling fun vilner yidisher arbeter-bavegung*. Vilna, 1926.

Gozhanskii, S. 'Evreiskoe rabochee dvizhenie nachala 90-kh godov.'

Bibliography

Revoliutsionnoe dvizhenie sredi evreev, S. Dimanshtein (ed.), Moscow, 1930, pp. 81–93.

Grinberg, Joseph. 'Erinerungen vegen bershter-bund.' *Der veker* (New York). Vol. VI, No. 309, 15 October 1927, pp. 19–21; No. 310, 22 October 1927, pp. 13–15.

Gurvich, E. A. 'Evreiskoe rabochee dvizhenie v Minske v 80-kh gg.' *Revoliutsionnoe dvizhenie sredi evreev*, S. Dimanshtein (ed.), Moscow, 1930, pp. 33–64.

[Hurvich, Zhenie.] 'Di ershte propagandistishe krayzl.' *Royte bleter*. Vol. I, Minsk, 1929, . pp 1–5.

Gurvich, Isak. 'Pervye evreiskie rabochie kruzhki.' *Byloe* (St Petersburg). No. 6, June 1907, pp. 65–77.

[Hourwich], Isaac A. 'Zikhroynes fun an epikoyres.' *Fraye arbayter shtime*. Vol. XXII, No. 49, 11 November 1921; Vol. XXIV, No. 21, 30 March 1923.

Ivensky, M. 'A. Valt (Liesin), der onfirer fun der ershter idisher natsional-sotsialistisher bevegung.' *Di tsukunft* (New York). Vol. XXIV, No. 4, April 1919, pp. 205–8.

Kahan, Isar. 'Bay Aleksandern in krayzl.' *Arkady, Zamlbukh tsum andenk fun Arkady Kremer*. New York, 1942, pp. 145–6.

Khaytovitsh, Y. A. 'Dos vos ikh vays vegn Hirsh Lekert, zikhroynes.' *Hirsh Lekert, tsum 20-ten yortog fun zayn kepung*. Moscow, 1922, pp. 58–60.

Kling, Lazar. 'Epizodn fun der amoliker bundisher tetikayt', *Buletin fun bund arkhiv* (New York). No. 3 (19), October 1964, pp. 10–13.
'Zikhroynes fun der amoliker bundisher tetikayt.' *Buletin fun bund arkhiv* (New York). No. 2 (18), May, 1964, pp. 4–9.

Kon, Feliks. 'Moi pervye vstrechi s evreiskimi rabochimi.' *Revoliutsionnoe dvizhenie sredi evreev*, S. Dimanshtein (ed.), Moscow, 1930, pp. 21–32.

Za piat'desiat let. 2 vols., Moscow, 1936.

Kopelman, Gedaliah. 'Der bund.' *Drohiczyn, finf hundert yor yidish-leben*, Dov B. Varshavsky (ed.), Chicago, 1958.

Kopelovich, Khanke. 'Der onhayb fun kampf.' *Royte bleter*. Vol. I, Minsk, 1929, pp. 1–5.

Kopel'zon, T. M. 'Evreiskoe rabochee dvizhenie kontsa 80-kh i nachala 90-kh godov', in *Revoliutsionnoe dvizhenie sredi evreev*, S. Dimanshtein (ed.), Moscow, 1930, pp. 65–75.

Kremer, Arkady. 'Mit 35 yor tsurik.' *Arkady, Zamlbukh tsum andenk fun Arkady Kremer*. New York, 1942, pp. 395–401.

Bibliography

Lev, A., 'Vospominaniia o tov. Sikorskom.' *Katorga i ssylka* (Moscow). No. 41, 1928, pp. 142–5.

Levin, Bentse. 'Di 5-te konferents fun bund, zikhroynes.' *Hirsh Lekert, tsum 20-ten yortog fun zayn kepung.* Moscow, 1922, pp. 58–60.

Levin, Shmaryahu. *The Arena.* Translated by Maurice Samuel. New York, 1932.

Levin, Sholem. 'Di ershte yorn fun der revolutsie.' *Royte bleter.* Vol. I, Minsk, 1929, pp. 1–8.

'Finf yor in di umlegale drukerayen.' *Royte bleter.* Vol. I, Minsk, 1929, pp. 1–7.

Untererdishe kemfer. New York, 1946.

Liesin, Avraham. 'Di amolike opozitsie in minsk.' **Liesin, Avraham,** *Zikhroynes un bilder.* New York, 1954, pp. 272–94.

Litvak., A, pseud. (Helphand) *Vos geven.* Vilna, 1925.

Martov, Iulii. *Zapiski sotsialdemokrata.* Berlin, 1922.

Medem, Vladimir. *Fun mayn leben.* 2 vols. New York, 1923.

Mikhalevich, Baynish. *Zikhroynes fun a yudishen sotsialist.* Vols. I and II, Warsaw, 1921; Vol. III, Warsaw, 1929.

'Erev "bund".' *Royter pinkes.* Vol. I, Warsaw, 1921, pp. 31–44.

Mill, John, *Pionern un boyer.* Vol. I, New York, 1946; Vol. II, New York, 1949.

Mitskin, Isak. 'Di vilner organizatsie fun bund un Lekerts attentat.' *Hirsh Lekert, tsum 20-ten yortog fun zayn kepung,* Moscow, 1922, pp. 42–6.

Nisenboim, Yitskhak. *Alay heldi.* Warsaw, 1929.

Notkin, Aleksandr. 'Otryvki vospominanii o pervom sotsial-demo-kratisheskom kruzhke v Gomele v 1894 godu.' *K dvadtsatpiatiletiiu pervogo s'ezda partii.* Moscow–Leningrad, 1923, pp. 160–5.

Pakovskii, M. 'Neskol'ko slov o Sikorskom.' *Katorga i ssylka* (Moscow). No. 41, 1928, pp. 146–7.

Paperna, A. I. 'Iz nikolaevskoi epokhi, vospominaniia.' *Perezhitoe* (St Petersburg). Vol. II, 1910, pp. 1–53.

(Pasakhson, Y. M.) 'An alter bekanter in varshe erev bund.' *25 yor zamlbukh.* Warsaw, 1922, pp. 35–50.

'Der onhayb fun der yidisher arbeter-bavegung in lodz.' *Royter pinkes.* Vol. II, Warsaw, 1924, pp. 159–64.

Pati, pseud. (Srednitskaia). 'Zikhroynes vegn Arkadin.' *Arkady, Zamlbukh tsum andenk fun Arkady Kremer.* New York, 1942, pp. 22–72.

Bibliography

Peskin, Jacob. 'Di "grupe yidishe sotsial-demokratn in rusland" un Arkady Kremer.' *Historishe shriftn.* Vol. III, Paris–Vilna, 1939, pp. 544–55.

'Di vilner grupe un Arkady Kremer.' *Arkady, Zamlbukh tsum andenk fun Arkady Kremer.* New York, 1942, pp. 112–22.

Peskovoi, Iv. 'V smorgoni (vospominaniia rabochego proshlom).' *Krasnaia letopis'* (Moscow). No. 8, 1923, pp. 77–95; No. 1 (10), 1924, pp. 222–5.

Pietkiewicz, Kazimierz. 'Mojżesz Łurje i "Raboczeje Znamia".' *Niepodległość* (Warsaw). VI, No. 1 (12), May–October 1932, 26–40.

Presman, Ezriel. *Der durkhgegangener veg.* New York, 1950.

Rabinovich, Sh. 'A. Valt (Liesin) un zayn kampf gegen kosmopolitizm, "ekonomizm" un broshurizm.' *Di tsukunft* (New York). Vol. XXIV, No. 4, April 1919, 208–11.

Rafes, Moshe. 'In lekerts tsayten (zikhroynes).' *Hirsh Lekert, tsum 20-ten yortog fun zayn kepung.* Moscow, 1922, pp. 34–41.

Memoirs in 'Vospominaniia o "evreiskoi nezavisimoi rabochei partii".' *Novoe o zubatovshchine.' Krasnyi arkhiv.* Vol. I, 1922, pp. 323–26.

Rappaport, Charles. 'Dos leben fun a revolutsionern emigrant.' *Historishe shriftn.* Vol. III, Paris–Vilna, 1939, pp. 283–309.

Raskin, Miriam. *Tsen yor lebn.* New York, 1927.

Raytshuk, Elie. 'Fun vaytn over.' *Royte bleter.* Vol. I, Minsk, 1929, pp. 1–10.

Rozental, Anna. 'Bletlekh fun a lebens-geshikhte.' *Historishe shriftn.* Vol. III, Paris–Vilna, 1939, pp. 416–37.

Sayman, Serere. 'Di ershte demonstratsie (erinerungen vegen der onhayb fun der revolutsionerer bavegung in bialystok).' *Bialystoker shtime* (New York). Vol. VI, No. 13 (March 1926), 37–9.

Shkliar, H. 'Onhayb fun der yidisher arbeter-bavegung in kovne.' *Lite.* Vol. II, Tel Aviv, 1965, pp. 181–228.

Shtern, Berl. *Zikhroynes fun shturmishe yorn (bielsk, 1898–1907).* New York, 1954.

Shtufler, Benjamin. 'Tsvay pionern fun der revolutsionerer bavegung in bialystok.' *Natsionale un politishe bavegungen bay yidn in bialystok*, Herman Frank *et al.* (eds.). New York, 1951, pp. 47–55.

Solomon, Saiman. *Derinerungen fun der yidisher arbeter bavegung.* New York, 1952.

Szuszkiewicz, Bronisław. 'Organizacja grodzieńska P.P.S. w latach

Bibliography

1898–1910.' *Niepodległość* (Warsaw). Vol. XVI, No. 3 (44), November–December 1937, pp. 513–64.

Tsipir, Boris. 'Zikhroynes fun a bialystoker bundist (1901–5).' *Natsionale un politishe bavegungen bay yidn in bialystok*, Herman Frank *et al.* (eds.), New York, 1951, pp. 38–46.

Vilenskii, Il'ia. 'Pionery vitebskogo rabochego dvizheniia.' *Revoliutsionnoe dvizhenie sredi evreev*, S. Dimanshtein (ed.), Moscow, 1930, pp. 96–9.

'Sotsial-demokraticheskaia rabota v Vitebske v 90-kh godakh.' *K dvadtsatpiatiletiiu pervogo s'ezda partii.* Moscow–Leningrad, 1923, pp. 149–60.

'Vospominaniia o "evreiskoi nezavisimoi rabochei partii".' Novoe o zubatovshchine.' *Krasnyi arkhiv.* Vol. I, 1922, pp. 315–28 (memoirs of Chemerinskii, Rafes, Frumkin).

Zil'berblat, I. F. 'Moi vospominaniia o tov. Simone Vul'foviche Sikorskom.' *Katorga i ssylka* (Moscow). No. 41, 1928, pp. 148–51.

Books

Agursky, Sh. (S) (ed.). *Di sotsialistishe literatur of yidish in 1875–97.* Minsk, 1935.

Ocherki revoliutsionnogo dvizheniia v Belorussii 1863–1917. Minsk, 1937.

Akimov, Vladimir pseud. (Makhnovets), *Materialy dlia kharakteristiki razvitiia rossiikoi sotsialdemokraticheskoi rabochei partii.* Geneva, 1904.

Ainzaft, S. *Zubatovshchina i Gaponovshchina.* Moscow, 1925.

Baron, Salo W. *The Russian Jew under Tsars and Soviets.* New York, 1964.

Batiushkov, P. N. *Belorussiia i Litva, Istoricheskiia sud'by severo-zapadnago kraia.* St Petersburg, 1890.

Belorussiia v epokhu feodalizma. Vol. III, Minsk, 1961.

Bershadskii, S. A. *Litovskie evrei.* St Petersburg, 1883.

(ed.). *Russko-evreiskii arkhiv, dokumenty i materialy dlia istorii evreev v Rossii.* Vol. I, St Petersburg, 1882.

Bliokh, I. *Sravnenie material'nago byta i nravstvennago sostoianiia naseleniia v cherte osedlosti i vne eia.* St Petersburg, 1891.

Brafman, Ia. *Kniga kagala.* Vol. II, St Petersburg, 1875.

Brenan, Gerald. *The Spanish Labyrinth.* Cambridge, 1962.

Bukhbinder, Nahum A. *Istoriia evreiskogo rabochego dvizheniia v Rossii.* Leningrad, 1925.

Burgin, Herts. *Di geshikhte fun der idisher arbayter bavegung in amerike, rusland, un england.* New York, 1915.

Bibliography

Cherniovsky, E. *Der yidisher arbeter in vaysrusland bam baginen fun der yidisher arbeter-bavegung.* Minsk, 1932.

Deutscher, Isaac. *The Prophet Armed: Trostky, 1879–1921.* London, 1954.

Dimanshtein, S. *Di revolutsionere bavegung tsvishen di idishe masn in der revolutsie fun 1905 yor.* Moscow, 1929.

Dokumenty i materialy po istorii Belorussii (1900–17). Vol. III, Minsk, 1953.

Dovnar-Zapolskii, A. V. *Narodnoe khoziaistvo Belorussii 1861–1914 gg.* Minsk, 1926.

Dubnov-Erlich, Sophie. *Garber-bund un bershter-bund.* Translated (from Polish) by L. Hodes and Kh. Sh. Kazdan. Warsaw, 1938.

Dziewanowski, M. K. *The Communist Party of Poland, an Outline of History.* Cambridge, Mass., 1959.

Eisenshtadt, Shmuel. *Perakim be-toldot tenuat ha-poalim ha-yehudit.* Vol. I, Palestine, no date.

Ekonomicheskoe sostoianie gorodskikh poselenii Evropeiskoi Rossii v 1861–62 g. 2 vols., St Petersburg, 1863.

Evreiskoe naselenie Rossii po dannym perepisi 1897 g. i po noveishim istochnikam. Petrograd, 1917.

Galenson, Walter (ed.). *Comparative Labor Movements.* New York, 1952.

Gessen, Iulii. *Evrei v Rossii.* St Petersburg, 1906.

Istoriia evreiskogo naroda v Rossii. Vol. I, Petrograd, 1916.

Gessen, I., (ed.). *Khrestomatiia po istorii rabochego klassa i professional'nogo dvizheniia v Rossii.* Vol. I, Leningrad, 1925.

Getzler, Israel. *Martov: a Political Biography of a Russian Social Democrat.* Cambridge, 1967.

Ginzburg, Saul M., and P. S. Marek. *Evreiskiia narodnyia pesni v Rossii.* St Petersburg, 1901.

Grinevich, V. *Professional'noe dvizhenie rabochikh v Rossii.* Moscow, 1922.

Hershberg, A. S. (ed.). *Pinkes bialystok.* Vol. II, New York, 1950.

Herts, Y. Sh. *Di geshikhte fun bund in lodz.* New York, 1958.

Hirsh Lekert. New York, 1952.

et al. *Di geshikhte fun bund.* Vol. I, New York, 1960; Vol. II, New York, 1962; Vol. III, New York, 1966.

Hofman, B. (ed.). *Toyzent yor pinsk.* New York, 1941.

Ihnatowicz, Ireneusz. *Przemysł Łódzki w latach 1860–1900.* Warsaw–Wrocław–Cracow, 1965.

Johnston, Robert. *Travels through parts of the Russian Empire and the country of Poland.* London, 1815.

Bibliography

Kastelianskii, A. I. 'Mebel'noe-stoliarno proizvodstvo v cherte evreiskoi osedlosti', *Materialy i izsledovaniia o evreiskoi remeslennoi promyshlennosti*. Vol. I, *Stoliarno-mebel'noe proizvodstvo*. Petrograd, 1915, pp. 1–190.

Keep, J. L. H. *The Rise of Social Democracy in Russia*. London, 1963.

Korev, A. (ed.). *Vilenskaia gubernaia. Materialy dlia geografii i statistiki Rossii, sobrannye ofitserami general'nago shtaba*. Vol. III, St Petersburg, 1863.

Korol'chuk, E. A. *Rabochee dvizhenie semidesiatykh godov*. Moscow, 1934.

Korzec, Paweł. *Pół wieku dziejów ruchu rewolucyjnego Białostocczyzny (1864–1914)*. Warsaw, 1965.

Kursky, Franz. *Gezamlte shriftn*. New York, 1952.

Landau, S. R. *Unter jüdischen Proletariern*. Vienna, 1898.

Leschinsky, Jacob. *Der idisher arbeter (in rusland)*. Vilna, 1906.

Dos idishe folk in tsifern. Berlin, 1922.

Levanda, V. O. (ed.). *Polnyi khronologicheskii sbornik zakonov i polozhenii kasaiuchshikhsia evreev*. St Petersburg, 1874.

Levita, L., and D. Ben-Nahum (eds.). *Borokhov, Ketavim*. Vol. 2, Tel Aviv, 1958.

Levitats, Isaac. *The Jewish Community in Russia, 1772–1844*. New York, 1943.

Lispet, Seymour, Martin Trow, and James Coleman. *Union Democracy*. New York, 1962.

Mahler, Raphael. *Yidn in amolikn poylen in likht fun tsifern*. Warsaw, 1958.

Malinowski, Aleksander (ed.). *Materiały do historii PPS i ruchu rewolucyjnego w zaborze rosyjskim od r. 1893–1904*. Vol. I, Warsaw, 1907.

Margolis, A. *Geshikhte fun yidn in rusland*. Moscow–Kharkov–Minsk, 1930.

Yidishe folksmasn in kamf kegn zayre unterdriker. Moscow, 1940.

Mezrich zamlbukh. Buenos Aires, 1952.

Montreuil, Jean. *Histoire du mouvement ouvrier en France, des origines à nos jours*. Paris, 1946.

Morskii, A., pseud. (von Stein). *Zubatovshchina, stranitsa iz istorii rabochego voprosa v Rossii*. Moscow, 1913.

Mysh, M.I. *Rukovodstvo k russkim zakonam o evreiakh*. St Petersburg, 1904.

Nedasek, N. *Bol'shevizm v revoliutsionnom dvizhenii v Belorussii (1863–1917)*. Munich, 1956.

Nettl, J. P. *Rosa Luxemburg*. 2 vols., London, 1966.

Orlov, Petr. *Ukazatel' fabrik i zavodov evropeiskoi Rossii s Tsarstvom Pol'skim i Vel. Kn. Finliandskim*. St Petersburg, 1881.

Bibliography

Orshanskii, I. G. *Evrei v Rossii, Ocherki i izsledovaniia.* St Petersburg, 1872.

Russkoe zakonodatel'stvo o evreiakh. St Petersburg, 1877.

Otchet I. I. Ianzhula po izsledovaniiu fabrichnozavodskoi promyshlennosti v Tsarstve Polskom. St Petersburg, 1888.

Patkin, A. L. *The Origins of the Russian–Jewish Labour Movement.* London and Melbourne, 1947.

Perl, Feliks (Res, pseud.) *Dzieje ruchu socjalistycznego w zaborze rosyjskim do powstania PPS.* Warsaw, 1958.

Piłsudski, Jósef. *Pisma zbiorowe.* Vol. I, Warsaw, 1937.

Pipes, Richard. *Social Democracy and the St Petersburg Labor Movement, 1885–97.* Cambridge, Mass., 1963.

Pogozhev, A. V. *Uchet chislennosti i sostava rabochikh v Rossii.* St Petersburg, 1906.

Prokopovich, S. N. *K rabochemu voprosu v Rossii.* St Petersburg, 1905.

Rabinowitsch, Sara. *Die Organisationen des jüdischen Proletariats in Russland.* Karlsruhe, 1903.

Rabochee dvizhenie v Rossii v XIX veke. Vol. II, *1885–94,* Part I, Moscow–Leningrad, 1952; Vol. IV, *1895–97,* Part I, Moscow–Leningrad, 1961.

Rafes, Moise (Moshe). *Ocherki po istorii 'bunda'.* Moscow, 1923.

Raisin, Jacob S. *The Haskalah Movement in Russia.* Philadelphia, 1913.

Rashin, A. G. *Formirovanie rabochego klassa Rossii.* Moscow, 1958.

Roth, Guenther. *The Social Democrats in Imperial Germany.* Totowa, N.J., 1963.

Rülf, J. *Drei Tage in Jüdisch-Russland.* Frankfort a/M., 1882.

Saladkov, I. I. *Sotsial'no-ekonomicheskoe polozhenie Belorussii do velikoi oktiabr'skoi sotsialisticheskoi revoliutsii.* Minsk, 1957.

Samuel, Maurice. *Prince of the Ghetto.* New York and Philadelphia, 1959.

Sbornik materialov ob ekonomicheskom polozhenii evreev v Rossii. 2 vols., St Petersburg, 1904.

Schwarz, Solomon. *The Russian Revolution of 1905.* Chicago, 1967.

Shelymagin, I. I. *Fabrichno-trudove zakonodatel'stvo v Rossii vo vtoroi polovine XIX veka.* Moscow, 1947.

Sliozberg, G. B. *Pravovoe i ekonomicheskoe polozhenie evreev v Rossii.* St Petersburg, 1907.

Soloweitschik, Leonty. *Un prolétariat méconnu, étude sur la situation sociale et économique des ouvriers juifs.* Brussels, 1898.

Sosis, Israel. *Di geshikhte fun di yidishe gezelshaftlekhe shtremungen in rusland in 19 y"h.* Minsk, 1929.

Bibliography

Di sotsial-ekonomishe lage fun di ruslendishe yuden in der ershter helft fun 19-ten yorhundert. Petrograd, 1919.

Stepniak, pseud. (S. Kravchinskii.) *The Russian Storm Cloud.* London, 1886.

Subbotin, A. P. *V cherte evreiskoi osedlosti.* Part I, St Petersburg, 1888; Part II, St Petersburg, 1890.

Sviatlovskii, V. *Professional'noe dvizhenie v Rossii.* St Petersburg, 1907.

Szmidt, B. *Socjaldemokracja królestwa Polskiego i Litwy, Materiały i dokumenty.* Moscow, 1934.

Tartakover, Arieh. *Toldot tenuat ha-ovdim ha-yehudit.* Vol. I, Warsaw, 1929.

Ustav remeslennyi, izdanie 1897 goda. St Petersburg, 1879.

Vandervelde, Émile. *Enquête sur les associations professionnelles d'artisans et ouvriers en Belgique.* Brussels, 1891.

Venturi, Franco. *Roots of Revolution.* Transalted by Francis Haskell. New York, 1960.

Vilenskii fabrichnyi okrug—otchet za 1885 g. fabrichnago inspektora okruga G. I. Gorodorka. St Petersburg, 1886.

Wasilewski, Leon. *Litwa i Białorus.* Cracow, 1912.

Webb, Sidney and Beatrice. *The History of Trade Unionism.* London, 1920.

Weinryb, S. B. *Neueste Wirtschaftsgeschichte der Juden in Russland und Polen.* Breslau, 1934.

Wildman, Allan. *The Making of a Workers' Revolution, Russian Social Democracy 1891–1903.* Chicago, 1967.

Wischnitzer, Mark. *A History of Jewish Crafts and Guilds.* New York, 1965.

Yidishe bal melokhe tsekhn in poylen un lite. Berlin, 1922.

Yakhinson, Y. *Sotsial-ekonomisher shtayger ba yidn in rusland in XIX y"h.* Kharkov, 1929.

Yasni, Volf A. *Di geshikhte fun bund in lodz.* Lodz, 1937.

Yeshurin, Yefim (ed.). *Vilne, a zamlbukh gevidmet der shtot vilne.* New York, 1935.

Yuditsky, A. *Yidishe burzhvasie un yidisher proletariat in ershter helft XIX y"h.* N.p., n.d.

Zelinskii, I. (ed.). *Minskaia Gubernaia. Materialy dlia geografii i statistiki Rossii, sobrannye ofitserami general'nago shtaba.* Vol. xv. St Petersburg, 1864.

Zeman, Z. A. B., and W. B. Scharlau. *The Merchant of Revolution, the Life of Alexander Israel Helphand (Parvus), 1867–1924.* London, 1965.

Bibliography

Articles

Ain, Abraham. 'Swislocz, Portrait of a Jewish Community in Eastern Europe.' *YIVO Annual of Jewish Social Science* (New York). Vol. IV, 1949, pp. 86–114.

Akimov, Vladimir pseud. (Makhonets), 'Stroiteli budushchago.' *Obrazovanie* (St Petersburg). Vol. XVI, No. 4, April 1907, pp. 91–118.

Aynzaft, Sh. 'Der ekonomisher kamf fun di holtsarbeter bizn 1905 yor.' *Visnshaftlekhe yorbikher.* Vol. I, Moscow, 1929, pp. 90–107. 'Ekonomicheskaia bor'ba Belostotskikh tekstil'shchikov v 80-kh i 90-kh godakh.' *Revoliutsionnoe dvizhenie sredi evreev*, S. Dimanshtein (ed.), Moscow, 1930, pp. 244–63.

Belostochanin. 'Iz istorii anarkhicheskago dvizheniia v Belostoke.' *Almanakh, Sbornik po istorii anarkhicheskago dvizheniia v Rossii.* Vol I, Paris, 1909, pp. 5–28.

Borokhov, Ber. 'Tenuat ha-poalim ha-yehudit be-misparim.' *Borokhov, Ketavim*, L. Levita and D. Ben-Nahum (eds.), Vol. II, Tel Aviv, 1958, pp. 260–320.

Brentano, Lujo. 'On the History and Development of Guilds.' *English Guilds*, Toulmin Smith (ed.), London, 1870.

Brutskus, B. 'Ocherk ekonomicheskago polozheniia evreev v Rossii.' In *Ocherki po voprosam ekonomicheskoi deiatel'nosti evreev v Rossii.* St Petersburg, 1913, pp. 3–68.

Bukhbinder, Nahum A. 'Evreiskoe rabochee dvizhenie v Gomele 1890–1905 gg.' *Krasnaia letopis'* (Moscow). Nos. 2–3, 1922, pp. 38–102.
'Evreiskoe rabochee dvizhenie v Minske 1895–1905 gg.' *Krasnaia letopis'* (Moscow). No. 5, 1923, pp. 122–68.
'Evreiskie revoliutsionnye kruzhki 80-kh i nachala 90-kh gg.: period propagandy.' *Evreiskaia letopis'* (Petrograd). Vol. I, 1923, pp. 52–8.
'Iz istorii evreiskogo sotsialisticheskogo dvizheniia v 70-kh gg.' *Istoriko-revoliutsionnyi sbornik*, V. Nevskii (ed.). Vol. II, Moscow, 1924, pp. 37–66.
'Nezavisimaia evreiskaia rabochaia partiia.' *Krasnaia letopis'* (Moscow). No. 2–3, 1922, pp. 208–84.
'O zubatovshchine.' *Krasnaia letopis'* (Moscow). No. 4, 1922, pp. 289–335.

Cahan, Ab. 'Bildung un sotsialistishe propagande bay yidishe bale melokhes in di litvishe shtet.' *Historishe shriftn.* Vol. III, Paris–Vilna, 1939, pp. 394–7.

Ch. (Cherikover?). 'Di lage fun di minsker handel-ongeshtelte in di 80-ker yorn.' *Tsaytshrift* (Minsk). Vol. IV, 1930, pp. 133–5.

Cherikover, E. 'Der onhayb fun der yidisher sotsialistisher bavegung.' *Historishe shriftn.* Vol. I, Warsaw, 1929, pp. 469–532.

'Yidn revolutsionern in rusland in di 60er un 70er yorn.' *Historishe shriftn.* Vol. III, Paris–Vilna, 1939, pp. 60–172.

Eidel'man, B. 'K istorii vozniknoveniia Rossiiskoi sots.-dem. rabochei partii.' *Proletarskaia revoliutsiia* (Moscow). No. 1, 1921, pp. 20–67.

Friedman, Phillip. 'A sotsialer konflikt in lodz onhayb 19-tn y"h.' *YIVO bleter* (Vilna). Vol. II, Nos. 1, 2, November–December 1931, 145–9.

'Rola Żydów w rozwoju Łódzkiego przemysłu włonkienniczego.' *Miescięcznik Żydowski* (Warsaw). Vol. I, Nos. 1–6, December 1930–May 1931, pp. 431–50.

Frumkin, Boris. 'Iz istorii revoliutsionnago dvizheniia sredi evreev v 1870-kh godakh.' *Evreiskaia starina* (St Petersburg). Vol. IV, No. 2, April–June 1911, pp. 221–48; No. 4, October–December 1911, pp. 512–40.

'Ocherki iz istorii evreiskago rabochago dvizheniia v Rossii (1885–97 g.)' *Evreiskaia starina* (St Petersburg). Vol. VI, No. 1, January–March 1913, pp. 108–22, 245–63.

'Zubatovshchina i evreiskoe rabochee dvizhenie.' *Perezhitoe.* Vol. III, 1911, pp. 199–230.

Giffin, Frederick C. 'The Formative Years of the Russian Factory Inspectorate.' *Slavic Review* (New York). Vol. XXV, No. 4, December 1966, pp. 641–50.

Gutman, Herbert G. 'Reconstruction in Ohio: Negroes in the Hocking Valley Coal Mines in 1873 and 1874.' *Labor History* (New York). Vol. III, No. 3, Fall 1962, pp. 243–64.

Halperin, Israel. 'Hevrot ba'alay melakhah yehudim be-polin ve-lita.' *Zion* (Jerusalem). Vol. II, No. 1, October 1936, pp. 70–89.

Ianovskii, Sam. 'Opisanie odnogo mestechka.' *Evreiskaia zhizn'* (St Petersburg). No. 4, April 1904, pp. 132–40.

'K istorii Zubatovshchini.' *Byloe*, Vol. I (23), July 1917, pp. 86–99.

Kalabiński, Stanisław. 'Początki ruchu robotniczego w białostockim okręgu przemysłowym w latach 1870–87.' *Rocznik Białostocki*

Bibliography

(Bialystok). Vol. II (1961), pp. 143–94; continued for years 1887–96, in Vol. III, (1962), pp. 97–145; 1897–1900, in Vol. IV, (1963), pp. 159–235.

Kamanin, I. 'Statisticheskiia dannyia o evreiakh v iugo-zapadnome krae vo vtoroi polovine proshlago veka 1765–91 gg.' *Arkhiv iugozapadnoi Rossii*. Part V, Vol. II, Kiev, 1890, pp. 1–239.

Kan, Pinkhas. 'Idishe tsekhen in vilna onhayb 19-tn yorhundert.' *Shriftn far ekonomik un statistik*, J. Leschinsky (ed.). Vol. I, Berlin, 1928, pp. 89–91.

Khoroshch, I. 'Po promyshlennoi cherte osedlosti.' *Voskhod* (St Petersburg). Vol. XX, No. 3, March 1901, pp. 50–65; No. 4, April 1901, pp. 134–55; No. 6, June 1901, pp. 37–54; No. 7, July 1901, pp. 32–48; No. 8, August 1901, pp. 37–56; No. 10, October 1901, pp. 23–49; No. 11, November 1901, pp. 45–64; No. 12, December 1901, pp. 100–20.

Korobkov, Kh. 'Ekonomicheskaia rol' evreev v Pol'she v kontse XVIII v.' *Evreiskaia starina* (St Petersburg). Vol. III, No. 3, July–September 1910, pp. 346–77.

'Perepis' evreiskago naseleniia vitebskoi gubernii v 1772 g.' *Evreiskaia starina* (St Petersburg). Vol. V, No. 2, April–June 1912, pp. 164–77.

Kossovsky, Vladimir. 'Zubatov "likvidirt dem bund"', in *Arkady, Zamlbukh tsum andenk fun Arkady Kremer*. New York, 1942, pp. 175–207.

Kotik, A. 'Proshloe i nastoiashchee belostotskoi evreiskoi tkatskoi promyshlennosti.' *Teoreticheskie i prakticheskie voprosy evreiskoi zhizni* (St Petersburg). Nos. 2–3, 1909, pp. 118–30.

Kramerówna, Perla. 'Żydowskie cechy rzemieślnicze w dawnej Polsce', *Miesięcznik Żydowski* (Warsaw). Vol. II, Nos. 7–12, July–December 1932, pp. 259–98.

Kremer, Moshe. 'Le-heker ha-melakhah ve-hevrot ba'alay ha-melakhah etsel yehuday polin ba-maot ha-17-ha-18.' *Zion* (Jerusalem). Vol. II, Nos. 3–4, July 1937, pp. 295–325.

Leschinsky, Jacob. 'Di antviklung fun idishen folk far di letste 100 yor.' *Shriftn far ekonomik un statistik*, J. Leschinsky (ed.). Vol. I, pp. 1–64.

Lev, Aba. 'Di yidishe arbeter-bavegung in minsk bizn yor 1900.' *Visnshaftlekhe yorbikher*. Vol. I, Moscow, 1929, pp. 108–17.

'Pervye shagi evreiskogo rabochego dvizheniia v g. Grodno.' *Revoliutsionnoe dvizhenie sredi evreev*, S. Dimanshtein (ed.). Moscow, 1930, pp. 264–81.

173

'Aynike bamerkungen tsu kh. Raytshuks zikhroynes vegen der arbayter bavegung.' *Royte bleter*. Vol. I, Minsk, 1929, pp. 1–3.

Mark, B. 'Proletariat żydowski w przededniu rewolucji 1905 roku.' *Biuletyn żydowskiego instytutu historicznego* (Warsaw). Nos. 13–14, January–June, 1955, pp. 3–72.

'Rzemieślnicy żydowscy w Polsce feudalnej.' *Biuletyn żydowskiego instytutu historicznego* (Warsaw). Nos. 9–10, January–June 1954, pp. 5–89.

Martov, Iulii. 'Razvitie krupnoi promyshlennosti i rabochee dvizhenie do 1892 g.' *Istorii Rossii v XIX veke*. St Petersburg, no date, pp. 114–62.

Mendelsohn, Ezra. 'Worker opposition in the Russian Jewish socialist movement, from the 1890s to 1905.' *International Review of Social History* (Amsterdam). Vol. x, Part 2, 1965, pp. 268–82.

'Jewish and Christian workers in the Russian Pale of Settlement.' *Jewish Social Studies*. Vol. xxx, No. 4, October 1968, pp. 243–51.

Menes, Avraham. 'Der onhayb fun der idisher arbeter-bevegung un ihr shoyresh in idishen folks-leben.' *Di tsukunft*, Vol. xl, No. 9, September 1935, pp. 539–44.

'Di yidishe arbeter-bavegung in rusland fun onhayb 70er bizn sof 90er yorn', in *Historishe shriftn*. Vol. iii, Paris–Vilna, 1939, pp. 1–59.

'Vegen der industrie-bafelkerung ba idn in rusland, 1897.' *Shriftn far ekonomik un statistik*, J. Leschinsky (ed.). Vol. I, pp. 255–6.

Mindel, Y. 'A historishe yubilii.' *Der Homer* (New York), No. 4, June 1926, pp. 46–8.

Mishkinsky, Moshe. 'Ha-sotsializm ha-mishtari u-megamot ba-mediniut ha-shilton ha-tsari legabay ha-yehudim.' *Zion* (Jerusalem). Vol. xxv, Nos. 3–4, 1960, pp. 238–49.

'Mekorotehah ha-ra'ayoniim shel tenuat ha-poalim ha-yehudit be-rusiah be-rashitah.' *Zion* (Jerusalem). Vol. xxxi, Nos. 1–2, 1966, pp. 87–115.

'Naselenie.' *Evreiskaia entsiklopediia*. Vol. xi, pp. 534–47.

Notik, R. 'Tsu der geshikhte fun hantverk bay litvishe yidn.' *YIVO bleter* (Vilna). Vol. ix, Nos. 1–2, January–March 1936, pp. 107–18.

Orinsky, G. 'Gezelshaftlikhe bavegungen in pruzhene.' *Pinkes fun finf fortilikte kehiles*, M. Bernshtein (ed.). Buenos Aires, 1958, pp. 117–26.

Rabinowitsch, S. 'Zur Bildungsstatistikder jüdischer Arbeiter in Russland.' *Zeitschrift für Demographie und Statistik der Juden*. Vol. ix, No. 11, November 1913, pp. 153–60.

Rafes, Moise (Moshe). 'Girsh Lekert i ego pokushenie.' *Krasnyi arkhiv*, Vol. II (xv), 1926, pp. 86–95.

Rimlinger, Gaston. 'The Management of Labor Protest in Tsarist Russia: 1870–1905.' *International Review of Social History* (Amsterdam). Vol. v, Part I, 1960, pp. 226–48.

Tidmarsh, K. 'The Zubatov Idea.' *American Slavic and East European Review* (Seattle). Vol. xix, No. 3, October 1960, pp. 335–46.

Tobias, Henry J. 'The Bund and Lenin until 1903.' *Russian Review* (Hanover, N.H.). Vol. xx, No. 4, October 1961, pp. 344–57.

and Charles E. Woodhouse. 'Primordial Ties and Political Process in pre-Revolutionary Russia: the Case of the Jewish Bund.' *Comparative Studies in Society and History* (The Hague). Vol. viii, No. 3, April 1966, pp. 331–60.

Tsitron, Shmuel L. 'Kehilat yisrael be-minsk.' *Knesset yisrael*. Vol. i, Warsaw, 1886, pp. 735–40.

'Tsu der geshikhte fun der "arbeter opozitsie".' *Yedies fun YIVO* (Vilna). Nos. 4–5, April–May 1937, pp. 7–10.

Tulman, Moshe. 'Di antshtayung fun "bund" un zayn untergang.' *Pinkas slutsk u-vnotehah*. New York-Tel Aviv, 1962, pp. 301–12.

Vishnitser (Wischnitzer). 'Di struktur fun yidishe tsekhen in poylen, lita, un vaysrusland inm 17-tn un 18-tn yorhundertn.' *Tsaytshrift* (Minsk). Vols. II–III, 1928, pp. 73–87.

Von Laue, Theodore. 'Factory Inspection under the Witte System', *American Slavic and East European Review* (Seattle). Vol. xix, No. 3, October 1960, pp. 347–67.

Wajner, Menachim. 'Do historii P.P.S. na Litwie.' *Niepodległość* (Warsaw). Vol. ix, No. 2 (22), January–June 1934, pp. 221–35.

Zaslavsky, David (F. P., pseud.). 'Di oppozitsie fun 1893 yor.' *Di hoffnung* (Vilna). Vol. i, No. 14, 22 September–8 October 1907.

'Zubatov i Mania Vil'bushevits.' *Byloe*, No. 3 (31), March 1918, pp. 99–128.

'Zhitel'stvo i peredvizhenie evreev po russkomu zakonodatel'stvu.' *Evreiskaia entsiklopediia*. Vol. vii, pp. 590–7.

Ziskind, A. 'Fun bialystoker arbayterleben: veber oif mekhanishe shtulen.' *Fragen fun leben zamlbukh* (St Petersburg). Nos. 2–3, 1912, pp. 112–20.

Index

Index

Index

Khoroshch, I., 13 n., 20, 22, 36
Kiev, 90 n., 121 n.
Kishinev, 94, 150
Kon, F., views on Jewish proletariat, 9, 18, 34
Kopel'zon, T., 79
Korolenko, V., 35
Kotik, A., 21
Kovno, x f., 4 f., 6 n., 12, 14 n., 15, 37, 45, 53, 59 n., 63 n., 64 n., 65, 67, 73, 80, 96, 102, 113, 121 n., 123, 124, 125 n.
Krapivnikov, K., 80 f.
Kremer, A., 35, 38, 40, 53 n., 92, 119 n., 129 n., 134; and agitation program, 52 f.; and attitude towards Jewish proletariat, 60 f., 85
Kreslavka, 83, 87, 90 n., 144
Krozhki, 124 n.
Krynki, 87, 90 n., 91, 106, 109

Lafargue, P., 121
Lassalle, F., 66, 121
Lavrov, P., 36, 56
Leipzig, 74
Lekert, H., 103, 122, 133, 134 n., 148 f., assassination attempt of, 131 f.
Lermontov, M., 72 n.
Leschinsky, J.: and attitude towards the Jewish labor movement, 22 n., 60
Levin, Shmaryahu, 25
Levin, Sholem, 33, 72, 101, 120, 127
Libau, 121
Liebermann, A., 13, 28 n.
Liesin, A., 62, 85, 116; and *opposition* in Minsk, 58 ff.
Lithuania, viii, xi, 2, 5, 76
Lithuanian Socialist Movement, 51 n.
Litvak, A., pseud. (Helphand), 81, 84, 118, 123
Liza 'the Tailor', 45, 154 f.
Lodz, xi, 10, 13, 17, 20 n., 23 n., 28 n., 42, 89 n., 90 n., 91, 92, 98, 99 n., 101, 106, 113 n., 130, 133, 135, 138
London, 46 n., 90
Lur'e, M., 37; and opposition in Bialystok, 58 f.
Lyon, 90

Machajski, J., 57
Martov, Iu., 10, 46, 49 n., 62; on Jewish and Christian workers, 33; on Polish socialist movement, 47; on Vilna *opposition*, 59
Marx, K., 35, 56, 57, 66, 121

Marxism, ix, 16, 30 f., 34, 36, 48, 53, 104, 130
Medem, V., 33, 70; on bristle-workers, 72; on hooligans, 101
Mendele Moicher, Sforim (Mendele the Book-Seller), 117
Mezrich, 86, 106, 108
Mill, J., 35, 61
Minsk, x, 4 f., 6, 7, 9, 10, 11 n., 12, 13, 14, 23 n., 25, 27, 30 n., 31, 39, 40, 41, 42, 46, 58, 59, 61, 63, 66 n., 68, 70, 71, 83, 84, 85, 86, 87, 88, 90 n., 95, 98, 102, 105, 109, 112, 116, 120, 121, 127, 128, 130, 136, 140, 154 n., 157 n., Jewish and Christian workers in, 33; beginnings of agitation period in, 50 ff.; as centre of the *Independents*, 143 ff.
The Minsk Worker (Der minsker arbayter), 119
Mogilev, x, 3, 5, 8 n., 10 n., 14, 24, 42, 51, 86, 90 n., 142
Mohilever, S., 106
Moscow, 139, 140 n., 144 n.
Moses 'the Binder', 39, 53
Motke 'the Tanner', 102
Mozir, 25
Mstislav, 105 n.

Nekrasov, N., 35 n.
New Russia, 3
New York, 90, 105
Nissenboim, Y., 21
Nodel, M., 46, 53, 69 n.
Northwest region, x, 11, 12, 53
Notkin, Y., 40

Ob agitatsii, 53
Odessa, 2, 145 n., 148 n.; as center of *Independents*, 150 f.
Opposition movements: Gordon's *Opposition* in Vilna, 55 ff.; spreads to other cities, 58 ff.; perseverance of, 61 f.; demand for more democracy, 126 ff.; opposition of terrorists, 130 ff.; opposition to politics, 134 ff.; Zubatovism and the *Independents* in Minsk, 139 ff.; Zubatism in Odessa, 150 f.; decline of Zubatovism, 151 f.

Pabjanice, 133 n.
Pale of Settlement, 85, 139; definition of, 3
Palestine, 150 n.
Parachi, 86
Pati, pseud. (Srednitskaia), 71 n.

179

Index